£7.50

Love For

PORTRAIT OF PERTH, ANGUS AND FIFE

Portrait of
PERTH, ANGUS and FIFE

by

DAVID GRAHAM-CAMPBELL

ROBERT HALE · LONDON

© *David Graham-Campbell 1979*

First published in Great Britain 1979

ISBN 0 7091 7550 7

Robert Hale Limited
Clerkenwell House
Clerkenwell Green
London EC1

PRINTED IN GREAT BRITAIN BY
LOWE AND BRYDONE LTD., THETFORD, NORFOLK
PHOTOSET AND BOUND BY
WEATHERBY WOOLNOUGH, WELLINGBOROUGH, NORTHANTS

CONTENTS

Author's Notes   7

Acknowledgments   9

I   Introduction   13

II   Perth   30

III   North from Perth   48

IV   West from Perth   78

V   South from Perth   104

VI   Angus – Strathmore   131

VII   Angus – The coast   151

VIII   North Fife   170

IX   South Fife   197

Further Reading   229

Index   235

AUTHOR'S NOTE

The district portrayed in this book is, as near as may be, that of
the newly-created Regions of Strathtay and Fife. The term Fife
is familiar to all, whether as a region, a county or a kingdom.
Not so Strathtay. Its older usage was to describe the valley of
the Tay from Aberfeldy to Dunkeld, at which point it merged
into Strathmore. Now, as a Region, it includes the whole of
Angus and most of Perthshire, but not Killin, nor Lochearnhead, nor Dunblane, let alone Callander, Doune and the
Trossachs. For the most part, I have managed to keep within its
boundaries, but I make no apology for including the Falls of
Dochart which feed Loch Tay, and Dunblane and Sheriffmuir,
without which the history of the area would be incomplete. As
for the title, it seems to me to be more euphonious, and also
more readily understandable to those living outwith Scotland,
than "Portrait of the Regions of Strathtay and Fife".

D.G.-C.

The Permanence of the Young Men

No man outlives the grief of war
Though he outlive its wreck;
Upon the memory a scar
Through all his years will ache.

Hopes will survive when horrors cease;
And dreaming dread be stilled;
But there shall dwell within his peace
A sadness unannulled.

Upon his world shall hang a sign
Which summer cannot hide:
The permanence of the young men
Who are not at his side.

from *The Expectant Silence,*
William Soutar, Perth 1898-1943

ACKNOWLEDGMENTS

I should like to express my thanks to those friends who have read various chapters in draft for their helpful suggestions; to Volie and Harry Wilson, Sandie Watt and Alan Elliott; and to Charles Millar who has also, once again, read proofs for me with endless patience, to him, to Roger Sylvester and to the staff of the Sandeman Library, Perth, for help in obtaining books; to Miss Smythe of Methven and to the Earl of Strathmore for leave to quote from their family papers, and to Mr J. A. McCowan for some notes on the history of John Dewar and Sons.

For the use of copyright material, I am indebted to the University of London Press for a passage from James Scotland's *History of Education in Scotland*; Messrs Barrie and Jenkins for three extracts from the *History of the Black Watch* by E. and A. Linklater; the National Trust for Scotland for a quotation from their *Guide to Killiecrankie*; Mrs Walker (Miss Alexandra Stewart) has kindly allowed me to quote from her *The Glen That Was* as have her publishers, the Club Leabhar, and from her father's *A Highland Parish*; Messrs Milne, Tannahill and Methven from *About Kinross and Its Folk* by Robert S. Young; Mr John Dunbar and Batsford Ltd from *The Historical Architecture of Scotland*; the Rev. D. Lister from Largo Kirk; the *Scots Magazine* for an excerpt from an article by Mr A. C. McKerracher in their issue for November, 1977; to Christopher Smith for the use of his mother's poem "Whit wey does the engine say toot-toot?" and for his hospitality and guidance in other matters. For the use of three passages from Mrs Maxtone-Graham's *"The Maxtones of Cultoquhey"* I should like to thank Mr James Maxtone-Graham.

The two poems of William Soutar "The Permanence of the Young Men" and "Ae' Nicht at Amulree" are quoted by permission of the holders of the copyright, the National Library of Scotland, and his literary executor, Dr W. R. Aitken.

ILLUSTRATIONS

Between pages 48 and 49

1 Perth: Rose Terrace and the old Academy building
2 The bull sales
3 Perth from the air
4 Pictish stone cross
5 Stone at Glamis
6 Stone with mirror symbol and 'elephant'
7 Dunkeld Cathedral
8 Blair Castle
9 The Soldier's Leap at Killiecrankie
10 Wade's Bridge, Aberfeldy
11 Loch Rannoch and Schiehallion
12 Stone circle at Croft Moraig
13 Loch Tay
14 Ben Lawers

Between pages 64 and 65

15 Fort at Dundurn
16 Dochart falls, Killin
17 Glamis Castle
18 Drummond Castle and its gardens from the air
19 Kirriemuir
20 Edzell Castle and garden
21 The round-tower at Brechin
22 Souterrain at Ardestie

23 Claypotts Castle
24 Arbroath smokies
25 Arbroath Abbey
26 Death catches up with old age, Arbroath Abbey Museum
27 Falkland Palace
28 Falkland Palace, the south range

Between pages 128 and 129

29 Clatchard Craig hill fort
30 Scotstarvit Tower
31 Norman church at Leuchars
32 The town house at Culross
33 St Andrews Abbey and St Rule's Tower
34 Culross
35 Dunfermline Abbey from Pittencrieff gardens
36 Inchcolm Abbey
37 Dunfermline Abbey, the nave
38 Inchcolm Abbey, the refectory
39 Burntisland Church
40 St Monance
41 Outside the Fisheries Museum at Anstruther
42 Crail harbour

	page
Line figure: Pictish symbols	16
Map	232-3

Picture Credits

Tom Berthon, 1, 3; John Watt, 2; Department of the Environment, 4, 5, 6, 20, 21, 22, 23, 25, 26, 30, 33, 35, 36, 37, 38; National Trust for Scotland, 9, 14, 27, 28, 32, 34; Scottish Tourist Board, 8, 10, 11, 12, 13, 17, 19, 24, 31, 40, 41, 42; Royal Commission for the Ancient and Historical Monuments of Scotland, 18, 29, 39; James Graham-Campbell, 7, 12, 15, 16; Tom Scott, 27.
Fig. 1 is reproduced from Isobel Henderson's *The Picts* by permission of Thames & Hudson.

I

INTRODUCTION

A general introduction to three regions as different as these is hardly possible. Perthshire, though much of it is Lowland, is Highland oriented; Angus has a Highland fringe but its outlook and its economy are Lowland; and Fife is – the kingdom of Fife, largely isolated from the rest of Scotland till recent times and fiercely independent – so much so that it successfully campaigned against being included in a larger region when local government was reorganized. The result is that 'Tayside' only includes one side of the Tay estuary.

Still, the three have a number of things in common. They all have much to offer the visitor – birds to watch and other forms of wild life to enjoy; hills to walk, or to climb, or ski on; golf and curling, sailing and bathing; sites to visit, prehistoric and historic in plenty. And, until the Reformation, the three were very much the centre of government and of trade in North Britain. For the remarkable geology of the area, the reader is directed to A. R. MacGregor's *Short Excursion Guide*, published for the University of St Andrews by the Scottish Academic Press, which includes not only a general outline but also a series of detailed itineraries for walks, to see unfolded the various developments in the evolution of the landscape and its rocks. From the earliest times of life, Angus has a fossil of one of the oldest known fish, and Fife has the (as yet) earliest dateable remains of Man, in Scotland. Food remains which were found at Morton Farm, Tentsmuir, show that Mesolithic Man found one of his stopping places there around 6000 B.C. – a hunter, living in rough shelters, always on the move in search of the boar, wild cattle, deer, shellfish and berries on which he lived. It is also possible that the heavy dug-out canoes now in the

13

Dundee and Perth Museums may date from this period. In Perthshire, there was a flint factory at Creag na Caillich near Killin in Neolithic times *c.* 2500 B.C., and stone circles are to be found in many places as, for instance, Croftmoraig at Taymouth. Some time between 700 and 300 B.C., hill forts became widespread, the stone walls of some being reinforced by timber, as at the Cathertuns, north-west of Brechin, at Normans Law and Clatchard Craig in Fife, and at Dunsinane and Barry Hill in Perthshire.

The Romans arrived in Strathearn and Strathmore in 83 A.D. and, if Agricola had not been so soon recalled, would no doubt have left an even greater mark than they did; as it is, there are notable sites within our area of each of the three periods of major advance – Inchtuthil was Agricola's, Ardoch chiefly Antonine (*c.* 142) and the fort of Carpow mainly Severan (between 208 and 211). The Roman armies were fighting against tribes that they called the Picts (from the belief that they painted or tattooed themselves) and this was the heart of Pictland – as Argyll was the heart of Scotland. Here is the greatest concentration of Pictish art in its most fully developed form. Little is known of its creators, not even their language or languages except that their main one was a form of Celtic.

Their souterrains – underground storehouses or refuges or cattle shelters, who knows? – are common in Angus, and occur in Fife and in one or two places in Perthshire. They are best seen in those cared for by the Ministry of the Environment at Ardestie and Carlungie, about seven miles east of Dundee and just north of the A92 road. Though we call them souterrains they were not always wholly below ground-level and can hardly have been intended as places of concealment for either man or beast. Nor can they have been built with defensive intent since nothing would have been easier than to smoke out anyone in them. Nor, so far as the Angus souterrains are concerned; is there any evidence that they were used as dwellings; such domestic debris as has been found has been from huts on the surface around them. They may have been used for herding cattle and sheep in winter and bad weather.

The really striking thing is the hard work and the stone-building skills which men devoted to them in the very early centuries A.D. As for the men themselves, we do not even know whether they really did tattoo themselves as the Romans believed, nor do we know what they called themselves, nor whether it had anything to do with the prefix 'pett' which, as 'pit', is so common in the place-names of Eastern and Central Scotland. What we do know is that they had forts stretching eastwards and northwards from Dundurn near Comrie, and that they were wonderful carvers. The stones that they erected are so beautifully executed and so fascinating that it is worth the initial effort to understand an art form that is unfamiliar and which presents problems which may indeed never be solved.

The earliest, or Class I, stones are unshaped, and largely undressed, boulders that were probably carved in the seventh century A.D. On these are incised animal figures and certain symbols, some of them pictorial, but others purely abstract, yet standardized and easily recognized (see Fig. 1 for some of the more common). Certain facts about their use are clearly significant, though we do not know of what; for instance, an animal may appear by itself but one symbol is never used alone; certain combinations of symbols commonly appear together, others never; animals and symbols regularly appear together. At this stage there is no evidence of Christian imagery (see plate 6).

Class II stones, in contrast, are carefully dressed and, on one side, have a cross, ornamented with interlacing patterns, and often with human figures or animals between the arms of the cross. On the reverse of the stone will be symbols and animals, and sometimes compositions including them, such as a hunting or a warlike scene. The technique passes from the incising of Class I to shallow relief sometimes quite exquisitely accomplished, as for instance in Eassie and Aberlemno churchyards – and finally to higher relief and a more plastic style as at the roadside at Aberlemno and in Stone 5 in the Meigle Museum collection. There is also a certain move southward to be detected; whereas the greatest concentration of Class I stones is

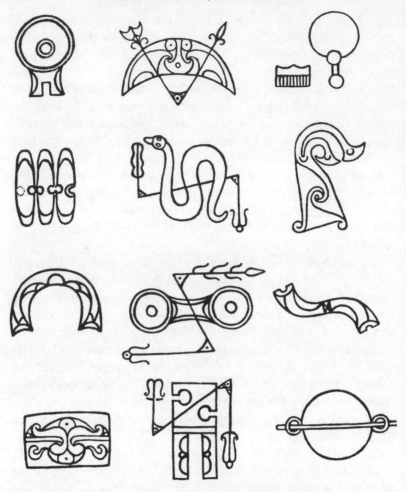

Fig. 1. Symbols commonly used on Pictish stones (reproduced from *The Picts* by I. Henderson, by courtesy of publishers Thames & Hudson).

further north than our area, Angus and Fife have the largest number of Class II stones. Class III stones drop entirely the purely Pictish symbols. We cannot be sure what lies behind the changes though presumably the development from Class I to Class II was connected with the adoption of Christianity; and the change to Class III may have coincided with the conquest of the Picts by the Scots, if indeed there was such a conquest. More important still, we do not know the purpose for which they were erected. Various possibilities have been suggested – gravestones, memorials to important individuals unconnected with burials, evidence of marriage alliances, boundary stones, evidence of personal possession – but none has been supported by sufficient evidence to win general approval (*see* plates 4, 5).

The prevalence of place-names including Pictish elements is matched by the scarcity of those of Scandinavian origin. In the ninth century, Kenneth MacAlpine had managed to unite Pictland with Scotland, and had moved his headquarters from the west where he was vulnerable to Viking attacks, to the neighbourhood of Scone and Forteviot. Here he was no longer on the main Viking trade route to Ireland, and he seems to have been strong enough to discourage any would-be settlers. He also transferred the relics of St Columba from Iona to Dunkeld, making it the religious and ecclesiastical focus of the new kingdom. And, though Scone had in due course to yield precedence to Dunfermline, and Dunkeld to St Andrews, all lie within our area. Right up to the time of the Reformation, there is no doubt where the nerve centre of Scotland lay. Kings lived and held their councils here, and, as late as the fourteenth century, more charters were issued from Perth and Scone than from Edinburgh and Holyrood, or indeed anywhere else. As late as the sixteenth century, Dundee was still third, and Perth fourth, city in importance.

So far as is known, the district was not the first to receive Christianity, whether at the hands of Ninian, Kentigern or Columba, but Culdee communities at Dull and at Abernethy date from the generation after Columba – and Dunkeld, Brechin, St Andrews, Dunblane and Muthill follow not long after. Dunfermline's great days date from its adoption by St Margaret, Malcolm Canmore's queen, in the eleventh century; those of St Andrews from the arrival of the relics of that saint and from the founding of its cathedral in the twelfth century. From the tenth to the twelfth centuries come the two Irish-inspired round towers of Brechin and Abernethy, and a number of square towers such as those at St Andrews, Resten-neth (where the lowest storey may be older still), Dunblane, Markinch and Muthill. Most of the monasteries, which in the twelfth century were concentrated in Fife and Angus, were effectively destroyed at the time of the Reformation but there are substantial remains at Dunfermline, Inchcolm and Arbroath.

Wallace, according to Blind Harry, was at school in Dundee, and certainly campaigned against Edward I in these parts. Bruce was crowned at Scone, defeated at Methven, signed the famous Declaration at Arbroath, and was buried at Dunfermline. The countryside has almost as many castles as Aberdeenshire, from the earliest and simplest to the Renaissance work of Elcho and Falkland Palace. Dunkeld and the little burghs of Fife flourished before Edinburgh, let alone Glasgow, grew – and their domestic architecture, preserved by the National Trust for Scotland, is part of our heritage.

At the beginning of the Reformation, John Knox first celebrated the Holy Communion service in public at Montrose in 1556; he preached his famous sermon against idolatry in St John's Kirk in Perth, and was present during the siege of St Andrews. But, with the growth of Edinburgh, and still more with the move of James VI to London, the district inevitably lost something of its importance. And it tended, for a time, to look back rather than forward. James Graham, the great marquis, was born at Montrose and educated at St Andrews, but the future lay with the other great marquis – of Argyll – who burnt the bonnie braes of Airlie because the Ogilvys were unquestioning in their support for the monarchy. Perthshire too provided many supporters for the Jacobite cause; Murrays and Drummonds, Stewarts, Robertsons and Oliphants among others, and many estates were forfeited in the eighteenth century as a result. Inverkeithing and Sheriffmuir were defeats, and the victory of Killiecrankie was hard paid for.

Eventually, during the later eighteenth century, the agrarian changes brought prosperity to potentially very fertile land, though the process involved, only too often, as much harshness for individual lives as did the industrial revolution for those of the cottage weavers displaced by the machinery in the factories of Dundee and Kirkcaldy. And, if actual slavery was abolished in the coal mines of Fife, that did not bring good wages, nor,

always, enlightened employers. But it was a time of great
wealth for the few, whether it came from agricultural rents or
from the profits of industry.

Another thing which Perth, Angus and Fife have in common is a history of excellence and of innovation in education.
Whatever may be thought of the tradition that there was a
college of some sort at Dull in the times of St Fillan, there is no
question of the primacy of St Andrews as Scotland's oldest
university, one much loved by its students. James Melville
"lyked the schollar's life the best" and, though it was no
luxurious one, the food in the early collegiate days compared
very favourably with that at many English places of learning at
the time: 4oz bread at breakfast and supper, with 8oz at dinner;
broth and a dish of meat, or on fast days fish, at dinner, and
vegetables and beer. There were certain restrictions on ostentation in dress (but no more than for other classes of young men)
and hair was not to be so long that it hid the ears; but
out-of-door recreation was encouraged with the exception of
football, a dangerous game, then as well as now, and one which
already led to violence on the terraces. Even a poor student
could say "I had my necessary of my father, but no more; for
archery and golf I had bow, arrows, club and balls, but not a
purse for Catchpull* and tavern, yet now and then I learned
and used so much both of the hand and racket catch as might
serve for a moderate and wholesome exercise of the body."
And he acted in plays and had musical evenings with his
friends. And, when he found the work hard, his regent gave
him a bed in his own chambers so that he could give him
private tuition in the evenings. With St Andrews in the
forefront of theological thinking and the first to introduce
Greek, it must have been exciting intellectually too.

Nor were the schools behindhand. Greek came to St
Andrews because Andrew Melville had learnt it at Montrose
which, like all the chief burghs had its Grammar School. Nor
were these Grammar Schools confined to Grammar, i.e., Latin;
James Melville learnt French at his. By the mid-seventeenth
century not only all burghs had schools but many villages. All
the parishes in the Dunfermline presbytery of Fife had a

* Real- or Royal-Tennis, from the Dutch word *Kaatsspel.*

schoolmaster: thirteen out of fourteen in the Kirkcaldy presbytery and seventeen out of nineteen in St Andrews and in
Cupar.*

By the mid-eighteenth century, some of the schools were
beginning to have a reputation outside their own locality.
Perth Grammar School had always drawn in the sons of
Perthshire lairds such as John Campbell of Carwhin later
chamberlain to the second Earl of Breadalbane, and his
kinsman John Campbell, an illegitimate son of the Earl's
younger brother, who was to become a power in the land as
the first Cashier of the Bank of Scotland. A few years later, the
village of Crieff was prospering (so the factor for the forfeited
estates after the 1745 wrote) because people were settling there
so as to send their children to its school. And this, in spite of
the fact that they had had a serious setback only a few years
before, when from 1723 to 1742 they had been unable to get
rid of a schoolmaster who was guilty of "drinking to excess,
enticing or forcing others to drink to excess . . . neglect of his
schools, ludicrous behaviour in them and cruel usage to their
scholars . . . coming drunk into school and ludicrously dancing,
fencing and tumbling and making the scholars dance, contrary
to their inclination and to the grief of their parents".

He was also a Jacobite in a town that was Hanoverian in
sympathy. His insobriety must have been a great grief to the
Jacobite laird of Gask, who was thus forced to send his son
away to board, aged eight, to another school with a high
reputation at Dunfermline; the terms are set out in the following letter:

Sir,
    I am very sensible of what I owe you for enclining to trust
me with the care of your only son, etc, of so tender an age; and if
he come here, I assure you he shall be very carefully looked after.
My conditions are six guineas a quarter, when they sleep with a
bedfellow; of which four go for their Entertainment, and two for
teaching. If you desire your son shall sleep alone, I think it would
be best to send the chair-bed with him, in case it should not be
made so right here. I have no room where it can stand just now,
but one where there are two beds already. After our next vacation,

* T. C. Smout, *A History of the Scottish People*, p.88.

which will be in August, I intend Lord Elcho's room for the Master of Nairn, provided he does not return, as I have reason to expect he will; and in that case your son's bed might stand there, and then he will have nobody at all in the room with him save the Master. I can only add with my humble duty to Mrs Oliphant, that I am

Sir,

Your most obliged and humble servant,

F. PATTERSON.

As your son's bed does not take up the room of another, you will pay no more than the rest.

Dunfermline, March 17, 1732

In this case, the choice may have been to secure a private school with a suitably Jacobite flavour.

At the turn of the century, Perth led the way in Scotland with the founding of an Academy to teach utilitarian subjects rather than Latin, while in some of the smaller villages, no praise could be too high for the schoolmasters at Aberdalgie (*see* p. 111) and Fearnan (*see* p. 71). At Perth, the first Prospectus

> . . . was extremely ambitious, including higher arithmetic, mathematics, geography, logic, composition, algebra, Euclid, differential calculus, plane and spherical trigonometry, mensuration of surfaces and solids, navigation, fortification, analytical geometry, conic sections; natural philosophy in the form of statics, dynamics, hydrostatics, pneumatics, optics and astronomy; and, later, chemistry – heat, light, the spectrum, chemical affinity, atomic theory, the laws of combination, nomenclature, notations, gases, acids, alkalies and so on. It claimed to have carried out most of its original intention and it is worth recording that the oldest Scottish science notebook in existence was written at the Perth Academy in 1777.*

By 1837, joined by the Grammar School, it had added Latin, Greek and Ancient Geography, Elocution, History, French, Italian, Spanish and German.

This was a time, too, for men of goodwill to leave substantial sums to endow schools. In 1804, Lieutenant Andrew

* James Scotland, *History of Scottish Education.*

Waid left all his money to found a school in his native Anstruther. Daniel Stewart's most famous benefaction was to Edinburgh, but he was born the son of a crofter in Strathtay and he endowed a village school there too. John Morgan left £70,000 to found his Academy in Dundee, and only a few years later William Harris of the same town left £20,000 to the High School there, and another £10,000 to found Harris Academy. Cupar got the Bell-Baxter High School, and St Andrews its Madras Academy, to put into practice the pupil-teacher theories worked out by Andrew Bell in India. Most of these have now passed to state control but without loss of their founders' intentions; Perthshire, Angus and Fife have all prided themselves on being in the forefront of educational advance.

If good schools abound, so do great gardens. The sixteenth century is represented by Edzell with its box hedges clipped into Latin mottoes and its flowers planted out in heraldic colours; the seventeenth by Sir William Bruce's gardens at Balcaskie and Kinross; the eighteenth by the Versailles-like Drummond Castle (*see* plate 18). More recent, but famous, are Glendoick, Keillour and Branklyn, while Falkland is in a category of its own. These are only a few of those to be seen, and the list published each year by the Scottish Gardens Opening Scheme is essential for anyone in the area.

So far as economic life is concerned, coal is confined to Fife, but textiles have always been a source of employment in towns throughout the area, and Aberdeen-Angus cattle in the country, the black polled breed which is such an efficient converter of pasture into the best beef. Though its strongest strain originally came from Buchan, its founding fathers were largely Angus men in the early part of the nineteenth century: Hugh Watson of Keillor, Lord Panmure, William Fullerton of Ardoe, and later of Ardestie, the Earl of Southesk; even the great W. McCombie, who farmed at Tillyfour in Aberdeen-shire, came originally of Angus families. And, when the Aberdeen-Angus Society was formed in 1879, Perth was chosen as its headquarters.

I wrote, in the companion book on Argyll in this series, that it would be unthinkable to write a Portrait of that county without mentioning their county regiment. The same is true of Perthshire, Angus and Fife, for they are the recruiting district of the Black Watch – 'Black' for no sinister reason, but for the darkness of the Government tartan which they have worn from their earliest days, and 'Watch' because their first duties were, as they have so often been since, in support of the civil power. The astonishing change which came over Argyll in the early part of the eighteenth century and only a little less immediately to Highland Perthshire, was due to the success of the Government in suppressing cattle thieving and similar forms of lawlessness; a success which was due, in no small part, to the Independent Companies of local men – Territorials to use a modern term – who were allowed to wear the kilt and to carry arms when those two cherished practices had been proscribed. Six companies of them were raised on the recommendation of General Wade in 1725 "of such Highlanders as are well affected to His Majesty's Government . . . commanded by officers speaking the language of the country . . . to be employed in disarming the Highlands, preventing depredations, bringing criminals to justice, and hindering rebels and attainted persons from inhabiting that part of the country".

When war came with Spain in 1739 the six independent companies, with four more newly raised, were embodied into a single regiment at Aberfeldy with Sir Robert Munro of Fowlis as their Lieutenant Colonel and effective commander. Scarlet tunics with buff facings now lightened their dark tartan. For a time their duties remained the same, but, as the war enlarged in scope and lingered on without success, the Government decided to use the Black Watch abroad. Common decency demanded that men, who had enlisted to keep the peace in their own country, should have been given some chance to withdraw, or, at least, have had the urgent needs of the country explained to them. Instead they were marched to London on the pretext that they were to be reviewed by the King, who in fact had already left for the Continent.

That in the circumstances, and under the impression that

they were going to be sent to certain death by fever in the West Indies, a few deserted, was only to be expected; that more did not do so is surprising. Three soldiers were shot in the Tower in front of their comrades and a number of others were deported to the fever ridden islands.

> It is impossible to avoid a belief that the Hanoverian Government's vindictive punishment of the mutineers did much to encourage, fortify and enlarge the menace to itself of the Jacobite Rebellion of 1745 . . . of the mutineers sent into exile, nine were Camerons, and four Stewarts . . . and among others were MacGregors, Macintyres, Grants, Robertsons, Macdonalds and Frasers; all of them belonging to the clans that supported Charles Edward . . . of the three shot, two were Macphersons.*

The astonishing thing was that, within months, the regiment had won its first honours by a magnificent rearguard action at Fontenoy. Munro proved to be a great trainer of men, the first of a long series. The next notable engagement was in 1756 against the French in North America. When General Abercromby launched them in a disastrous frontal attack on the fortress of Ticonderoga, they lost, in a day, two-thirds of their strength either dead or badly wounded.†

From 1775 to 1789 the regiment was continuously abroad, fighting throughout the War of American Independence, and they did not have long at home, when they got there, before they were again committed to battle on the Continent and in Africa. By now they had become the 42nd (the Royal Highland) Regiment of Foot and had adopted the famous 'red hackle'. At Alexandria, their gallantry in a landing operation earned them the Sphinx in their regimental badge.

Incidentally, it was not only their fighting record which had earned them tributes but their reputation for sobriety, discipline and fitness; but sobriety was not easy to maintain under the appalling conditions and injustices which soldiers had to suffer in the nineteenth century, especially during long periods of inaction in isolated garrisons overseas. Nor was the situation improved by the need to rely increasingly on recruits from Lowland towns, and by a temporary influx of officers less

---

* E. and A. Linklater, *History of the Black Watch*.
† Those who were killed included Duncan Campbell of Inverawe whose well-authenticated ghost story is told in *Portrait of Argyll* in this series.

devoted to the service, less imbued with the spirit of comrade-
ship between commanders and commanded when both spoke
the Gaelic. Even where this still existed, the right example did
not always come from above. The latest history of the regiment
has a delightful story of "Colonel Dickson of Kilbucho, who
was known as a toper of such generous appetite that one of his
men, sentenced to be flogged for drunkenness and already
strapped to the halberds, was said to have shouted out 'Hey,
Kilbuckie, you're no going to let them flog an auld drunken
loon, just like yourself'. According to the legend, Colonel
Dickson had him released at once."*

The Peninsular War restored discipline, and the 42nd
displayed it in the Retreat to Corunna – incidentally their men
carried their fellow-countryman Moore when he was wounded – and in all the major engagements including Burgos and
Salamanca, and the march into France, and then notably at
Quatre Bras and Waterloo. At the former, the controlled fire
of an uncompleted square beat off a charge by the French
cavalry. The Battle of Alma claimed its casualties in the
Crimea – and disease, less so, though, than in many regiments,
but it was a very tough time. One of the worst chores was
having to manhandle supplies and ammunition and even the
guns themselves up from sea-level to the high ground above
Sebastopol – being turned into what the men called "damned
commissariat mules". A lesser annoyance came after a brief rest
away from Balaclava:

> Characteristically, Colonel Cameron did not allow the regiment
> to relax in the warmth and quiet of Kertsch; he drilled a different
> company each day, so that efficiency did not slip, and insisted that
> the men be as immaculate as though they were in Edinburgh
> Castle. Their anger, therefore, was justifiable when they returned
> to Sebastopol in July to discover that their feather bonnets, which
> had been left there, had been used by the sacrilegious French to
> make feather beds, and were squashed flat. However there was no
> end to the qualities of that excellent headgear, and, with the wire
> frame straightened out, and the hackle cocked out, it was as good
> as new though no doubt suffused with a garlic scent.†

Sir Colin Campbell who commanded the Highland Brigade

* Linklater, op. cit.
† Linklater, op. cit.

of the 42nd, 73rd (and the 93rd) was told by General Pelissier that he thought the Highland soldiers the best in the world, a view with which Sir Colin's staff officer, an Englishman, agreed.

Service in India brought eight V.C.s but many deaths from cholera, in spite of heroic efforts by those in command to improve conditions by providing libraries and coffee rooms for off-duty times; and the sinking of the *Birkenhead* in 1852 cost the regiment fifty-six lives, as the soldiers on board remained at their stations as the ship went down lest the boats with the women and children in them should be over-crowded. The regiment was at Tel-el-Kebir, and right through the mis-management of the South African War. In the First World War, of the 50,000 who served with the Black Watch, 8000 were killed and nearly 20,000 wounded.

From the Second World War, as from the First, it is impossible to select names or incidents without being unfair. The 6th Territorial Battalion, detached from the 51st High-land Division in order to accommodate the 1st Battalion, saved the 5th Division by seizing and holding a bridge over the Lys Canal. Of the splendid fight of General Fortune's Division and the subsequent long years in a Prisoner of War Camp, it is still difficult to read without tears. The other regular Battalion, the 2nd, fought in the early days in Somali-land under General Wavell's command – the best known of all Black Watch officers, and the most courageous. "A large butcher's bill," he wrote to Churchill "is not necessarily evi-dence of good tactics", and he was never forgiven. The regiment was in Crete, in Tobruk in 1941, at Cassino – only those who were in those battles can fully appreciate the continued drain on resources. Meanwhile an entirely new 51st Division had come into being, with a new 1st Battalion who were joined by the 5th and the 7th (Territorial) Battalions. Highly trained but without any previous exposure to actual war, they were given pride of place in the first assault on the German minefields at Alamein. It was not their fault that a whole armoured corps was pushed up into their midst to complicate their operation before the break-through had been completed. But in the end, they had the satisfaction of chasing the enemy back all along the north coast of Africa and crossing to Sicily.

In the Far East, a Black Watch officer, Bernard Fergusson (later Lord Ballantrae), commanded one of the Chindit Columns with great personal distinction; and the 2nd Battalion found itself flown in behind the Japanese lines, "regular troops in a hazardous situation for which specialist volunteer units are generally called"; after which they showed further versatility by converting into a parachute Battalion. At the end, the 51st Division returned to Northern Europe to share in the crossing of the Rhine and the final defeat of tyranny.

Each of the Highland regiments would claim, I think, to be a family, but the Black Watch most of all; a family in which son succeeds father but also a family which accepts as sons all who serve in it, wherever they may come from. Something of how that spirit of family appears to outsiders who have served alongside them may be seen in books such as Ian Hay's *First Hundred Thousand* and a lesser known successor from the Second World War, *Men of Alamein* by Colonel Denholm Young, Chief Signals Officer to the 51st Division in that battle. Much to be recommended, too, is a visit to the Regimental Museum at Balhousie Castle in Perth, recently reopened after a serious, but fortunately not disastrous, fire.

Other regiments which have local connections are the Fife and Forfar Yeomanry, the Scottish Horse and the Cameronians. Yeomanry regiments were raised in both Fife and Forfar during the Napoleonic Wars, but the joint regiment really dates from the South African War in which about 500 officers and men took part. The regiment was still horsed when it went to Gallipoli in 1915 but later fought as infantry on the Western front. By 1939 they had been mechanized, fighting as part of the Royal Armoured Corps with the B.E.F. and in the later campaign to recover France. Their regimental march is "Wee Cooper o' Fife".

The origins of the Scottish Horse are unique in that they were first raised, not in Scotland, but in South Africa. When, towards the end of that war, Kitchener needed more mounted troops, the Highland Society of Johannesburg suggested that they should raise a body of cavalry from those of Scottish origin. Under the energetic leadership of the Marquis of Tullibardine, who had been seconded from the Horse Guards with whom he was serving, one regiment was soon raised in South Africa, and then another of volunteers from Australia and Scotland, especially from Perthshire, his own home. They saw extremely distinguished service both in that war and in the First World War, being rewarded in each case by immediate disbandment; in each case, too, this was followed by resurrection within a year. Some of its service in France had been as infantry but it was still fully mounted as late as 1936, only to be mechanized in 1940 and converted to medium artillery, one of its regiments serving in the Normandy landings and the other in Sicily and Italy. Its pipers wear the Tullibardine tartan and the family of the Dukes of Atholl have maintained their close connection; Lieutenant Colonel G. A. Murray, father of the present Duke, was killed serving with the regiment in Italy in 1945.

The Cameronians owed their Perthshire connection to the Cardwell reforms of 1881 when the 26th Regiment, the descendants of the Covenanters of the south-west – called after the Fifer, Richard Cameron – received as their second battalion the 90th Regiment, the Perthshire Light Infantry, and became the Scottish Rifles. Up to that time they had had little in common save an admiration for Sir John Moore. The 90th had been raised by Thomas Graham of Balgowan (later Lord Lynedoch), desperate after the loss of his deeply loved wife and vengeful against the French revolutionaries who had insulted her memory by breaking open her coffin as Graham was bringing it back to Scotland for burial at Methven. In 1794, he issued a Proclamation:

> To the Inhabitants of the County of Perth
> Being desirous that the regiment I have undertaken to raise and which I have the honour to command should bear the name of a country I am so much attached to I have obtained His Majesty's leave that it shall be called 'The   ᵔ Volunteers'. While I

flatter myself that the corps will prove worthy of such a distinguished name, allow me to hope that it will find in the spirit of the young men of the County, and in the zeal of the recruits, that preference and support which may make up for the want of the extensive influence and patronage which patronizes the other corps now recruiting. I need not assure all able-bodied volunteers that they will be received by the C.O. at the headquarters at Perth with the greatest attention and will meet with the most liberal treatment.

In fact, neither this battalion nor a second one which he raised were confined to Perthshire men. From the beginning the regiment was a light infantry, no doubt because of Graham's admiration for Moore, to whom he shortly afterwards became A.D.C., and with whom he was when the general was killed. They also acquired the nickname of the Greybreeks from the colour of their pantaloons. Up to the time of their linking, their most famous exploits had been at Alma and Sebastopol in the Crimean War and at Lucknow in the Indian Mutiny; in the former, they won two, in the latter six Victoria Crosses. As Cameronians they served in South Africa, and from 1914 to 1918 in France and the Middle East. At Neuve Chapelle in March 1915, one morning, twenty-three officers and 597 other ranks went into battle; by the end of that day, twenty-two officers and 447 other ranks had been killed or wounded. After comparable service at Dunkirk and Anzio and in Burma 1939-1945 and then in Aden in 1968, the Cameronians were disbanded at an intolerably moving ceremony recalling the traditions of the 26th. There had been no Scottish regiment with which they could share either their Covenanting background or their Riflemen's traditions.

II

PERTH – "THE FAIR CITY"

PERTH – formerly St Johnstown – is a fair city to live in. It is true that it might have been even fairer, had more been done to preserve the treasures of the past. Many fine buildings have been allowed to fall into decay and then have had to be pulled down, because they had become dangerous; or to make way for something more habitable, or more useful, or just more in keeping with passing fashions. What would one not give to have the sixteenth-century Gowrie House back again, or the Blackfriars' Monastery or the Charterhouse? One splendid medieval building remains, the High Kirk of St John's, "one of the noblest burghal churches that have survived to us in Scotland"; and there is much of interest from the eighteenth and early nineteenth centuries: the King James Hospital, the façade of the Salutation Hotel, the Waterworks (now imaginatively converted into a well-equipped Information Centre), Marshall Place overlooking the South Inch, and, beside the North Inch, Rose Terrace with the well-proportioned Old Academy building as its centre piece (*see* plate 1).

Yet it is not for its old buildings, as a rule, that a man chooses his home town, for few people can actually live in old houses; it is rather for the situation and the friendliness of its people. The casual tourist passing hurriedly through may find the High Street crowded on a Saturday afternoon, especially in the height of the summer, or the motorist be confused by its complex system of one-way streets, but he should wait till Sunday morning, and stand at the west end of South Street and look down its wide spaciousness to the trees of Kinnoull Hill; or, from the other end, on the Queen's Bridge, look back along South Street, again to green fields; or up the broad Tay to

30

Smeaton's Bridge (1766-1771) and the North Inch beyond; or downstream to Moncrieffe Island and the King James VI golf course. One of the great attractions of Perth, as of the larger Aberdeen, is its compactness, so that the countryside is always close at hand, and, because Perth like Aberdeen is embraced by hills, the green is visible from nearly everywhere. Perth's crowning glory is, of course, its river and the two open spaces that complement it, the South Inch astride the road to Edin-burgh, and the North Inch with its magnificent beeches and elms and chestnuts.

If Perth has a past to live down, it has a strong social sense today. Its Civic Trust and the Friends of St John's and its own Local Authority have done much to see that its citizens should be aware of, and preserve, their heritage; and their publications are a model of what such things should be – short, authori-tative, yet easily understood and a delight to look at: *Perth. A Town Survey by the Civic Trust*, 15p; *A History of St John's Kirk* by the late Dr W. Douglas Simpson; *Walks in Perth*, 10p. Value for money indeed. But vigilance is still necessary: an elected councillor was recently reported as saying that the Civic Trust "is as outmoded as the House of Lords".

The same civic sense is evident in private life too, in, say, the little gardens of Florence Place or the aptly named Rose Crescent, and in the enthusiasm which gives Perth not only a fortnight's Festival of the Arts but, throughout the year, thriving amateur orchestral and choral societies, and a profes-sional repertory theatre company with a deservedly high reputation. The local ice rink is the home of international curling; and the swimming baths and Bell's sports centre, the river and the Inches provide facilities for every sort of rec-reation.

As we saw in the first chapter, Perth lay on the line of the Romans' advance, but little is known of it in the following millennium and no definite date can be given for its beginnings as a centre of commercial exchange and industrial specializa-tion. Many factors must have contributed but especially its geographical position which makes it a natural centre of communications. Religion and politics played their part, too.

From the days of Kenneth MacAlpine, Scottish Kings were ceremonially enthroned on the Stone of Destiny at Scone nearby, and, from Bruce to James I, they were crowned there too. The King's presence at Scone or at Forteviot or, later on, at other castles in the neighbourhood, led to the granting of rich lands round about to his faithful followers. They, in their turn, provided the demand which would help a trading centre to grow. No less important would have been the needs of the religious communities.

Scone was an ecclesiastical centre before Kenneth MacAlpine arrived, and remained so, even though the great abbey was not founded until 1115. But it was Perth's geographical position which was paramount; the Tay was navigable up to Perth, and at Perth it was first possible to ford and indeed later, to build a bridge, and thus to facilitate north-south communications. Unfortunately a flood swept the bridge away in 1210, the same flood which swept away the king's castle just outside the city's boundaries. Only the year before, the town had received the official status of a royal burgh by a charter from King William, but, long before that, foreign merchants had been trading there. Its two broad parallel arteries, High Street and South Street (see plate 3), go back at least as far, and probably further. By the middle of the thirteenth century, "Perth was the second town in Scotland; second that is to Berwick and far ahead of Edinburgh, Aberdeen or Stirling in importance."*

In this thriving city were four great monasteries. Alexander II founded a Dominican or Blackfriars House in 1231, near the North Inch; Alexander III a Carmelite or Whitefriars House, and James I a Charterhouse in 1425, near the railway station, where King James's Hospital now stands. The fourth, the Franciscan or Greyfriars was founded by Laurence, first Lord Oliphant, and stood where a burial ground adjoins the South Inch. Not a stone of any of them survives. In their day, they had done the good work for which they had been founded, and the Blackfriars had, in addition, been a building of architectural distinction and had provided James I not only with comfortable lodgings but with a "fair playing place for tennis". But, as elsewhere, they declined and a description of

* Prof. A. A. M. Duncan, *Perth, the First Century of the Burgh* (Transactions of the Perthshire Society of Natural Science, 1973).

them by a distinguished traveller, who saw them just before
their destruction at the hands of the Reformers, is highly
critical. He and his companion are supposed to be looking
down over the town from the south-west shoulder of Kinnoull
Hill:

> The warden of the Franciscan or Greyfriars Monastery, that
> building you see nearest us outside the walls, is well known to be
> the favorer of the new doctrines. There are but eight of them in
> that huge house – good canty fellows, all of them, – known to
> keep an excellent table, and willing to let all the world alone, so
> that they are not disturbed at dinner-time. But then they are in
> constant dread of the firebrands in that princely building you see
> on the same side of the town farther to the west, who can write,
> though their rules forbid them to speak. Austere fellows they are,
> those Carthusians, and pride themselves not a little on this their
> only establishment in Scotland and on the odour they and it are in
> with the Queen Regent. But for all their austerity, there are queer
> stories told of them and the nuns in the convent of St Leonard's
> and the Magdalenes, both of which are a short distance to the
> southward. Certain jolly skippers, too, from the coast, under cover
> of a few oysters or haddocks, wink and glance knowingly at this
> *monasterium vallis virtutis,* as the monks call it, while they hint
> about the many good and ghostly customers they have in Perth.
> Then there are those Dominicans – beggars they profess themselves
> to be, like the Franciscans, and sturdy ones they are. See how
> comfortably they have set themselves down in that palace you see
> without the walls on the north side of the town just over by the
> castle there. Ah, these Blackfriars are your men for the pulpit. If
> you want a good easy confessor, go to the chapels of St Paul's or St
> Catherine's you see peering above the trees, on the west side of the
> town, and there find one of the Carmelites or Whitefriars from
> Tullilum, a monastery still farther to the west, hid from us by the
> wood; but if you want a discourse that will keep you quaking for
> a week, go to the church of the Dominicans. And well worthy it is
> of a visit – such walls, such aisles, such windows; the gardens, too,
> and the gilten arbour. No wonder our monarchs forsook that old
> gloomy palace [the castle] at the end of the bridge for the sweet
> arbour and the soft beds of the Blackfriars.

It was from the gardens of the Blackfriars that the ailing

Robert III watched the Battle of the Clans in 1396. His method of trying to end the perpetual feuding between Clan Chattan and Clan Kay was to arrange a grand trial by combat between thirty contestants on either side, who were to fight to the death. £14 2s. 11d. was spent on building, on the North Inch, the enclosure within which they were to fight, and in that barbarous age this Roman carnival attracted lusting spectators from as far afield as England and France. Clan Chattan turned up one man short, but a local man volunteered to step into the breach on condition that, if he survived, he should have his keep for life – Hal o' the Wynd of Scott's *Fair Maid of Perth*. One version of the story has it that the King ended the ghastly spectacle when only one Kay remained alive; another that, when that stage was reached, the single survivor escaped by swimming the Tay, while all eleven remaining of Clan Chattan were too badly wounded to pursue. Both agree that Hal survived, though some say that, afterwards, he could not say which side he had been fighting for. And accounts differ as to whether the feuding ceased thereafter.

It was in his lodgings at the Blackfriars that James I died. His arbitrary acts had made him enemies among the more powerful of his subjects, amongst whom were his uncle, James Stewart, Earl of Atholl, and Atholl's grandson, and Patrick Graham of Kincardine. Stewart opened the doors one night in February 1437 to admit Graham and a party of desperate men. The King was prevented from escaping by the fact that the windows of his chamber were barred; one of the ladies-in-waiting tried to keep the murderers out by thrusting her arm through the sockets of the door but it was easily broken; the King felled two men in self-defence but was eventually struck down by Graham, who denied him even the consolation of a confessor. The Queen, who had witnessed the scene and had herself been hurt, extracted a barbarous revenge. Atholl was tortured for two days before being disembowelled on the third. Graham was nailed naked to a pillar and then pulled to pieces with pincers.

James VI, too, was nearly murdered in Perth. In 1600, the most magnificent private house in Perth was that of the

Ruthvens, Earls of Gowrie, down on the waterfront where the
Sheriff Court now stands. They also owned Huntingtower on
the road to Crieff. Of this family, William, fourth Lord
Ruthven, was a builder, a collector, and a great planter of trees,
and, as a thinker in advance of his contemporaries, was
suspected of witchcraft; he was also one of those concerned in
the murder of Rizzio, Mary Queen of Scots' secretary and
favourite. He was pardoned but again fell foul of authority in
the person of the Regent Lennox, controller of the fifteen-
year-old King. Gowrie, with the Earl of Mar and others,
including the Master of Glamis, induced the boy to spend the
night at Huntingtower, where they worked on him to banish
Lennox and then made it quite clear that he was now their
prisoner. When James burst into tears, the Master of Glamis
bluntly told him that it was better that "bairns greet than
bearded men", as they were doing under the oppression of the
Regent. But the King's captivity only lasted ten months and,
though there was another pardon, it did not last long and this
Lord Gowrie was executed at Stirling Castle 1585.

The third Earl also met an untimely end, after the incident
of the Gowrie Plot in the family's Town House. Again James
was returning from his favourite occupation of hunting when
he was persuaded (or decided) to go to dinner with the Earl
and his brother. They dined without other companions, after
which the King disappeared, and some thought he had left the
house and went out to see if they could find him. To their
horror they suddenly heard a shout from an upper turret and
the King crying out "I am murdered! Treason! Treason! My
Lord of Mar, Help! Help!" They burst back into the house and
eventually into the upper turret where the King claimed that
Gowrie's brother Alexander Ruthven had attacked him. In
the resulting fracas, both Gowrie and his brother were stabbed
to death. Even at the time, there were those who disbelieved
the King's story and declared that the whole thing was a
carefully planned scheme of James's to eliminate the Ruthvens
from the political scene, and, on the whole, modern historians
seem to agree. Nearly as many books have been written about
the incident as about the Casket Letters, and the whole truth

will never be known. To my mind, it is improbable in the extreme that James, who was so terrified of being assassinated that he always wore a thickly quilted doublet, should have had the iron nerve to have put himself so completely in the hands of men whom he believed to be so dangerous that they had to be murdered; he was not a shedder of blood anyway. It seems to me much more likely that the Ruthvens were in truth seeking control of the King's person to exact some concession and that their plot misfired.

Other neighbouring landowners were closely connected with the city's history and had large houses in the Watergate, but it was those who made their fortunes by commerce who were the benefactors, from the Mercers in the Middle Ages to the Bells and the Dewars in the nineteenth and twentieth centuries.

John Mercer, the first of whom we have record, is said to have given three mills in the city to Malcolm Canmore in the eleventh century which Malcolm's successor Robert III gifted back to the inhabitants; the water to power them came from the River Almond by a lade which fed the wash-houses near the bus stance and is still open alongside West Mill Street; it is also visible (and more comfortably) from the foyer of the City Mills Hotel, a skilful conversion of an eighteenth-century mill built on the old site.

Another John Mercer acquired the lands of Meiklour in 1162 and these are still in the hands of a direct descendant 800 years later. Another was Provost of Perth in the fourteenth century and one of the richest merchants in the kingdom. Yet others, in due course, gained possession of Huntingtower, Gorthy and Aldie, the last also having a house on the corner of the High Street and the Watergate, and a burial vault in St John's Kirk. There is an old tradition that it was a Mercer who gave the North Inch to the burgh; certainly it was a Mercer who handed over Huntingtower to be preserved and opened to the public by the Ministry of the Environment (or the Office of Works as it then was).

In the early days, Perth was primarily a market town for the sale of local produce, that of the fields around, and that of the burgh's artisans, weavers, dyers, smiths and other craftsmen;

but so long as ships were small enough to navigate the river, the big money came from commerce further afield. Merchants were not, on the whole, specialists but would import and export a wide variety of goods. Later, as capitalism led to the organization of the textile industry on a larger scale, with one man buying the raw materials and employing many craftsmen to process them for him to sell, manufacturers might become rich too, and the line between merchant and manufacturer become less clear than it had been earlier, in the days when the latter had been wholly excluded from the government of the burgh.

Much light has recently been thrown on the development of Perth in the fourteenth century by excavations on a large site adjoining the High Street. Some of the finds are on view in the Perth Museum and include everyday utensils such as bone combs and wooden bowls, and rarer objects including a gilded spur of the twelfth century and an ornate ampulla of the thirteenth century depicting the death of St Thomas of Canterbury. But, because textiles perish so quickly and are rarely found in any state of preservation, it is the fragments of all sorts of stuffs that have given most pleasure to the archaeologists, especially the fourteenth-century lace.

A Perth merchant whose name has become a household word was David Sandeman who came to Perth from Alyth in 1681. One of his sons, William, built up a dyeing business at Luncarty, where in summer the fields would be white with cloth, bleaching in the sun, a process helped in those days by spreading cow dung on it! His descendants continued in that business until it was merged with Pullars* in the nineteenth century, and they also included the distinguished mathematician Professor Archibald Sandeman, to whom we owe the Sandeman Free Library. George, another son of David, lived in the Watergate and was the father of the founder of the wine firm which did so much to make port popular in the eighteenth century. It is remarkable that between 1765 and 1923 the firm had only three heads, George until 1841 (he was one of the principal raisers of money for the Old Perth Academy), his nephew till 1868 and then Albert Glas Sandeman till 1923.

* 'Pullars of Perth' really fathered the dry-cleaning industry and at one time were the largest employers in the town, with 2000 employees.

The Glas name was introduced to the family when two other of David's sons married daughters of the Rev. John Glas, evicted minister of Tealing and founder of a somewhat exclusive Secession sect the Glassites; in it, unanimity was secured "in all proceedings by the simple expedient of expelling any member who obstinately differs in any opinion from the majority". So many of the family joined, that the members of the sect were locally known as Sandemanians, though sometimes less politely as Kail Kirkers because of the substantial meal with which they followed their weekly Communion. The old building in which they worshipped still stands, opposite St Paul's Church at the west end of the High Street.

Another civic benefactor was Thomas Hay Marshall, Provost at the turn of the eighteenth and nineteenth centuries. During his time, the size of the North Inch was doubled, Rose Terrace and Marshall Place were built by the North and the South Inches and the Old Perth Academy for which he gave the site. Grateful citizens subscribed for a memorial to him in the form of a statue in George Street and a building which houses the museum.

About the time that Marshall died, Arthur Bell was born, founder of the whisky firm. Arthur K. Bell, his son, turned a fairly small family firm into a great exporting concern and amassed a fortune which was the origin of the Gannochy Trust. His benefactions started with the building of a model housing estate, round which he used to walk every morning before going to work. Then, as a keen cricketer himself, he made a cricket ground, Doocot Park, adjoining the house where he lived. The young and the old were his special concern, and, when his widow died, his house was made into a home for old folk. Recently, a book *Pride of Perth* by Jack House has told how the business was further expanded by his successors, and has listed some of the Gannochy Trust benefactions: £600,000 for a new sewage system for Perth and £125,000 to build an indoor Sports Centre for every sort of activity; £500,000 for twelve flatlets and work centre for spastics; £125,000 for a new hall of residence at St Andrews University, and gifts to Stirling and Strathclyde. And these are

only a part of a wide range of gifts to schools and to organiz-
ations helping the elderly as well as the young.

Just about the same time that the first Arthur Bell started up
on his own, John Dewar, a joiner who came from Dull near
Aberfeldy, opened up his wine and spirit shop at 111 High
Street, where Woolworths now stands. "The duty on whisky
in those days was 18d. per proof gallon (£27,09 now) and this
was thought to be so iniquitous that whisky smuggling was
prevalent, and this made legitimate trading difficult. The
whisky itself was immature and raw as no attempt was made
to age or blend it; and it was very strong, round about 10 o.p.
It was sold from kegs or jars since no one had yet come up with
the idea of putting whisky up in bottles."* For many years the
business was largely local, but by the time that John took his
eldest son John Alexander into partnership, orders were coming in regularly from Inverness, Edinburgh and Glasgow.
When John died in 1880, J. A. took in his brother Thomas
who did much to expand the trade from a London office. In
1915 they merged with Buchanans and ten years later joined
the Distillers Co. The elder brother became Lord Forteviot and
the younger Lord Dewar and both followed the Perth tradition of benefaction. Lord Dewar, though he had spent most of
his life in England, had not forgotten his days at the Old Perth
Academy, and bought Kinnoull Hill for the city in 1924. Lord
Forteviot's gifts included a new wing at the Perth Royal
Infirmary, a model lodging house in Skinnergate, considerable
help with the restoration of St John's Kirk, and the founding of
a charitable trust for local purposes.

The founders of the two whisky firms had been contemporaries as well as rivals, and there is an apocryphal story about
them which is too good to omit. They were both due to attend
a church meeting one morning and, finding themselves too
early, decided to have a little refreshment. "What will you
have?" said Bell (or Dewar, according to your sympathies). "A
Bell's", replied Dewar. "It would not do to go into the meeting
smelling of whisky."

More recently, the third giant (and now the largest single
employer in the town), the General Accident Assurance

---

* From notes on the history of John Dewar & Sons for which I am obliged
to Mr J. A. McCowan.

Company have beautified the left bank of the river with gardens above and below Smeaton's Bridge; above the bridge is an extension to their offices; below is a riverside walk and garden, gifted to the public in memory of their chairman, Sir Stanley Norie-Miller.

He and his father Sir Francis Norie-Miller managed the company from 1887 to 1971, and the story is a remarkable one. When the Employers' Liability Bill was made law in 1880, a number of local people – an estate agent, a lawyer, a banker, an agricultural auctioneer, and several land-owners – determined that if premiums had to be paid, they should not go out of the neighbourhood. They issued their first policy in 1885 but, since none of them had any experience of insurance, and their capital was limited, their beginnings were not very successful, until, two years later, they invited a young man of twenty-seven to be secretary; although he was assured of a steady future with the company he was serving as Accident Manager, he left it for this small ailing company in distant Perth, overruling his father's protest with – "I feel I can control; I want a whole company to control."

Francis Norie-Miller could not only control; he could infuse his own tremendous energy into all he worked with. Within a year, he had opened a number of branches throughout the country and secured 800 agents. Within four years the capital of the company had increased from £2,500 to £100,000. He travelled untiringly all over Britain, 25,000 miles in the first year, and he had a flair for seeing lines of new business which might prove profitable. He was first into the field of burglary insurance in 1890; motor insurance in 1896; and later in no-claims bonuses, and was among the first in householders' comprehensive insurance. In early days, he insisted that every claim should be settled on the day that it was adjusted, and accompanied it with a personal letter. Later, he travelled all over the world to establish General Accident, so that now two thirds of their premium income comes from overseas.

Sadly, his eldest son was killed in the First World War, but the second, Stanley, returned safely, with a Military Cross, and changed from a career at the Bar to join the company. In due course, he succeeded his father as General Manager and then as Chairman. Now, General Accident is the third largest U.K. company in terms of non-life business – half of it in the motor class – and has a very large life business too. And all the while its head office has remained firmly in Perth – and will do so. Only recently has a new site been obtained at Cherry Bank on the western outskirts of the town for a new building to get all their departments under one roof.

One last gift may be mentioned, that of Branklyn Garden to the National Trust for Scotland. Created by Mr and Mrs John Renton between 1922 and 1967 it lies on the south-eastern outskirts of the town and has been called "the finest two acres of garden in the country". For the layman, the rhododendrons and the blue meconopsis, followed by the great range of lilies and hydrangeas, the *Pieri forrestii* and the lovely eucryphia, are the most exciting, but its countless rarities also make it a garden for the expert. And it is not just a spring garden; it is designed to carry on throughout the high summer to the autumn foliage.

In business, it is not only the giants who make Perth notable. There are an unusually large number of smaller firms which have remained in the day to day control of the same families through several generations, and where one may be sure of an old-fashioned welcome. Proudfoot's the watchmakers is one, and Hume's the ironmonger; and though Garvie and Syme has moved from the High Street to the southern outskirts it is still run by the Garvies. McEwen's in St John Street is a family firm, and Caird's and Rattray's. Love's have been furnishing for more than a century and there is still a Mr Fraser at Macdonald Fraser, the auctioneers who preside over the famous bull sales each February and October. Ex-Lord Provost David Thomson is Chairman of Peter Thomson; Gloag's have sold wines and spirits since 1800 and there has been a Gloag as proprietor or director ever since. These are but some of the names that have long served Perth.

Another recent centenary was that of Alastair and James Cairncross in the silversmith's business founded by their grand-father. People come from far to buy their own-designed jewellery and to see the Abernethy pearl, the finest freshwater pearl found in recent history – so named because it was fished from the Tay by William Abernethy, a full-time local professional pearl fisherman. The Tay, which has been known for its pearls since Roman days, is one of the few rivers still clean enough to provide a home for the mussel which forms these jewels to protect itself against irritant grains of sand. They range from white, through grey, to gold and lilac, and

> when compared with natural or oriental pearls, the Scots pearl is like a plum still on the tree with the bloom on it, whilst the former are plums picked from the tree, polished and put in the shop window. There is a lovely untouched quality about them which is highly distinctive so that they are obviously real and cannot be mistaken for anything other than what they are.

These family businesses are what have made Perth, but in order to keep unemployment down (the rate at present is below not merely the Scottish average but the U.K. average) the Local Authority has pursued a policy of building advance factories on the southern, and more recently the northern, edges of the town, and a number of light industrial concerns have been attracted.

Of the buildings which the visitor will wish to see, St John's Kirk must take precedence. Apart from its situation in its square, it is not particularly striking from outside, except for the tower and graceful spire, but inside one is immediately struck with its size and a feeling of awe. Its modern glass would make it dark but for the skilful lighting which brings out very successfully the vaulting of the central tower. Apart from this and Halkerstone's tower, the roofing is wooden, old in the choir, modern in the nave. The latter is part of the skilful restoration work done in the 1920s by Sir Robert Lorimer, as a memorial to those who fell in the First World War.

In the south transept is a display of the chief treasures of the church plate, a baptismal basin of *c.* 1590, a sixteenth-century Nuremberg cup said to have been gifted by Mary Queen of Scots, and two seventeenth-century English Steeple cups, together with some lovely modern work. In this transept too are fifteen of the outstanding collection of bells, some sixty-three in all. Those now in use are a carillon of thirty-four modern bells with one 28-cwt bourdon of the early sixteenth century. They chime the quarters and the hours, and can play airs. Seven others date from before the Reformation – more than in any other church in the British Isles – and one from the time of Bannockburn. But the greatest glory of the building is the choir "which gives a splendid impression of spaciousness, comparable to a cathedral, a characteristic due mainly to the perfect proportion". So, Dr W. Douglas Simpson in his *Brief History* of the church which combines, as one would expect from its distinguished author, learning with clarity and ease of understanding, and not only describes the church but places it firmly in its historical context. On this site, though in an earlier building, Edward I celebrated St John's Day in 1296 "with circumstances of high feudal solemnity, regaling his friends in the city, creating new knights, and solacing himself with his barons. In the midst of these rejoicings, messengers arrived from the unhappy Balliol, announcing his submission and imploring peace".*

In the building which we can see today, John Knox preached the sermon on 11th May 1559 and set off the outburst of image-breaking. He and others had been summoned to Stirling by Mary of Guise, the Regent, to abjure their doctrines but he preferred to issue a defiant challenge, choosing Perth as the site, partly because it had city walls, unlike most Scottish towns. Unfortunately he aroused passions that he could not control, and an incident followed, as far-reaching as when Jenny Geddes threw her stool at the preacher in St Giles's.

> The multitude was so inflamed, that neither could the exhortation of the preacher, nor the commandment of the magistrate, stay them from destroying the places of idolatry. The manner whereof was this: . . . it chanced next day, which was the eleventh of May, after that the Preachers were exiled, after the sermon, which was vehement against idolatry, that a priest in contempt would go to the Mass. And to declare his presumption, he would open up an Altar-piece which stood upon the High Altar. There stood beside certain godly men, and among others a young boy who cried with

* P. F. Tytler, *History of Scotland*, Vol. I, p.45.

a loud voice, "This is intolerable that when God by his word hath plainly damned idolatry, we shall stand and see it used in despite." The priest hereat offended, gave the child a great blow; who in anger took up a stone, and casting it at the priest did hit the tabernacle and brake down the image; and immediately the whole multitude that was about, cast stones, and put hands to the said tabernacle and to all other monuments of idolatry; which they dispatched before the tent men in the town were advertised (for the most part were gone to dinner). Which noised abroad, the whole multitude convened, not of the gentlemen, neither of them that were earnest professors, but of the rascal multitude, who finding nothing to do in that Church, did run without deliberation to the Black and Grey Friars; and notwithstanding that they had within them very strong guards kept for their defence, yet were their gates incontinent broken open. The first invasion was upon the idolatry; and thereafter the common people began to seek some spoil; and in very deed the Grey Friars was a place so well provided, that unless honest men had seen the same, we would have feared to have reported what provision they had. Their sheets, blankets, bedding and coverings were such as no Earl in Scotland hath better; their napery was fine. There were but eight persons in the convent, and yet had eight punscheons of salt beef (consider the time of year May 11th), wine, beer and ale, besides all store of victual. The like abundance was not in the Black Friars and yet there was more than became men professing Poverty. The spoil was permitted to the poor: for so had the preachers before threatened; . . . their conscience so pricked them that they permitted those hypocrites to take away what they could, of that which was in their places. The Prior of Charterhouse was permitted to take away with him even so much gold and silver as he could carry . . . they had no respect to their own particular profit but only to abolish idolatry, the places and monuments thereof; in which they were so busy and so laborious that, within two days, these three great places, monuments of idolatry, to wit, the Black and Grey Friars and the Charterhouse monks (a building of Wondrous cost and greatness) were so destroyed that the walls only did remain of these great edifications.*

Knox himself had not wanted damage to the buildings, only to remove the images within them, and the fabric of St John's was not damaged at that time; it was later neglect that

* Knox's own account, the spelling modernized.

rendered necessary so much restoration by Lorimer – neglect and incidents such as Montrose using the nave as a camp for his prisoners after Tippermuir, and the Cromwellians using it as a court house. Charles I was a reluctant listener to Presbyterian sermons in the Choir when he was in the hands of Argyll and the Scottish army; the Young Pretender, as a Roman Catholic, must have been almost as ill at ease when his Perth supporters arranged an Episcopal service for him there; more happily our present Queen gave thanks there at the time of her Silver Jubilee.

Having seen St John's, one cannot do better than spend a day following the guidance of the pamphlet *Walks in Perth*. Architecturally it is the eighteenth-century districts which are the most rewarding: Rose Terrace with the Old Academy in the centre and a house where Ruskin spent part of his childhood (he also contracted his ill-starred marriage in the town at Effie Gray's home, Bowerswell, now an Eventide Home); Atholl Crescent adjoins it at one end, Barossa Place at the other, both having some gems of little houses. Southwards runs George Street with the George Hotel. This has an early Victorian front and a modern addition behind, looking across the river. Not everyone will admire the new houses going up on the far bank, and it is sad that the old buildings there had to go, but the architects have taken a great deal of trouble with the grouping and the silhouette of the roof lines to form a pleasing composition. Opposite to the hotel is the museum and the art gallery. Not far away, in Tay Street, is St Matthew's Church with its dominant spire.

The other Regency terrace is Marshall Place facing south over the South Inch, not far from which the poet William Soutar spent part of his long illness, writing with equal facility in English and in Scots. One of his poems stands as the dedication to this book, another on page 65. Near the river is the Round House, the former waterworks, a graceful building designed by a gifted amateur, Dr Anderson, Rector of Perth Academy. Between the Inches, the High Street and South Street follow the medieval lay-out of the city (*see* plate 3). The former has not much to interest anyone other than the shopper, but the western end of Mill Street leads past an old mill. South Street starts from the old Watergate, now largely derelict but with fragments not to be missed, and leads eventually to the second most distinguished building left, the King James Hospital. The site is that of the Charterhouse; the original endowment, that of James I, who was buried here, while James VI made a further grant to build and maintain a hospital (or place to care for the poor as well as the sick); the building which survives dates from 1750 with a cupola added in 1764. Later converted into flats, it was restored by the Gannochy Trust in 1973. The main modern hospital is the Perth Royal Infirmary, higher up the hill.

In earlier days, the only transverse streets, at right angles to the High Street, were narrow passage ways or vennels (from a French word *venelle*; some of these survive, of which Oliphant's Vennel is one of the more picturesque; there is a key to them on the wall in Fountain Close, off the east end of South Street.

On the far side of the river is Kinnoull Hill, with some of the pleasantest houses in Perth, looking west, but also north away to the Grampians and south to the Ochil Hills. Above them are the woods, given to the townspeople by Lord Dewar, extensive walks, a nature trail, and, at the top, a superb view with a mountain indicator. Below, at the foot of Manse Road which leads up to the nature trail, is a burial ground, and in it the old church, famous for a life-size memorial to Sir George Hay, 1st Earl of Kinnoull, the redoubtable Lord Chancellor who refused Charles I's demand that he should yield precedence to the Archbishop of St Andrews at the coronation, provoking Charles's irritable outburst "I will not meddle further with that old cankered goutish man". Unfortunately, the burial ground is not very easy of access, being only open on Sundays and Wednesdays, and by application to the custodian.

Golf has always figured largely in the life of Perth. According to the kirk records of 1604, one Robertson had to sit in the seat of repentance for "playing at the gowf on the Sabbath on the North Inch at the time of preaching afternoon", and the game has been played there ever since. The Royal Perth

Golfing Society, now combined with the City and County Club, was founded in 1824 and has comfortable premises in Atholl Crescent. The King James VI club also played on the North Inch at first. This club was founded in 1858 by the Rev. Charles Robertson, 'Gowfing Charlie', who had been licensed for the ministry but declined the cares of a parish because they would have interfered with his more serious passion for golf. But he had very strict views on alcohol: "If ye're playing well, dinna taste. But if ye're no playing well, ye may take a drappie." Eventually, a grazing dispute caused them some inconvenience and they created a new course for themselves on Moncrieffe Island. Yet another course was made on Craigie Hill where Joe Anderson presided, father of Mrs Jessie Valentine, British Woman Champion more than once, and good friend to many young golfers; and, at the time of writing, there is another course being made just north of Perth, at Murrayshall, former home of the Norie-Millers.

Horse racing goes back as far as golf on the North Inch, but today it takes place at Scone, the autumn meeting being followed by the hunt ball. Also on the North Inch are the headquarters of the Perthshire Cricket Club, and the Perth Rugby Football Club, while not far away is Muirton Park, the St Johnstone football ground. The club had a good run in the sixties and had a great goal-getter in Henry Hall, but the reorganization of the leagues caught them at a bad moment, and, having lost their place in the premier league the first year, they narrowly escaped further relegation the next.

One last, and rather picturesque, feature of Perth is its company of uniformed high constables, an institution shared only by Holyrood, Edinburgh and the Port of Leith. They were in existence before 1466 as a sort of police force to enable the city magistrates to enforce law and order, but they have not been called out in that capacity since 1843 when some soldiers ran amok. Now, like the Queen's Bodyguard for Scotland, theirs is a dignified rather than a martial role.

III

NORTH FROM PERTH

OF THE roads running north from Perth, the A94 is described in the chapter on Strathmore; the other two, the A93 to Blairgowrie and Braemar, and the A9 to Inverness, embrace between them some of the most magnificent and the most varied scenery in Scotland. The southern tip of the inverted triangle is well wooded lowland along the Tay, which is best followed on foot, but the road bridges at Kinclaven and at Dunkeld both yield good vistas; the beech hedge at Meiklour is unique, and the conifers at Dunkeld House are more than 200 years old; the string of lochs between Blairgowrie and Dunkeld are noted for their bird life.

North of this line, trees yield to heather as the country becomes ever higher and more mountainous – and as the Grampians force the A9 more and more westwards past Ben-y-Gloe and Beinn Dearg, with Glen Tilt between them, and, on the left, Loch Tummel, and the Queen's View, Loch Rannoch and Rannoch Moor. By the time the road reaches its highest point at over 1200 feet, the country has turned desolate indeed, and would be lonely but for the tremendous efforts of men and machinery to improve this trunk route. Lochs Tummel and Rannoch are as different as could be from Loch of Lowes and Loch of Clunie. Here is the land of the red grouse, the blackcock, the capercailzie and the red deer; of great skylines and swift streams in sudden spate, and falls such as those at Tummel and Moness, and, formerly, at Bruar – where the rest of Scotland gathers much of its hydro-electric power; the wild land of the Murrays and the Robertsons, Stewarts and Drummonds; the progression is from the un-

1 & 2.   Perth (*above*) Rose Terrace and the old Academy building and (*below*) the bull sales

3. Perth from the air, showing the medieval layout of High Street and South Street

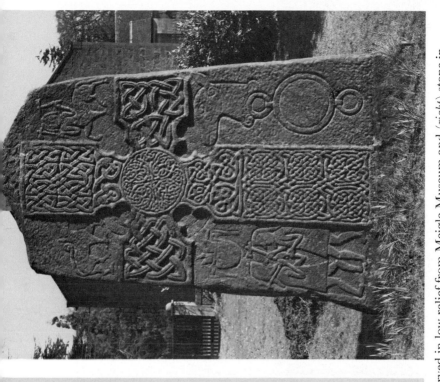

4 & 5. (*Left*) reverse of Class II Pictish stone cross carved in low relief from Meigle Museum and (*right*) stone in the manse garden at Glamis with symbol, animals and human figures

6. Class I stone with mirror symbol and 'elephant' in Meigle Museum

7. Dunkeld Cathedral with eighteenth-century houses in front

8 & 9.   (*Above*) Blair Castle and (*below*) the Soldier's
Leap at Killiecrankie

10 & 11.　(*Above*) Wade's Bridge, Aberfeldy and (*below*) Loch
Rannoch and Schiehallion

12 & 13.   (*Above*) stone circle at **CroftMoraig, near Taymouth and** (*below*) **Loch Tay**

14. Ben Lawers

defended Scone Palace and Meiklour House in the south to Blair Castle astride the route to Inverness, and Newton Castle and Ardblair guarding the exits from the mountains at Blairgowrie.

It is sad that so much has gone at Scone – a royal abbey, a medieval bishop's palace with its attendant village, and a sixteenth-century house built by the Gowries. But, though so much has been lost, Scone is a *must*.

The lovely park lands with their highland cattle (still horned) and the Jacob's sheep, the trees and shrubs of the immediate policies, the Pinetum and the woodland garden, would be reason enough. So would the sanctity of the place. It is impossible to stand on the low mound opposite the house without awe and a sense of sharing in the past – in the old gatherings on the moot-hill under the Pictish kings; in the enthronement of subsequent Scottish kings on the Stone of Destiny, from Kenneth MacAlpine to John Balliol, until it was removed to Westminster (or as some would have it, substituted and hidden away); in the coronations from Robert the Bruce to James I and James IV, and then that of Charles II as of one born out of time. Bruce was indeed crowned twice in three days, the first time by the Bishop of St Andrews, and then again by the Countess of Carrick as representative of her more cautious brother, the Earl of Fife, whose hereditary right it was. Charles II was crowned by the Marquis of Argyll, an event which can have given little pleasure to either. Above all, there is the palace to see, from May to September.

The present palace dates from 1802 but even those most prejudiced against the Gothic revival need not be put off; the outside has dignity without ostentation, and the colour of the local stone gives it warmth. Inside the house, too, the clever use of colour on the walls and in the carpets distinguishes every room, and helps to set off the wonderful collection of eighteenth-century furniture. Few houses can contain such a variety, or are able to display so much beautiful china, Meissen, Sèvres, Derby and Chelsea. The visitor's direct entry into the dining-room prepares him for what is to follow, a long table set with a Worcester dessert service, and Chippendale chairs, the blue walls showing off a priceless collection of ivories. The drawing-room has golden silks on the walls and French embroidered chairs and a little desk made for Marie Antoinette; the library, the main porcelain; the ambassador's room, a magnificent four-poster bed with hangings made for the second Earl of Mansfield when he was ambassador in Paris, and a delightful Zoffany. The long gallery houses a host of treasures including a large table given by James I and VI to the first Lord Stormont.

He was the first Murray to own the lands of Scone. As Sir David Murray he was lucky enough to be on the spot, with his cousin Lord Tullibardine, at the moment of the Gowrie Plot, and in return for the aid then given, Sir David received the Gowries' estates and their house and the Barony of Scone;* Tullibardine was made hereditary Sheriff of Perth, whence in due course the dukedom of Atholl. The earldom of Mansfield was created for the remarkable William, third son of the fifth Viscount Stormont. A great orator in the courts and in the House of Commons, he became one of the most distinguished Lord Chief Justices of England. As Solicitor General, he prosecuted the Jacobite Lords Balmerino, Kilmarnock and Lovat (in spite of his own family's strong Jacobite sympathies); as Lord Chief Justice, he delivered the famous judgement declaring that the whole conception of slavery was repugnant to the common law, and that therefore William Somerset, a negro slave who had been brought to England, must be set free. His nephew and successor was ambassador to France just before the Revolution and collected many of the treasures to be seen.

An ancient custom of the parish is described in the Old Statistical Account:

Every year on Shrove Tuesday, the bachelors and married men drew themselves up at the cross of Scone on opposite sides. A ball was thrown up, and they played from two o'clock till sunset. The game was this. He who, at any time got the ball into his hands, ran with it till overtaken by one of the opposite party, and then, if he could shake himself loose from those on the opposite side, who seized him, he ran on; if not, he threw the ball from him, unless it

* He was later created Viscount Scone for the rather more doubtful service he rendered in getting the unpopular, somewhat episcopalian Articles of Perth through the Scottish Parliament in 1618.

was wrested from him by the other party; but if no person, he was allowed to kick it. The object of the married men was to hang it, i.e., to put it three times into a small hole in the moor, the dool or limit on the one hand; that of the bachelor was to drown it, i.e., to dip it three times into a deep place in the river, the limit on the other. The party who could effect either of these objects won the day. But, if neither party won, the ball was cut into equal parts at sun-set. In the course of play one might always see some scene of violence between the parties; but, as the proverb of this part of the country expresses it, "all was fair at the ball of Scone". This custom is supposed to have had its origin in the days of chivalry. An Italian, it is said, came into this part of the country, challenging all the parishes, under a certain penalty in case of declining his challenge. All the parishes declined his challenge excepting Scone, which beat the foreigner; and in commemoration of this gallant action the game was instituted.

The last of these games was played in the 1830s according to J. D. Urquhart in his Historical Sketches of Scone:

About fifty years ago Lord Stormont, the present Earl of Mansfield, arranged a football match on a large scale, with the Lord Provost of Perth, the players on each side to number fifty. Previous to the match, a good deal of hard training was undergone by the Scone men in the parks close by the palace. . . . On the day fixed for the match the men came to Perth shod in tackety boots, their maxim "A's fair at the Ba' of Scone" fully justifying them in so preparing themselves for the fray. The rendez-vous and the battleground was the North Inch of Perth, on which were assembled several hundreds of spectators to watch the 'grand match' as it was very appropriately named. Mr Kemp, Writer, led off for the Perth team, by kicking the ball up the Inch, where soon ensued a general mêlée. The ball getting into the river, one of the Scone team, James Loudfoot, ran in up to the armpits and brought it ashore, whereupon he was allowed the privilege of a free-kick. The game having continued for some time, with prospects of success for each side hanging in the balance, the bulk of the spectators, being inhabitants of Perth, crowded in past the goal and prevented the strangers from scoring, and also did everything in their power to assist the home team. At the end of the first hour matters had assumed so serious an aspect that the game was abruptly stopped, and the strangers stoned off the pitch, some taking refuge in the offices of Mr Condie, North Port, and others where they could best find shelter. . . . Shortly after this, a challenge was sent by Lord Stormont to the Lord Provost to play forty-nine men a side, at any given place seven miles outside of Perth, when there might be a fair field and no favour, but the challenge was never accepted. Lord Stormont shortly afterwards entered into Parliament as the member for Perthshire and the game fell rapidly into disuse on his withdrawal from the post of Captain.

When the custom continued, every man in the parish, the gentry not excepted, was obliged to turn out and support the side, and the person who declined to do his part on this occasion was fined.

From Scone, the road north is pleasant enough through rich farm land, with occasional glimpses to low hills on either side. A few miles brings you to an interesting group of medieval buildings, at Stobhall, high above the Tay, but these are privately inhabited and only open under the Scottish Gardens Scheme. They were the home of the Drummond Earls of Perth (and are again, now) but passed for a time to the female line and the Earls of Ancaster by forfeiture after 1745. Otherwise the road lacks any special interest till the 110-foot high beech hedge at Meiklour. Nowadays, when it has to be trimmed, every six years or so, an outsize mechanical lift can be used, but the mind boggles at the work which must have been entailed before such devices (and mechanical trimmers) were invented. In the village, just to the west, is a seventeenth-century mercat cross and a joug stone nearby. And just to the north, the Cleaven Dyke was constructed by the Romans, less as a military barrier than as a sort of fence to demarcate their limits. Mercers have lived here since the twelfth century, but the lands have passed through the female line more than once, as when Jean Mercer married Robert, son of the second Lord Nairne (who was killed at Culloden); and when a later heiress married Lord Shelburne in 1843; the house is still the home of his descendant, George Mercer-Nairne, Marquis of Landsdowne.

Nor is Blairgowrie, as a town, of special interest except to the industrial archaeologist, though it must be a pleasant place to live in; and it is an excellent centre for the holidaymaker bent on exploring the neighbouring glens and such places as Glamis and Blair Castles, Dunkeld and Kirriemuir. It is really a fusion of several settlements west of the river with the Rattrays on the east bank. In the days when the economy depended on agriculture and weaving was organized on a cottage basis, this was convenient but when the flax looms were concentrated in mills so that they could be powered by lades from the swift flowing Ericht, the population increased and needed to live nearer their work. For the story, and a description of the various processes of sowing (a skilled job this) and gathering, scutching and heckling, bleaching, weaving, calendaring and packing, there is an excellent brief guide-book called *Old Blairgowrie – Tours, History, Memories, Tales* – published in the town and available at the Tourist Information Centre. Incidentally, it reveals that child labour lingered on long after the history books tell us that it had been abolished. An entry in the Rattray School Log Book tells us in 1903: "I find that the half-timers employed in the Keithbank Mill are at present working on their schoolday before and after school; that is to say a boy spends one day in the mill from 6 a.m. to 6 p.m. and the next day in the mill from 6 a.m. to 8.30 a.m., at school from 9.30 to 4.15. and then in the mill from 4.30 to 6 p.m. As a result, such a boy is quite unfit to make progress in his studies."

Another disadvantage of the mills was the pollution of the river – though this might come about by other means too. The Old Statistical Account reported that the local "method of fishing is curious. They make what they call a drimuck, resembling thin wrought mortar, which they throw into the pool to disturb the clearness of the waters. The fishers stand on the point of the rock with long poles and nets on the end of them, with which they rake the pool and take up the fish" – an art at which an eminent English bishop was caught red-handed not so long since, on another Perthshire river. His plea that "it was only a little one, and that anyway he had always meant to put it back" was fortunately accepted.

Eventually the linen industry and its blue flax fields gave way to jute, introduced to the town by David Grimond, even before it had reached Dundee. Today, the mainstay is the growing and processing of the strawberries and raspberries which grow so well in the district.

The three interesting old buildings nearby are all in private occupation, but it is worth climbing the hill to Newton Castle, home of the Chief of the Clan Macpherson, a Z-shaped sixteenth-century tower house, not so much for a glimpse of it, because it is well sheltered by trees, but rather for the view back over the houses and the mills to distant fields beyond. Craig Hall of Rattray, to the north, was a castle but was rebuilt on its precipitous site in the nineteenth century.

Ardblair to the west is a house of the greatest interest. From the fourteenth to the eighteenth centuries, it belonged to the Blairs, passing then by marriage to the Oliphants of Gask, becoming their main home when Gask was sold. But there is evidence of occupation as far back as Pictish times. Though on no natural eminence, it was secure because water used to surround it on three sides. The basis of the present building is an L-shaped tower house of the sixteenth century possibly incorporating part of a previous twelfth-century castle, with additions of various dates, forming a complete courtyard – the whole structure having a pleasing unity. Over the much eroded entrance doorway is an inexplicable stone arch, carved in deep relief with a multitude of strange beasts, some of them playing musical instruments. The work is not thought to be native, but when it was placed there or where it came from, nobody knows.

If the building itself is interesting, its contents are even more so. From Blair days, there is a copy of the National Covenant, and many weapons of various dates, but the real treasures are the Jacobite relics brought from Gask by the Oliphants. They include the Prince's garter, of a paler blue than that worn by the Hanoverians; an unusual bonnet of his; his gloves and spurs; some rough, thin leather shoes he wore when he was passing as Betty Burke; his crucifix and the little table at which he breakfasted at Gask. A number of his letters include a long one

to his father, telling him of the success at Prestonpans, but
saying that he could take little pleasure in a victory over men
who were his fellow-countrymen.

The house is also a museum of Oliphant family history, with
portraits of all the lairds from the seventeenth century onwards, and of the second Lord Nairne whose daughter married
an Oliphant - and a whole room is furnished with possessions
of Carolina Oliphant, the poetess Lady Nairne, who began and
ended her days at Gask. Only towards the close of her life, did
she admit authorship of works which included not only
Jacobite songs such as "Will ye no' come back again?" and
family pieces such as "The Auld Hoose", but "Caller Herrin' "
and "The Laird of Cockpen". This is a family house, still very
much lived in, although open to the public by previous
arrangement.

Alyth is another weaving town and also makes carpets. It
has a mercat cross, the ruins of an old church, and within its
modern successor, a Pictish stone and the hatchment of the
Ramsays of Bamff. One of the latter, Sir Gilbert Ramsay, died
in a duel here in 1790. Lady Ramsay's footman had been
insolent to a Captain Macrae, who in his turn had cudgelled
him soundly "on which Sir Gilbert challenged the Captain but,
not undeservedly, bit the dust".

A century before, the Kirk Session had had strong views
about the value of tobacco (probably as a preventive against
the plague) so that they ranked it with bread as being essential
to life. In 1675, "this day the merchants in Alyth being
charged, were called and compeired and promised not to sell
any wares to any person on the Sabbath, between or after
sermons except it be upon necessity, and that to any sick person
nor to sell unnecessarie things as they did formerly upon the
Sabbath, except needful, tobacco or bread".

Barry Hill, a mile and a half north-east of Alyth, has a
vitrified fort. These were Iron Age forts built of stones, laced
and strengthened with timbers. If these were subsequently set
on fire, either accidentally or deliberately, the heat could be
great enough to fuse the stones together.

Further to the north, the remarkable scenery along the

Ericht and its tributaries, the Ardle and the Shee, and the two roads, one through Strathardle to Pitlochry, and the other up to the Spittal (hospital or rather hospice) of Glenshee, have been described for this series by Dr W. Douglas Simpson in *Portrait of the Highlands.*

The other road to the north from Perth goes out past the St Johnstone football ground, the new industrial estates and the still expanding headquarters of Dewar's. Just beyond, where the Almond joins the Tay, lay a Roman fort which, in the fourteenth century was given the name of 'Bertha'. Though much ploughed down, and now bisected by the road, the ramparts are still visible; a stone with *"DISCIPLINAE AUGUSTI"*, from over the door of its headquarters, is in the Perth Museum.

At Luncarty, the Danes were given a bloody nose in 990 and the story goes that the adoption of the thistle as the Scottish national emblem dates from this occasion. It is said that the Scots would have been surprised sleeping, had not an unwary Dane exclaimed when he stepped barefooted on a particularly prickly specimen. The building of the new road here led to the discovery of a souterrain and its emergency excavation before it was destroyed for the sake of the surrounding gravel. Either from this road or from the A93, a detour should be made to take in the view from Kinclaven Bridge, and, for those interested, the Roman legionary fortress at Inchtuthil, the site of one of the most important excavations in Great Britain – by Professor Richmond in the 1960s. The east ditch and the south rampart are the best preserved, but the ploughed-down rampart gives an idea of the size of the work; round the fortress, beside the rampart, there was originally a five-foot-thick stone wall. The most extraordinary find was a hoard of nails, 11 tons in weight, which had been carefully buried and hidden, to prevent the valuable iron from falling into the hands of the enemy when the fort was evacuated. Specimens, some of them as much as 10 inches long, may be seen in the National Museum of Antiquities in Edinburgh.

The new A9 by-passes both Birnam and Dunkeld and must be a tremendous boon to the inhabitants, as it is to the motorist;

no longer do you have to reconcile yourself to the fact that if you get behind a lorry just north of Perth, you will still be behind that vehicle till you are well north of Blair Atholl. It has opened up wide views over the Tay between Dunkeld and Logierait.

Birnam Woods would be impressive even without their Shakespearian associations with Dunsinane ten miles to the east – in fact, of course, Macbeth was killed not here but at Lumphanan in Aberdeenshire. Dunkeld is the smallest of cathedral cities but it has a great deal to offer. One could do without the pretentious gateway to the hotel, but the grounds of Dunkeld House have some magnificent larches and contain the remains of a Pictish fort. Neil Gow, most famous and most beloved of fiddlers, was born at Inver. Just to the west is the Hermitage, an eighteenth-century folly overlooking the gorge of the Braan, given to the National Trust for Scotland in memory of the eighth Duke of Atholl by his widow; just to the east is the bird sanctuary of the Loch of Lowes, with one of only two osprey observation posts in Scotland.

But the treasure of Dunkeld is its cathedral (*see* plate 7) and the little houses around it. The saving and rehabilitation of these latter would justify the existence of the National Trust for Scotland if nothing else did, and the former Perthshire County Council has matched them in far-sightedness. Between them they have made habitable two shops and forty houses, the eighteenth-century appearance of which makes an ideal approach to the cathedral itself. For a time the home of the sacred relics of St Columba from Iona, it was subsequently outstripped by both Dunfermline and St Andrews, but it remained a very large diocese, and its bishops were important people. One of them, William Sinclair, a friend of the Bruce, repulsed an English raid which had defeated the Earl of Fife in 1317.

> The King thatfor, ay for that day
> Hym lufit, honorit, and prisit ay,
> And held hym in-to sic daynte
> That 'his awne bischop' hym callit he.

Another bishop – John – at the very end of the twelfth century was esteemed as being one of the few medieval prelates who voluntarily agreed to reduce the size of his diocese, and therefore his revenues, by asking the Pope to create a diocese of Argyll. However, since he was an Englishman and spoke no Gaelic – and anyway, the teinds of Argyll were minimal and very difficult to collect – his unselfishness may have been more apparent than real. It was not long after John's death that the building that we can see today was started – the choir as usual first. This part, now the parish church, retains much of the cathedral's original dignity in spite of its stripping at the Reformation and its restoration during the nineteenth century. It still houses Bishop Sinclair's sedilia, and his tomb, though not in its original place in front of the high altar. Ironically, the magnificent tomb that does stand in its original site is that of the sacrilegious destroyer of Elgin Cathedral, the Wolf of Badenoch, son of Robert II. Earlier than anything, even the choir itself, is an upright cross slab, carved with a number of biblical figures including Daniel in the lion's den.

The nave dates from the fifteenth century; though open to the skies, it has peace and an undeniable grandeur, with its massive pillars supporting pointed arches with triforium and clerestory above. The destruction wrought was not intended – was indeed directly contrary to Argyll's orders. The lairds of Arntilly and Kinvaid were to "cast down the altaris, and purge the kirk of all kind of monuments of idolatry" but "fail not, but see ze take guid heyd that neither the dasks, windocks, nor durris, be ony ways hurt or broken – eyther gassin wark or iron wark".

At any rate the tower survived even if not entirely un-altered, and its vaulted ground floor is particularly interesting because of its rare pre-Reformation paintings – of the Judge-ment of Solomon, and the story of the woman taken in adultery.

North of Dunkeld, the new road takes you swiftly on to Pitlochry. Just why a town of that size should have grown up there rather than at Blair Atholl or Ballinluig, or by increasing the size of Dunkeld, is not obvious. But it makes an excellent centre for all kinds of outdoor activities, which would please the writer of the Old Statistical Account for the parish (that of Moulin):

> It is observable [he bewailed] that those gymnastic exercises, which constituted the chief pastime of the Highlanders forty or fifty years ago, have almost completely disappeared. At every fair or meeting of the country people, there were contests at racing, wrestling, putting the stone etc; and on holidays, all the males of the district, young and old, met to play at football, but oftener at shinty. These games are now only practised by schoolboys, having given place to the more elegant though less manly amusement of dancing, which is becoming very common. . . . A shooting match for some small prize occupies part of the day, and in the evening they repair to a ball, in a barn or tap-room where they enjoy all the pleasures of rural felicity.

When its promised by-pass comes, Pitlochry may even be a pleasant place to live in again, but the traffic is appalling in the summer. However its excellent hotels and other accommodation do not lack for business, and it supports a repertory theatre of national reputation. Within easy reach are stretches of National Trust land along the Garry in the Pass of Killie-crankie, and along the Tummel – the latter given by the late Dr Barbour of Bonskeid. Bonskeid House itself went to the Y.M.C.A. But his son still has Fincastle – an unusual laird in that he is also a minister, a Professor of Divinity, and this year (1979) Moderator of the General Assembly of the Church of Scotland. Another place of beauty, the hill of Craigower with a view over all the countryside, was given to the National Trust for Scotland by Mrs M. D. Fergusson of Baledmund in memory of her husband. There have been Fergussons of Baledmund and Stewarts of Balnakeilly since long before the Victorian doctors decided that there was something special in the air of this part of the world. For the historically minded there is the Pictish stone at Dunfallandy House*, one of the finest both in its cross and in the fantastic beasts surrounding it and on the reverse; for the natural historian, the fish ladder where the salmon can be watched making their way up the

---

* Boarded up and not visible during the winter months.

river to spawn; for the romantic there is Killiecrankie. The narrow gorge with its sheer wooded sides is tremendous, and the wishing well and Balfour's Stone and the Soldier's Leap and the notion of kilted Highlanders defending their rightful king, their faith and their way of life against an incoming tyrant. But Bonnie Dundee was bonnie only in his looks, and the king, and the cause for which he was fighting, were in fact far from romantic, and little understood by the men who were taken to fight there. He had been the agent of the ministers of Charles II in their dragonnades in the south of Scotland against all who refused to accept the bishops. To preach at a conventicle was a capital offence and the hills were scoured by 'Bloody Clavers' for offenders in 'the killing times'.

Not even the accession of James VII and II, and his Declaration of Indulgence, helped the Cameronians, though it led some Episcopalians to think that they might have more to gain by supporting him rather than the Dutchman whom the English had invited over. But James cut the ground from under their feet by departing, and they failed to win the day in Edinburgh. The Lords of Convention declared for William and they controlled the Lowlands. It was in this situation that the newly ennobled Viscount Dundee induced some 2500 Highlanders with promises of plunder to fight for James who neither understood nor liked his Scottish subjects, whether Highland or Lowland, and whose chief aim was to force them into a Roman Catholicism for which they had no yearning, not even Dundee himself. Against them was moving General Mackay with 4000 troops also Scottish. His aim was not only to bring Dundee to battle but also to recover Blair Castle which was being held for James by Steuart of Ballechin, against its owner's wishes. To reach Blair Castle, Mackay had to pass through the defile of Killiecrankie, an ideal place for the irregular type of warfare at which the Highlanders excelled. In fact, he got through safely, though stalked throughout by Ian Ban Beag Macrath, while Dundee was marching his force round the back of Lude, to take up favourable ground at Urrard. Here he might hope to destroy Mackay's troops rather than merely prevent their passage through the defile. On his right were the Macleans under their chief; in the centre, his cavalry and the Camerons under their chief; on the left, the Macdonalds. The fight did not begin till half an hour before sunset but it was over in daylight. A headlong charge downhill by the Highlanders suffered inevitable casualties but carried all before it in hand-to-hand fighting. The losers were out-weaponed when they had no time to fix their plug bayonets, and outspirited, and they fled in disorder. Only about a tenth of Mackay's men got away over the hills to Aberfeldy, but Dundee was dead. In his absence, the victors failed to capture Dunkeld and soon dispersed, as Highland levies were apt to do.

Balfour's stone is where Brigadier General Balfour, at bay against Alastair Ban, Ballechin's brother, spurned mercy with insults and was cleft from collar bone to thigh. At the Soldier's Leap, Donald MacBean saved himself by an enormous jump:

> The sun going down caused the Highlanders to advance on us like madmen, without shoe or stocking, covering themselves from our fire with their targes; at last they cast away their musquets, drew their broadswords, and advanced furiously upon us, and were in the middle of us before we could fire three shots apiece, broke us, and obliged us to retreat. Some fled to the water, and some another way (we were for the most part new men). I fled to the baggage, and took a horse in order to ride the water; there follows me a Highlandman with sword and targe, in order to take the horse and kill me. You'd laugh to see how he and I scampered about. I kept the horse between him and me; at length he drew his pistol, and I fled; he fired after me. I went above the Pass, where I met with another water, very deep; it was about 18 foot over betwixt two rocks. I resolved to jump to it, so I laid down my gun and hat and jumped, and lost one of my shoes in the jump. Many of our friends were lost in the water.

In a visit, time must be left to take the path down to the river, not so much to see these two particular spots, as to walk along the old road by the river, the route that the Government troops took. Between the sheer sides of the wooded hills, one can sense again the blind terror that must have been in the hearts of all at the thought of the unseen Highlanders who might fall on them at any moment – and then the sense of relief when they emerged into the open ground beyond, and felt (all too wrongly) that they could now engage the enemy on equal terms. And, forgetting your history, it is a lovely walk, especially in spring before the season starts, and again in autumn when the colours defy description and salmon may be seen jumping at the Soldier's Leap. And, if you have more time, take the little road which goes west from the village and gives a fine view back over the site of the battle, which cannot be seen from the main road.

Blair Castle, though its exterior has been altered and re-altered a number of times, looks exactly what a Scottish castle should look like.* The earliest part, Cumming's Tower, goes back to the thirteenth century, the great hall range to the sixteenth. Inside, it is a great eighteenth-century house packed with treasures of every sort; surely there is something here for everybody. By and large, the Murrays who have held the castle since 1629, were supporters of the Stewart Kings, they themselves being Stewart in the female line and heirs to their Stewart predecessors as Earls of Atholl. They were out with Montrose in 1644 and paid for it by a Cromwellian occupation of the castle in 1652. Thereafter the family was often divided. The first Marquis protested against the persecution of the Covenanters and supported William and Mary. His son, the first Duke, supported the Hanoverians in 1715, but not so his eldest son, the Marquis of Tullibardine who thereby forfeited his right to succeed and had to go into exile as did two of his brothers, Lord Charles and Lord George Murray. When 1745 came, Tullibardine landed with the Prince in Moidart and Lord George was his principal general. As such, he besieged Blair Castle which he claimed as his own – the last siege of a castle in this country. Meanwhile the second son of the first Duke had succeeded to the title and it was he who carried out the chief re-modelling of the house.

There is, as I have said, something for everyone. The close connection of the Stewart earls with the royal family in the

* Open Easter and May–October.

fifteenth and sixteenth centuries is shown in the first room which has delightful double portraits of James V and his queen, and of Mary Queen of Scots and her son, James VI. The Civil War royalists are in the next room where there is contemporary furniture, a portrait of Montrose, the helmet and breastplate of Claverhouse, and one of the original signed copies of the Covenant of 1638. The later Jacobite Murrays have their memorial upstairs, the Tullibardine room, with a bed covered with tartan hangings 200 years old, said to have been formerly on a round bed in which slept all seventeen sons of Sir David Murray of Tullibardine.

For the lover of furniture, it would be simply a matter of taste which room he would most like to transfer to his own home – few houses can have such a wealth of Scottish, English, French and Dutch work, all set off in rooms with splendid fireplaces and plaster ceilings, spacious and well-lit by the large eighteenth-century windows. And the interest is much enhanced by the photostats, everywhere, of the accounts for the original purchase of the items. All the dukes must have been relentless collectors of pictures, too. There are portraits of everyone who was anyone, as well as some charming family pieces such as those of the third Duke with his children, of the Hon. James C. P. Murray, and of James Moray younger of Abercairny. There are weapons of all sorts in the entrance hall, some remarkable pistols in the terrace room, and even the suit of armour worn by the sixth Duke at the 1839 Eglinton Tournament. One could very happily spend days, not hours, going round, seeing new things – the china, the embroidery on the chairs and on the bed in the Derby Room (worked by the first Marquis's mother-in-law while besieged in Latham House during the Civil War), the incredibly fine modern lace in the china room, the uniforms and the costumes and the stuffed birds; and there are curiosities too, such as the gruesome prints of the execution of the three Black Watch soldiers in the Tower of London in 1743 and of the Jacobite Lairds after the forty-five – and the coin cabinet of broomwood, made by Sandeman of Perth in the form of a Greek Temple.

One of the most famous incidents in the history of the castle was the entertainment there of James V and the Papal Legate by the third Earl of the Stewart line.

An elaborate rustic pavilion had been prepared for them built of timber, in the midst of a quiet meadow, and surrounded by moats or fosses, full of the most delicate fish. It was enclosed and defended by towers, as if it had been a regular castle, and had within it many apartments, which were decked with flowers and branches, so that in treading them one seemed to be in a garden. There were all kinds of game and other provisions in abundance, with many cooks to make them ready, and plenty of most costly spices and wines. The Italian ambassador was most surprised to see, amongst rocks and wildernesses, which seemed to be the very extremity of the world, such good lodgings and so magnificent an entertainment. But what surprised him most of all was to see the Highlanders set fire to the wooden castle as soon as the hunting was over and the King in the act of departing.

Mary Queen of Scots also visited Blair, for a hunting party, and Queen Victoria.

To the north and south of Blair were Robertsons, at Struan and at Lude, both unquestioning Jacobites. Their clan is the Clan Donnachaidh and their name derives from one Robert, a fifteenth-century chief, from whose exploits the family coat of arms also derives. He earned the gratitude of James I's family by capturing one of his murderers; a hand holds up the crown and a chained man lies below the shield. On the shield are wolves, signifying the responsibility of the Robertsons for clearing the Atholl Forest of these beasts. The chiefs had one specially prized possession, the Clach na Brataich, a clear crystal ball which could both foretell the fortunes of war and also cure epidemics. When, in 1715, the thirteenth chief took it out, it was not only clouded - the bad omen - it was cracked internally, and the end was not far off. This remarkable man had been out in 1689, and thus in exile till 1702; on his return, he built himself a house which he called the Hermitage, between Loch Rannoch and Loch Tummel, and allowed no woman ever to cross its threshold, neither relation or guest nor servant. In 1715 he took a vigorous part at Sheriffmuir and so

15. Timber-laced fort at Dundurn near Comrie

16. The falls at Dochart, Killin

17. Glamis Castle

18. Drummond Castle and its gardens from the air

19 & 20.　(*Above*) Kirriemuir, the birthplace of Sir James Barrie and (*below*) Edzell Castle and garden

21. The round-
tower at Brechin

22. Souterrain
at Ardestie, just
north of Dundee

23. Claypotts Castle

24. Arbroath smokies

25. Arbroath Abbey

26. Death catches up with old age, in Arbroath Abbey Museum

27 & 28.   Falkland Palace (*above*) from the garden and (*below*) the
south range from the inner court

had another spell in France till 1725. By 1745 he was 75 years old but that did not deter him until, after Prestonpans, Prince Charles Edward managed to persuade him to return home in the captured carriage of Sir John Cope. This time, he was not exiled but his house was burnt to the ground and he was compelled to spend his last few years with one of his sisters. The family never really recovered, but of recent years a clan society has been formed, and in its little museum* near the Falls of Bruar are some of its relics, including the Clach na Brataich.

West of the A9 lies Breadalbane, pierced but not directly traversed by a number of roads. From Dunkeld a famous scenic way runs through Strathbraan to Amulree and the Sma' Glen.

> Whan Little Dunnin' was a spree
> And no a name as noo,
> Wull Todd wha wrocht at Amulree
> Gaed hame byordinar fou.
>
> The hairst had a' been gethered in;
> The nicht was snell but clear;
> And owre the cantle o' the mune
> God keekit here and there.
>
> Whan God saw Wull he gien a lauch
> And drappit lichtly doun;
> Syne stude ahint a frostit sauch
> Or Wull cam styterin on.
>
> Straucht oot He breeng'd, and blared: "Wull Todd"
> Blythe as St Johnstoun's bell;
> "My God!" gowped Wull, "Ye'r richt" says God.
> "I'm gled to meet yersel."

William Soutar (*Collected Poems*, 1948)

From Amulree, you can also take the A826 to Aberfeldy, or an adventurous track from Loch Freuchie over the hills, to descend on to Loch Tay at Kenmore. This is really best for walkers – and Upper Glenalmond, above Newton Brig, is *only* for walkers. This last is, for those who know it, a very special

* Open during the summer months.

place. "It ranks", says one who really does know it "very high among the truly Highland glens of Scotland, and comprises one way or another the very essence of good walking, with one 'Munro', Ben Chonzie, not an exciting hill but a pleasant scramble rewarded by a good view at the top". The Auchnafree range to the north of the river is impressive too.

Returning to the A9, we can reach Aberfeldy by the little road from Ballinluig along the Tay, past Grandtully old church and castle. The church is clearly signposted on the main road but, up the track which is perfectly feasible for cars, it is not so easy to find. Persist through the first farm, and a few hundred yards beyond, stop at the second; behind it is a long low building without windows, looking like a barn. Unusual as could be, it is now in the care of the Ministry of the Environment. Its interest lies in the seventeenth-century paintings on the ceiling, ordered by Sir William Stewart of Grandtully who restored the church in 1636; they include his own arms, his wife's, the royal arms and pictures of the four Evangelists. The panels do not quite fit in the centre and may have been designed for the private chapel of the castle nearby. The latter – a superb example of sixteenth- and seventeenth-century work – is the successor to an earlier castle near the church. Being still a Stewart family home, it is not open to the public.

Aberfeldy is another of the delightful small towns of Perthshire. Surrounded by heather-covered hills, it has the Tay running beside it, and from its High Street in the very centre of the town, there is a footpath through the Birks of Aberfeldy to the Falls of Moness. On the northern outskirts are lawns extending to the bridge designed by William Adam and built by General Wade in 1733, the only Scottish one chosen by the Post Office for its issue of stamps illustrating British bridges. Overlooking it is a statue of a Highland soldier for it was here that the independent companies were embodied as a regiment, the Black Watch, seven years later.

One of Aberfeldy's most beloved sons was a Dr Munro who practised in the district in the middle of the nineteenth century, walking each day to all his patients carrying his lunch of oatcakes and home-made cheese. It is said that, after putting right a boy's leg which had been mis-set, he subsequently visited the patient sixteen times to make sure that the recovery was proceeding as it should, walking seven miles on each occasion – for which he charged a total of £3. Another was Daniel Stewart, son of a crofter in Strathtay; he founded not only his famous school in Edinburgh but also a little village school in the parish of his birth, where the beloved doctor got his early education.

Across the Wade bridge is a region of many historic associations. The old church at Weem (in the graveyard of the church in present use) is sixteenth century. It has an ancient octagonal font and contains graves of the Menzies family, three very primitive stone crosses moved here for safety, and a graceful monument erected in 1616 by Sir Alexander Menzies to his two wives, his mother, grandmother, great-grandmother and great-great-grandmother. The family – probably of Norman origin (Anketillus de Maynoers is mentioned in the reign of William the Lion, and Robert was Chamberlain to Alexander II) – came to Weem in 1266. Their first castle was plundered and burnt by a descendant of the Wolf of Badenoch in 1502; the chief part of what can be seen today is that which was built in its place. It unfortunately fell into decay when the main line died out some fifty years ago, but the Menzies Clan Association has been doing wonders in restoration and conservation since 1972, and the castle may be visited on Saturdays and Sundays in the summer. Particularly notable are the iron yett of the old main entrance, the vast hearth in the kitchen, and the first floor which has graceful eighteenth-century decoration in the hall and a plaster ceiling commemorating the union of Scotland with England. In the south tower is the room occupied by Prince Charles Edward on the nights of 4th and 5th February 1746, during his retreat northwards. On Jacobitism, the clan had been somewhat divided, with Menzieses fighting on both sides in 1689 and 1715 and 1745; on this last occasion the chief's sympathies had been Hanoverian but that did not prevent him giving the Prince shelter when it was needed, with the result that Cumberland seized his home and garrisoned it with Government troops.

Another primitive cross and another octagonal font, similar to those at Weem, stand outside a modern church at Dull; the Pictish stone which once also stood here has been transferred to the National Museum of Antiquities in Edinburgh. That is all that is left now of a site of great sanctity where St Eonan (or Adamnan - St Columba's successor and biographer) was buried. He had been priest at Fortingall where he is reputed to have miraculously stayed a plague that was moving up into Glen Lyon.

Glen Lyon is narrow and almost claustrophobic at times so sheer are the hills on either side, but it is incredibly beautiful in autumn with the vivid red sycamores and the geans, and the varied browns of the beeches, birches and oaks. The road is narrow but well supplied with passing places. For 200 years, this was Campbell country, the inheritance of a younger son of Sir Duncan Campbell of Glenorchy. His son Duncan the Hospitable had two children, Colin who started the building of Meggernie Castle, and a daughter who married Gregor MacGregor of Glenstrae, of whom presently. The castle was considerably added to by a great-grandson, the notorious Robert Campbell of Glenlyon, the thriftless, dissipated instrument of "Slaughter under Trust" at Glencoe. Although he had already sold his lands before that event, it may be said of the glen, as it was said of him for the rest of his life, that "Glencoe hangs about him day and night". Not surprisingly, Meggernie Castle is haunted, though tradition makes the ghost a Menzies rather than a Campbell. Fortunately not all the family were as weak as Robert, and three grandsons, the last of the line, did something to retrieve the family name. Colonel John was a distinguished officer in the Black Watch, David a doctor in the West Indies, and Archibald, having fought on the opposite side to John at Culloden, later also joined the Hanoverian army and was wounded with Fraser's Highlanders in the defence of Quebec. Later he became factor to the Earl of Breadalbane in Lorn where he was equally popular with the gentry and the poorer tenants. When he died, he was accorded a funeral "so extraordinary that, for a generation or two, it formed a fixed date from which the lapse of time was calculated. The gentry of Argyll and the tenants of Lorn carried the coffin, Highland fashion, that is, shoulder high, towards the Perthshire march. They were reinforced by the men of Glenorchy before they reached the border; and on Drumalbane they were met by the men of Glen Lyon and Breadalbane. Thence they marched, such a funeral having rarely been seen, to the family burial place at Fortingall, where he was laid beside his Jacobite father".

Today, the things to see in the glen are this church (Meggernie Castle is in private occupation and well secluded by trees), MacGregor's Leap, a mile to the west, and the little church at Innerwick. Both the churches are comparatively modern but they are beautifully kept, and they both have rare Celtic hand bells of the seventh or eighth centuries, perhaps even going back to the time of Adamnan. Fortingall also has its very ancient yew tree, an eight-sided font, outside the church door as at Dull, and, of course, associations with the oldest collection of Scottish Gaelic songs, the Book of Lismore. Its compiler was parish priest of Fortingall as well as titular dean of Lismore. The village has also a standing stone and, just above it, a dun. Though one of the best preserved, with walls a foot thick and four courses high, it is (except for the expert) more interesting for its situation and for its view than for what actually remains.

According to Stewart's *A Highland Parish*, the story of MacGregor's Leap has been much elaborated, but stripped of its accretions is as follows: On 27th July 1565, Alexander MacGregor of Glenstrae killed one James McGestalcar and his accomplices in revenge for their having murdered Gregor son of the Dean of Lismore and Robert McConil or Gregor. Unfortunately, McGestalcar was in the pay of the Campbells of Glenorchy and from that day, MacGregor was doomed:

> The rocks and the woods were his abode, and on many occasions his agility and endurance alone saved him from his pursuers. Sometimes, he managed to visit his Campbell wife at her father's castle at Carnban. There he many a time managed to

remain concealed for days until an unfriendly visitor appeared. On some occasions however his visits to his wife were made known to his enemies, and he had at once to flee for his life. It was on one of these occasions that, pursued by his enemies' bloodhounds, he made the daring leap across the Lyon at the place which still bears his name. It is not known whether he leapt from the higher or the lower part of the rock. Both are equally difficult and dangerous. If he leapt from the higher part, one would think that all his bones would be broken. From the lower part the distance is so far that it seems almost incredible that anyone would attempt it. . . .

Even this wonderful feat did not avail to save the devoted MacGregor for long. In 1569, while on another visit to his wife at Carnban, he was captured and taken to Balloch (now Taymouth) Castle. After some months of imprisonment there, the unfortunate Gregor was beheaded in April 1570. His sorrowing wife bewailed his fate in a most pathetic ballad; four stanzas may be quoted in translation:

> I was daffing with my loved one
> Early on the Lammas morn,
> But ere noontide I was weeping,
> For my heart with grief was torn.
> Ochain, ochain, ochain darling
> Thy father hears not our cry . . . .

> Had my Gregor of his clansmen
> Twelve good men and true brave,
> I would not now be shedding tears
> His kin my babe would save
> Ochain, ochain etc . . . .

> On oaken block they laid his head,
> and made his blood to flow;
> Had I there a cup to hold it
> I'd sip of it I know.
> Ochain, ochain etc . . . .

> O that Finlarig were blazing
> And Balloch burning low

And that I round my Gregor
  My arms could fondly throw
Ochain, ochain, ochain my darling
  Sad at heart am I.
Ochain, ochain, ochain darling
  Thy dad hears not our cry.

From Inverar there is a pass over the hills to Dall on Loch Rannoch, which the Fearnan people used when going to their shielings for the summer grazing. It was last used, according to Miss Alexandra Stewart in *The Glen that Was*, when wood was taken from Rannoch for the additions to Taymouth Castle at the time of Queen Victoria's visit. The horses were changed halfway at a large stone where the men rested. Club Leabhar are owed a debt of gratitude for printing these reminiscences, which bring to mind vividly what life must have been like in her childhood, and which supplement, for a later date, Duncan Campbell's *Reminiscences of an Octogenarian Highlander* and her own father's *A Highland Parish*. The former was a much loved schoolmaster at Fortingall until he took up journalism in 1857, one of a number still remembered. One, Dugald Buchanan, 1712-1768, poet and peacemaker as well as teacher, even has a statue to him, at Kinloch Rannoch. Indeed the more remote the district, the higher the value that was placed on schooling. In 1786 the tenants of Fearnan petitioned Lord Breadalbane for help to maintain a school. They stated that since 1761 they had themselves provided a teacher for their children, to whom they paid £1 6s. 8d. sterling for the half year from Martinmas to Whitsunday yearly without any other payment "except his chance at Handsel Monday [the first after the New Year] and at Cockfighting [early in February when he also got the cocks that did not survive], together with his maintenance which he got by going from house to house regularly with the scholars, which was an advantage as he teached the children at night in every house he came to".

Not the least evocative of Campbell's writings is his description of life in the shielings of Glenlyon from 1837 to 1841, the year in which he reached adulthood at the age of 13.

"There was always plenty of work for the shieling lads, who had to keep the young and the yeld stock up the corries and hill-sides and to separate below on their different grazings, cows and calves. The latter always got the finer parts of the lowest grazings. They needed the preference, for they were, when too young, put on short rations of milk, and soon as ever they could be trusted to feed themselves they were weaned altogether. There were few of the shieling boys who could not milk cows, goats, and sheep, but they said it was women's work, and they deemed it derogatory to their own sex either to help at the milking or the making of cheese, although they had no such objection to churning. The shieling boys were not about the huts much in the day. They left for their own work in the morning, and came home late. The social life of the shielings, when the women were in possession of the huts, was enlivened with songs, tales and merriment, mingled with constant work. The herding lads shared in all that, and had besides hill amusements of their own, but their solitary communion with nature gave them a contemplative gravity which formed a sort of religious training, independent of all dogmatic or written forms of faith.... I feel certain that the two huts with which I was acquainted were typical of all those which had fallen into ruin before I was born. They were not much to look at on the outside, but they were rather substantial roomy edifices, which were built of stone, thatched with heather, and well constructed for dairy purposes. Recesses, or rather cupboards, were built in the thick walls, with flags for shelves, on which the vessels for milk were placed. Planks were placed at intervals across the building from one top of the side wall to the other on which the cheese taken out of the presses was placed to harden, and to be partially smoked with the reek of the peats and the birns or the stalks of heather which had been burnt on the ground a year or two before. There might not be much in it, but this sort of smoking was a sacred tradition. The chimney was a hole or barrel with its ends knocked out, placed in the middle of the roof, and so the smoke, which always rose well up from the floor, perambulated among the cheese-bearing planks up near the roof before it got out into the blue.... There was a small flitting and a big flitting to the shielings. Whenever spring grass began to sprout freely on the hill-grazings, the young and the yeld animals, and the horses which were not wanted for the farm work, were sent to the shielings, with boys to herd them, under the direction of provisional or permanent '*airidhichean*' or caretakers. Men too went up to prepare and to thatch huts and to see that the supply of last year's peats would do until the new peats came into use. The boys pulled heather, which, when packed close, standing right end uppermost, within board frames, or borders of stone on the beaten clay floors, was as good to lie on as a spring mattress and far more fragrant. This first preparatory flitting made no noise compared with the great flitting – '*latha dol do'n ruighe*' – when the milk cows, and the women with their plenishings, went on migration. On that occasion universal excitement prevailed. Children and dogs went crazy. Horses caught the infection. Mothers were harassed with many cares, and father sympathized. It looked too as if the slow bovine intelligence was stirred with memories and anticipations which added to the general turmoil. Milk vessels, churns, cheese presses, pots, pans, meal bags, salt arks, rennet apparatus, blankets, clothing, shoes and stockings – which were little used – spinning wheels, spindles and distaffs, flax and wool, with many other things, had to be packed on to the carts which looked not unlike big baskets on low wheels, that sure footed horses could haul almost anywhere. When they had settled the women in their respective huts and enjoyed a feast of cream and crowdie, the men returned home – peradventure rather gloomily – to the farming work which was their allotted portion. . . . Parish ministers looked after the shieling population and by field preachings at convenient stations afforded opportunities for general gatherings of the flitted and those left behind. But in the opinion of an old Chesthill woman who could not say her catechism questions, and was bothered with sermons, the glory of Finglen in the forest was that it was beyond the religious pale. Her hail to it was '*Fionna Ghleann mo chridhefar nach bitheadh Di-domhnaich*' (where there be no Sunday)".

Alexander Stewart was a shoemaker as well as a scholar and a poet, and another story his daughter tells of the time of the royal visit is of Callum Dubh,

a broken old man who had once learned shoemaking. After passing his seventieth birthday, he came to my father asking for a job as a shoemaker's assistant. . . . In his younger days he had seen more of life than was often experienced by young people at that time. Callum was of medium height, was well formed and hardy, and sound of constitution. He had learned to play the fiddle and was an experienced dancer. His neat feet and well formed legs suited the Highland dress admirably. When Queen Victoria and the Prince Consort visited Taymouth Castle in 1842, Callum and three other dancers were chosen to give exhibitions of Scottish dances before the royal visitors and nobility assembled, amid the fairy-like scene which hundreds of Chinese lanterns suspended from giant trees presented. So well did the dancers acquit themselves that Highland dancing in costume became the rage. The quartette were taken to London theatres to demonstrate the dexterity and grace with which the dances could be performed by qualified experts. In London they got a great reception; their performance created such a sensation that they were taken over to Paris where they had the honour to appear before King Louis Philippe. Although they knew nothing of the French language, they were well treated by the French and taken to see the sights. From the time that they were taken south to the time that their engagement in France came to an end they lived like lords; but every good thing comes to an end too soon. During the time of their fleeting fame their earnings were no doubt very good, but little of these were put to good use. On their return from France they landed at Liverpool, and being flush of money, they stayed at one of the hotels until their money was nearly all gone. In Callum's case his exchequer was exhausted so that he had to raise the wind by playing the fiddle in the street and dancing a few steps to amuse the passers by. He had many strange adventures after that. He often taught dancing classes in the winter. He was married and had four daughters, but never did much for them. He had been brought up by pious parents. He knew his Bible well and had wonderful memory. When he was in his cups he used to bemoan his prodigal career. His tears were copious, while he would quote passages from sermons of famous preachers. Callum always maintained that he would finish his career as a good Christian. In the end his friends took him in hand; he was well fed and clad but no money was allowed him. In old age, like the jackdaw of Rheims, he passed away in an odour of sanctity.

If Glen Lyon is remote as suited the MacGregors, the country to the north is wild indeed. At Garth a castle has been restored for private use that has seldom brought good fortune to its owners. It was originally built in the fourteenth century by Robert II's son Alexander, Earl of Buchan, Wolf of Badenoch, plunderer of Elgin Cathedral. His descendant, 200 years later, was not much better. Neil the Doomed burnt down Castle Menzies in 1502 and followed this up by murdering his wife Mariota. General Stewart of Garth's accuracy as a historian and his romantic view of the Highlands in the old days have come in for a good deal of criticism, but we should know a great deal less without his *Sketches* of the manners and customs of the Highland people, and his *History of the Highland Regiments*; and he was certainly a more congenial character than some of his forbears.

Schiehallion at 3547 feet is not the highest but it is one of the best-loved mountains in Perthshire; its conical peak stands up so well from all round, it is graceful and easily recognizable. The minor road which skirts its lower northern slopes, and, still more, its continuation north of Dunalastair to Trinafour, not only reaches actual heights of over 1000 feet but gives you the feeling that you are actually on top of the world. Dunalastair and most of the southern shore of Loch Rannoch was Robertson country, but Bunrannoch belonged to Stewarts whose banner was known as *'bratach na mogan'*, the 'stocking-legged banner' ever since the women of the clan had, in the absence of all their men at a cattle tryst, driven off armed raiders by belabouring them with stockings filled with stones.

Further along the lochside is the Black Wood of Rannoch, a remnant of the natural pine forest that once covered the Highlands. In the midst of it is Dall. Here new life has recently been brought to the site of an old house by the courageous founding of a school. Less orthodox in many ways than some, it owes much to the ideals of Kurt Hahn, the founder of Gordonstoun. Its story has been of remarkable success in the face of the difficulties that such a remote situation might be thought to present, and it is ideally placed to provide adventure training and every sort of variety of outdoor activity as well as a sound academic education. And in view of its remoteness, it is able to put back something of what it gains from its environment by operating an emergency ambulance service and the use of its fire service for the district, and help with mountain rescue, and also rescue on the loch itself, where many sail besides the school.

At the very head of Loch Rannoch are the remains of the barracks, built after 1745, in the region where the celebrated Sergeant Mor Cameron operated, and the road to Rannoch station. Beyond that no road runs, and the land is lonely indeed, but no less precious to some for that very reason.

Cameron had been a sergeant in the French service and had come over to Scotland in 1745.

Having no settled abode, and dreading the consequences of having served in the army of France, and of being afterwards engaged in the rebellion, he formed a party of outlaws, and took up his residence in the mountains between the counties of Perth, Inverness and Argyll. While he plundered the cattle of those he considered his enemies, he protected the property of his friends, and frequently made those on the borders of the Lowlands purchase his forbearance by the payment of Black Mail. Many stories are told of this man. On one occasion he met with an officer of the garrison at Fort William on the mountains of Lochaber. The officer told him that he suspected he had lost his way, and, having a large sum of money for the garrison, was afraid of meeting with Sergeant Mor; he therefore requested that the stranger should accompany him on his road. The other agreed; and, while they walked on, they talked much of the sergeant and his feats, the officer using much freedom with his name, calling him robber, murderer. "Stop there," said his companion, "he does indeed take the cattle of the Sassenachs and the Whigs, but neither he nor his kearnachs ever shed innocent blood; except once," added he, "that I was unfortunate at Braemar when a man was killed, but I immediately ordered the creach [spoil] to be abandoned, and left to the owners, retreating as fast as we could after such a misfortune." "You," says the officer, "what had you to do with the affair?" "I am John Dhu Cameron – I am the Sergeant Mor; there is the road to Inverlochy – you cannot now mistake it. You and your money are safe. Tell your Governor in future to send more wary messengers for his gold. Tell him also, that though an outlaw, and forced to live on the public, I am a soldier as well as himself, and would despise taking his gold from a defenceless man who confided in me." The officer lost no time in reaching the garrison, and never forgot the adventure which he frequently related.

Sometime after this, the Sergeant was betrayed by a treacherous friend ... and was carried to Perth, and tried before the High Court of Justiciary for the murder in Braemar, and various acts of theft and cattle stealing. ... He was executed at Perth on 23rd November 1753, and hung in chains.

IV

WEST FROM PERTH

Our last Highland chapter covers ground hardly less steeped in history, and certainly no less majestic in scenery – the two largest lochs, Tay and Earn, and two of the best mountains, Ben Vorlich and Ben Lawers, both over 3,000 feet, the latter unmatched in Britain for its alpine flora. Even the lesser hills astride the Sma' Glen yield a distinguished skyline and some of the best walking. And we are still in the upper reaches of the Tay which, in its immense length, is fed by streams from the west as well as from the north. Men may now be few and far between over much of the area but stone circles, and legends of Celtic missionaries, and Gaelic poetry, bear witness to past occupation.

But the approach is at first prosaic; the road to the west leaves Perth through its two least inspired housing estates but, in less than a mile, Ruthven Castle comes into view, and then Methven Castle and Methven village, and a signpost to Tibbermuir – all familiar names. Of these, only Ruthven Castle (or Huntingtower) is worth a visit. There is nothing to see of the battlegrounds at Methven, where Bruce was beaten in 1306 or at Tibbermuir where Montrose swept away some feeble defence by the citizens of Perth in 1644; and Methven Castle, though it is impressive when viewed from the road, has been much altered over the years. The two sturdy towers of 'the Place of Ruthven' are a different matter. All that has been done to them is to link them together and to enlarge some of the windows in the sixteenth century. The eastern tower is the older of the two; it dates from the fifteenth century and has an early painted ceiling in its first-floor hall and a good fireplace on the second floor. The west tower is rather larger and a little later but, being of the same height, does not throw the composition out of balance. Both have attics with corbelled roofs. They are in the custody of the Ministry of Environment and are open all the year round.

The story of the Ruthven raid and that of the Gowrie conspiracy have been told in the chapter on Perth but there is a third story, more charming, which we owe to Pennant who heard it when he visited the castle in 1769:

> A daughter of the first Earl of Gowrie was addressed by a young gentleman of inferior rank, a frequent visitor of the family, who never would give the least countenance to his suit. His lodging was in the tower, separate from that of his mistress.
> [*Sed vetuere patres quod non potuere vetare.*]
> The lady, before the doors were shut, conveyed herself thither into her lover's apartment; but some prying duenna acquainted the Countess with it; who, cutting off, as she thought, all possibility of retreat, hastened to surprise them. The young lady's ears were quick; she heard the footsteps of the old Countess, ran to the top of the leads, and took the desperate leap of 9 feet 4 inches over a chasm of sixty feet, and luckily lighting on the battlements of the other tower, crept into her own bed, where her astonished mother found her, and of course apologized for the unjust suspicion. The fair daughter did not choose to repeat the leap; but, next night, eloped and was married.

Methven Castle is not open to the public but it has an interesting history. Queen Margaret Tudor, widow of James IV, lived here after her third marriage and till her death in 1544. In 1664 it was bought by Patrick Smythe of Braco whose descendant, Miss Smyth of Methven, still lives in the neighbourhood. This Patrick's wife was a formidable lady who once drove a party of Covenanters off her husband's land, pistol in hand. She reported to her husband in October 1678:

> [For my heart-keeper.]
> My precious love,
>
> A multitude of men and women, from east, west, and south, came, the 13th day of this October, to hold a field conventicle, two bows draught above our church. They had their tent set up before the sun, upon your ground. I, seeing them

flocking to it, sent through your ground and charged them to repair to your brother David, the bailie and me, to the castle hill, where we had sixty armed. Your brother with drawn sword and bent pistol, I with the light horseman's piece bent, on my left arm, and a drawn tuck in my right hand, all your servants well armed, marched forward, and kept the one half of them fronting the other, that were guarding their minister, and their tent which is their standard. That rear party which we yoked with, most of them were St Johnston people. Many of them had no wish to be known, but rode off to see what we would do. They marched towards Busby. We marched betwixt them, and gained ground before they could gather in a body. They sent off a party of a hundred men, to see if we meant to hinder them to meet. We told them that, if they would not go from the parish of Methven presently, it would be a bloody day, for I protested, as did your brother, before God, that we would wear out our lives upon them, before they should preach in our regality or parish. They said they would preach. We charged them either to fight or to fly. They held a counsel amongst themselves what to do. At last, about two o'clock in the afternoon, they said they would go away, if we would let the squadron that was above the church, with the tent, march freely with them. We were content, knowing that they had ten times as many as we were ... and so we went to church and heard a feared minister preach. They have sworn not to stand such an affront, but have resolved to come back next week; and I, in the Lord's strength, intend to accost them with all who will come to assist us. ... I have written to your nephew, the treasurer of Edinburgh, to send me two brass hagbutts if found, and that by the bearer. If they come next Saturday, I shall have them with us. My love, present my humble duty to my Lord Marquis of Montrose, and my Lady. Likewise all your friends. And, my blessed love, comfort yourself in this – if the fanatics chance to kill me, it shall not be for nought. I was wounded for our gracious King; and now, in the strength of the Lord God of Heaven, I'll hazard my person with the men I may command before these rebels rest where ye have power. Sore I miss you, but now more as ever. ... I wrote to you formerly to expect me up if ye would not come [her husband was in London]. Now I have engaged with the conventicles from whom I would not flee. I'll do your will. God give the blessing is the prayer of your

Anne Keith

The castle in which this good lady lived looks large enough and had housed a queen, but it was summarily dismissed by a nineteenth-century writer as a residence which might fit a baronet – or, he added somewhat half-heartedly, "even a peer".

The village of Methven is small but growing, with a wide main street. It once had a Collegiate Church but of this nothing remains but a small aisle with decorated tracery in its window – enough to show what has been lost. In the graveyard, General Sir Thomas Graham of Balgowan, Lord Lynedoch, is buried in a huge unadorned vault. Balgowan House is gone, and Keillour Castle, just further on, is now a ruin, but round the modern house there is a garden of European renown, created by Mrs Knox-Finlay and her late husband, an expert in Alpines, Himalayans and in shrubs. Even if it is not a day on which the garden has been opened to the public, as it is from time to time, it is still worth diverging from the main road at Balgowan School, past Craigend and Wester Keillour and Fornought Farms, for the sake of the wide views over Strathearn and, in the high summer, for the sake of the wild roses that profusely line the hedges. Then, a sharp drop down from Pitlandy brings you to Fowlis Wester and two great Pictish crosses. One stands on the village green; it is the more vigorous of the two, with human figures and animals, and is unique in that the arms of the cross extend beyond the slab. The other is inside the well restored thirteenth-century church and depicts two ecclesiastics, possibly St Anthony and St Paul, and Pictish beasts, one of them swallowing a man. There has probably been a church here since the eighth century when St Bean, to whom the church is dedicated, worked in these parts. A finely carved stone survives, dated 1644, probably intended for the place where a modern replica has been placed over the entrance to the churchyard: "Take heed to thy foot when thou enterest the hows of God." The little houses on the other side of the green are most attractive, especially, the old inn, which has been saved and put in good order by the National Trust for Scotland.

In this parish, and just across the road, Morays have lived at

Abercairny for over 600 years. Sir Andrew Moray of Bothwell was the first knight to join Wallace, and it was his son Sir John who acquired lands in Perthshire in 1290. Two descendants fell at Flodden and one at Pinkie. And in the seventeenth and eighteenth centuries, all fought for the Stewart cause, though they managed to escape forfeiture. The ruse by which this was achieved was preserved for posterity by Ramsay of Ochteryre who was an old family friend:

> In the autumn of 1746, Clerk Miller of Perth, a very able but unpopular man, much trusted by the King's servants at Edinburgh, seeing Mr Anderson, factor to James Moray of Abercairny, on the street, beckoned to him. Taking him aside, he said, "Anderson, do you not remember being in the town a year ago when the Highlanders were here?" "Really, George, my memory is not as good as it has been." Said the other, "I will refresh it. Do you not remember carrying 1000 guineas to the Prince and making a speech to him in your master's name?" Mr Anderson, who was a shrewd business man, got away as soon as he could, and galloped home. On hearing what had passed, Abercairny said, "Let my horses be saddled; I will set out directly for France or Holland." "That I hope will be unnecessary. Take your bed, and play the part of a sick man, to which your friend Dr Smith of Perth will give countenance, and leave the rest to me." The good Dr readily entered into the plot, and pronounced his patient to be in great danger. Meanwhile Abercairny directed George Miller to be sent for in great haste. On his entering into the bedchamber, the supposed sick man addressed him thus, in a very quavering voice, "My dear George, thinking myself a dying man, it is most proper I should settle my worldly affairs. In your ability and integrity I have full confidence; let bonds of provision to the younger children and a nomination of tutors and curators be drawn as soon as possible. I mean to make you factor on the estate till the heir be of age. Nor shall it be in the power of the tutors to remove you from office." The deeds were drawn for which Miller received fifty guineas and then went home. In a competent time, the laird recovered and it may well be thought that for some months George was a frequent and welcome guest at Abercairny. Anderson judged soundly. Miller, who was sheriff as well as town clerk, and supposed to be vicious as well as harsh, took no steps to investigate Abercairny's conduct in September 1745. When the

Act of Indemnity was passed, in which he was *not* an excepted person, he sent for his friend Miller and, after giving him a good dinner and plenty of wine, loaded him with abuse, and kicked him to the door. The person from whom I heard this, had good access to know. On my asking Abercairny if it was true, he laughed and said, "Hypocritical scoundrel! He went and said no man had ever used him so ill as I did."

In the nineteenth century the old house was pulled down and replaced with a vast Gothic mansion – hopelessly impracticable. This, in its turn, had to be demolished, but its gardens survive and are open to the public every Wednesday in summer under the Scottish Gardens Scheme.

Marching with Abercairny were the lands of Cultoquhey. These too were held by the same family – the Maxtones – for six centuries. They have recently been sold, but a delightful book of memories by the late Mrs E. Maxtone Graham enshrines what the house stood for. Its best known laird was Mungo in the early eighteenth century who used to intone daily at a well near the house, surrounded by his family:

> From the greed of the Campbells,
> From the ire of the Drummonds,
> From the pride of the Grahams,
> From the wind of the Murrays,
>   Good Lord deliver us.

a litany aimed not really at those clans in general, but against the particular owners of the considerably larger estates immediately surrounding him, all of whom he felt were ever ready to pounce. Desperate measures were sometimes needed, as may be seen from this letter written by the ever-scheming Earl of Breadalbane to the Duke of Atholl: "There is ane old little family ther, related to your Grace, readie to perish presently if it be not prevented: it is Cultewhay. All the cuntree has kindness for him, except such as covets his little vine yaird. I remember that your father preserved him once. It is debt that is lyk to swallow him up. The remedie proposed to me was that Balgown, having a very lame daughter, would bestow on him that was willing to accept of her, he giving 10 or 12 thousand marks with her, which would preserve him. This I only inform your Grace of, without making any application: it is thought Balgown may be the more neir altho his daughter be not mercat ware, that if lands must go, his son in law Abercairny is to be the merchant."

In fact, Mungo did marry a Graham, probably the girl referred to in the letter. He also kept up with the Duke, to whom he wrote to London:

> I have the infinit pleasure to tell you that my Lady Dutchess was safely delivered of a son, my young Marquis, this night a quarter after nine o'clock at night. My Lady Dutchess is very safe and the child a thumping boy.
>
> I desire that the Captain and your Grace may get as drunk as your humble servants shall do. My hand shakes so for joy that I cannot write.
>
> My Lord Duke, Your Grace's most humble servant, etc,
> 28th March 1735.

In spite of the Litany, the Graham connection was always close. The sixth, eighth, tenth, eleventh and twelfth lairds all married Graham neighbours, the sixth's wife being of Inchbrakie. This family, like that of Balgowan, is also no more – as was foretold by a witch, as she was tied to the stake for burning. The Inchbrakie family tradition was recorded in 1895 by Miss L. Graham

> My mother was the wife of the second son of Inchbrakie, and I have often heard her relate how, on her home-coming as a bride, my grandfather on one occasion told her the story. He spoke of a witch being brought to the notice of the authorities by Monzie. She was being burnt on the Knock of Crieff above Monzie, when the Inchbrakie of the day, riding past, did all in his power to prevent the matter from being concluded, without avail. Just as the fire was being lit, she bit a blue bead from off her necklet, and spitting it at Inchbrakie, bade him guard it carefully, for so long as it was kept at Inchbrakie the lands should pass from father to son. Kate McNiven then cursed the Laird of Monzie.
>
> My grandfather had the stone set in a golden ring and kept it in a casket, and his own daughter was not allowed to touch it, only his daughters-in-law. On my mother's presenting my grand-father with his first grandson, he bade her slip it on her finger, as

the mother of an heir. Nearly forty years after, when I was a young girl, I well remember my mother's horror and dismay when my cousin Patrick, the head of the family, opened a box of papers which, during the family's absence abroad, had been left in her care; for there was the ring in which the stone was set, no longer guarded within the walls of Inchbrakie. A few years after this, the first acres were sold; now there is not one of them left.

Before going west to Crieff, or north through the Sma' Glen, mention must be made of three places of interest on the little road running parallel to the main east-west road and north of it. The village of Harrietfield has associations with the Kailyard School of Scottish writing. Towards the end of the nineteenth century the Rev. John Watson, otherwise Ian Maclaren, was minister of the Free Church at Logiealmond and drew, from his time there, the material for "Beside the Bonnie Brier Bush" – as, earlier, he had drawn from his schooldays at Perth Academy for "The Young Barbarians".

At Buchanty Spout, there is a fall where salmon may be seen leaping in autumn as they make their way up the Almond to spawn, while between Buchanty and Logiealmond, is Trinity College Glenalmond, which shares with Plockton High School and Rannoch the three finest sites for a school in Britain. Founded in 1841 by W. E. Gladstone when he was still a young man, it has, over the years managed to combine academic distinction with the fullest possible use of the outdoor facilities which its position so lavishly supplies. Its chapel is one of the few successful and not over-ornate buildings of the Gothic revival, and, music being one of the school's traditions, boasts a fine organ. Another cherished tradition is that of Saturday dockets – free time on Saturdays in the summer to explore the surrounding hills.

The Sma' Glen needs no description. With its steep sides thick with heather, traces of Wade's old road, and the Almond flowing along its bottom, it is justly one of the most visited beauty spots in Scotland. South of Dallick, at its entrance, are the faint contours of a Roman auxiliary fort at Fendoch. This had a signal station and look-out post in the form of a platform surrounded with a small circular embankment; it can be found by going 150 yards along the road north from a stone drinking trough for horses (known to generations of Glenalmond boys as the Temperance Hotel) and then striking up into the heather.

A few miles north at Newton Brig, a public right of way (on foot) leads up the secluded Upper Glen Almond, offering also superb walking in the hills on either side, or over to Ardtalnaig on Loch Tay. Ben Chonzie to the south is a Munro.

Back on the main road, there are usually a few Highland cattle to be seen near Corrymuckloch, and sometimes a hen-harrier. At Amulree, a road runs up the deserted Glen Quaich, and from its head another right of way over to Loch Tay. After Amulree the road rises and the country becomes bleaker, though no less heather covered, and just before you start to descend to Aberfeldy, the little Loch na Craige adds a touch of variety. Then comes a view totally different from but as fine as anything in the Sma' Glen itself – green and fertile Strathtay with Farragon Hill beyond, and, to the west, the shapely cone of Schiehallion. From Aberfeldy to Tyndrum is Breadalbane.

> From Kenmore
> To Ben Mohr
> The land is a' the Markiss's
> The mossy howes
> The heathery knowes
> And ilka bonnie park is his
>
> The bearded goats
> The toozie stots
> And a' the braxy carcasses.
> Ilk crofter's rent
> Ilk tinker's tent
> And ilka collie's bark is his.
>
> The muircock's craw
> The piper's blaw
> The gillie's hard day's work is his
> From Kenmore
> To Ben Mohr
> The World is a' the Markiss's.

was Punch's verdict – not its first nor its only comment on the vast lands acquired by the Campbells of Glenorchy. In fact, they stretched far beyond Ben More into Nether Lorn and to the islands of Luing and Seil on the Argyll coast.

Not an acre of that now belongs to the family of Breadalbane, and there is no need to detail the harsh way in which the empire was built up. Even Glenorchy itself involved the eviction of Macgregors from Glenstrae. Then the Menzieses and the MacNabs were driven out of Glen Dochart, the Drummonds from Finlarig, the Chalmerses, the Napiers, the Haldanes and the Robertsons from the shores of Loch Tay until, finally, the eastern end of the loch was reached. Here was another possession of the MacGregor and it was seized by Grey Colin, sixth of Glenorchy, in the middle of the sixteenth century in spite of the fact that he had been fostered by the MacGregors and owed them special protection. Thereafter the family feud was pursued with the same senseless disregard for human life, let alone human rights, that can only be paralleled in Northern Ireland today. Castles were built first on a little island which had once held a priory founded by Alexander I, and then at Balloch, now Taymouth. This completed a string of castles which included Edinample at the head of Loch Earn, and Kilchurn at the head of Loch Awe, with Finlarig and Castle Dochart guarding the narrows of the east-west route – to say nothing of Barcaldine and Ardmaddy in Argyll. Black Duncan 1583-1631 had some merits; he had great energy and planted trees and built embankments, repaired Finlarig and built a chapel there; but he was deep in the plots which led to the murder of Cawdor, and the execution pit at Finlarig was also his, and the "warm hose" – an iron splint which could be heated to extract confessions. He was the first baronet and the great-grandfather of the most famous of all the family, Iain Glas, the First Earl, the most hated man of his day. He had waged war, out of time, to seize Caithness, which brought him no joy. He had disinherited his eldest son, quarrelled with the second whom he had chosen as his successor, and nagged at his youngest when the latter was dying. The Macdonalds and the other supporters of the Stewarts believed that he had engineered the Massacre of Glencoe, and had made off with a large sum of Government money intended for them. The Government believed with equal probability that he was in fact intriguing with the Jacobites. By his costly efforts to increase yet further his vast estates, he had ruined himself and his heir, and he ended his life a pitiable pensioner of his creditors. Only on his deathbed did he attain a semblance of dignity. At the time of the 1715 Rebellion, a garrison had been sent to Balloch as a precaution against his raising his people for the Old Pretender, and the officer in command touched the eighty-one-year-old Earl on the shoulder. "Sir, you are my prisoner," to which the Earl replied "Your prisoner? I am the prisoner now of Almighty God. Duncan, take that poor man away and get him out of the country before my people hear of the insult he has offered me."

"Grave as a Roman, cunning as a fox, wise as a serpent and slippery as an eel", was Mackie's verdict on him.

The earl who showed most concern for his tenants was the fourth, who later became the first Marquis and died in 1834. His motives may have been tinged with out-of-date ideas of keeping as many people as possible on his land – a relic of the days when a chief's importance was measured by the number of fighting men he could bring into the field – but he did impress on his chamberlains their responsibility to look after the widow, and the soldier returned from the wars, and one at least he dismissed summarily for oppression. But it was he who pulled down the old Balloch Castle which from a surviving drawing looks as though it must have been almost the ideal house – a sixteenth-century tower flanked by two dignified and comfortable-looking eighteenth-century wings. A Marquis needed something more, and the second Marquis who was also Lord Chamberlain needed a palace in which he could entertain his queen. The result was the empty Gothic shell which stands today in fallen grandeur in the middle of a golf course. It is not open to the public but once a year a ball is held there and guests may walk up the vaulted stairway with its elaborate plaster work to reach the heavily over-ornate Banner Hall.

The financially ruinous entertainments laid on by the

Marquis of Breadalbane for Queen Victoria's first visit to Scotland, in 1842, make odd reading today but they were in keeping with the age. The official record is dedicated to:

THE MOST HONOURABLE
JOHN, MARQUIS OF BREADALBANE ETC ETC ETC
WHOSE MAGNIFICENT RECEPTION OF HIS SOVEREIGN
AND HER ROYAL CONSORT
ON THE OCCASION OF
THE ROYAL VISIT TO SCOTLAND IN 1842
did equally honour to himself, his country, and his order, and has won the grateful admiration of Scotsmen.

On arrival the Queen was received by 200 of the Marquis's tenants dressed as Breadalbane Highlanders, at the expense of their chief, by the 93rd Highlanders, and by uniformed boat-men and other retainers. If we may believe the record, they were called to attention, after having stood at ease on parade for an unspecified time, as soon as a message was received that the Queen "was approaching the Castle", i.e. was nine miles off. She did not arrive for another hour! Then there was a grand dinner off gold and silver plate "the former predomi-nating", followed by a firework display in the grounds which were illuminated by literally thousands of fairy lights, after which Her Majesty retired to rest in a new wing which had been added to the castle for the occasion.

Next morning, His Royal Highness went out on the hill, he alone shooting while his host and the other gentry supervised the work of the beaters, and, on his return, was able to lay out for the Queen's inspection twenty-two roe-bucks, four and a half brace of black game, three brace of grouse, one brace of capercailzie, one partridge, one wood pigeon, twelve hares, one owl, and several rabbits. The Prince went out shooting again on the third day but its highlight was a grand ball in the evening for which there were more illuminations. On her last day, the Queen was rowed down Loch Tay all the way to Auchmore in a royal barge, the inside of which had been painted to resemble the Breadalbane tartan. It was steered by Captain MacDougall of Lorn and Dunolly R.N. and accompanied by four other barges containing notabilities, and two gigs with some pipers and the band of the 66th Highlanders.

An earlier and simpler form of life is revealed at Croftmoraig (*see* plate 12), a mile to the north-east of the castle, just by the road-side. Here there was first a circle of wooden posts – then an inner ring of stones, surrounded by a bank – and finally about 2000 B.C. an outer circle of stones. Given the lack of tools and means of transport, these circles must have involved human effort comparable to that involved in building Taymouth Castle.

As at Inveraray, an eighteenth-century village was created from nothing at Kenmore in order to remove the villagers out of sight of their chief and his guests – and the church was removed at the same time. From the square, roads run down both sides of Loch Tay; on the north, the faster; on the south the narrower but preferable way, with better views of Ben Lawers. Much of the mountain to the north is now the property of the National Trust for Scotland owing to the generosity of Percy Unna, that benefactor who was also responsible for securing much of Glencoe and Kintail and Torridon for the nation. Here is something for everyone – an Information Centre at the car park (by which time you are already at 1400 feet) – a Nature Trail on the lower slopes – walking and skiing above – and, for the botanist, an alpine flora unequalled in Britain. The trust have published an *Introduction* to the area, describing the geology in terms that even the layman can understand, the climate on the mountain, its vegetation with drawings of the rarer plants, and the ski-runs – the whole illustrated with four photographs at the various seasons of the year. From the car-park, the road continues to 1800 feet before dropping down to Milton Eonan and Innerwick in Glen Lyon (*see* page 14).

At the western end of Loch Tay, you cross the River Lochy, its stream and falls now much depleted by hydro-electric schemes, and almost immediately there is a signpost to the left to the pier. This used to serve a steamer by which those at the eastern end of the loch could reach the railhead at Killin. This side-road passes the rock on which stands the burial place of the Campbells of Glenorchy and the ruins of their favourite Finlarig. If Taymouth is sad, the remains of Finlarig are depressing beyond belief. The mausoleum is a heap of crumbled masonry surrounded gloomily with damp trees and is adjoined by an all-too-well preserved execution pit. The ruins them- selves are dangerous and not even the fine site can be ap- preciated, because the undergrowth obscures the views which the castle must once have had.

Killin is somewhat shut in by hills but is, none the less, an attractive place with a view up the loch from one end of the village and the Falls of Dochart at the other (*see* plate 16) – tremendous when in spate; Kinnell, the home of the MacNabs, with its vine that is said never to miss fruiting, and the little island of Inch Buie which is their burial place. The giant sixteenth laird is the best known of the line – from the Raeburn portrait of him – a superb portrayal of what a chief thought he ought to look like in the age of Sir Walter Scott. He was an eccentric and proliferous bachelor, the father of 32 children and, no doubt, an enthusiastic believer in the *droit de seigneur*. As the distiller of the best whisky in Scotland, he had a great hatred of excisemen, and on one occasion put to flight a posse of them when they were trying to intercept a consign- ment of illicit spirits that had been captured by MacNab's own company of the Breadalbane Highlanders.

Earlier, the MacNabs had tended to support the traditional but losing side. They backed the Macdougalls against Bruce, and, in the seventeenth century, the Stewarts against Par- liament, with the result that they fell increasingly into the hands of the Campbells of Glenorchy – and that, in the days of Iain Glas, was disastrous. Not content with persuading Monk to burn down Ellanrayne Castle, the Campbells continued to harry the MacNabs and the Government had to intervene: "Understanding that by virtue of my late orders for your having satisfaction out of the estates of the McNabs you are proceeding against the widow of the Laird of McNab deceast [he had been killed in the Civil Wars in 1653] I desire you will forbear to trouble her, in regard she has paid cesse, and lived peaceably since her husband's death: nor would I have you extend that order to any that live peaceably at home; but such as are obstinate and continue in arms against the Commonwealth," and the author adds significantly, "I desire you also to forbeare to meddle with any of the Magrigors." For all that, the family became increasingly in debt to Breadalbane, and they had a further misfortune when they did decide in the end to support the House of Hanover. Alan MacNab died in 1735 at the early age of nineteen when serving with one of the Independent Companies:

Humanity with Pity, both virtues shining clear
And those indeed are in a youth of birth and worth lies here.

And the fifteenth laird was taken prisoner by the Jacobites at Prestonpans in 1745. The sixteenth laird was not the sort to tailor his life style to his penniless situation, and the story of the seventeenth laird who had to flee to Canada is broad farce. He persuaded the Governor to grant him 81,000 acres so that he could persuade MacNabs to emigrate and settle on virgin land, two months journey up the Ottawa River. The land had to be cleared, there was no food for the winter, the settlers were cold and hungry and soon disillusioned. When they further discovered that MacNab was charging them rent for land that was supposed to be free, they sent a complaint to the Governor. MacNab thought that he knew who was responsible and wrote to the suspect:

Degraded Clansman,
                    You are accused to me by Sir John Colburne [the Governor] of libel, sedition and high treason. You will therefore compeir before me at my house of Kinnell and there make submission, and if you show a contrite and repentent spirit, and confess your faults against me your legitimate Chief and your crime against His Majesty King George I will intercede for your pardon.
Your offended Chief
MacNab.

He could not get away with that in Canada but he did manage to hold on in some sort of state for another ten years, until

Lord Durham, equally high-handed in his own way, arrived to deal with Mackenzie's rebellion. Then he was compelled to return all the rents he had exacted, and was finally ruined. Kinnell had already passed to the chief creditor – Breadalbane. Only recently, in 1949, was the house repurchased.

From Killin, our route must now take us south via Glen Ogle, and then back along Loch Earn to Comrie and Crieff, but others may prefer to follow the main road to the west past Castle Dochart on its island to Crianlarich and Strathfillan. Here St Fillan worked at the same time as St Adamnan was teaching in Glen Lyon. His name means Little Wolf. "One day, while the saint was ploughing, a wolf came and attacked his yoke of oxen, killing one of them; but no sooner had the saint invoked the power of heaven than the repentant wolf returned and submitted itself to the yoke, and so supplied the place of its victim." More historically he had a wooden crozier, which was preserved after his death, and most beautifully decorated with silver, and then enclosed in an even more intricately chased outer case. For centuries this was cared for by a family of Deuchars (Dewars) who received land in return as an inheritance. In time, this land was lost and the Dewars became simple labourers. But they kept possession of their precious relic, even when they had to emigrate to Canada. Eventually it was purchased and brought back and now, with St Fillan's handbell, it is among the most treasured possessions of the National Museum of Antiquities in Edinburgh. The saint also had eight stones which are still preserved in the old mill at Killin, each of which was used for healing different parts of the body.

Another alternative to our route back along Loch Earn is to take the Glasgow road at Lochearnhead to visit the Trossachs or to turn aside to Balquhidder to explore the braes by the footpath via Kirkton Glen over to Lecharrie in Glen Dochart. At Balquhidder is a ruined chapel and Rob Roy's grave. It is said that, as he lay on his deathbed, he was told that one of his enemies wished to speak with him. He would not be seen in a state of weakness and insisted on being dressed and armed. When the interview was over, he sought absolution from the church for his past sins, only to be abused by his wife and exhorted to die as he had lived. "You have put strife between me and the best men of the country, all my life," he replied, "and now you would place enmity between me and my God." With equal right the chiefs of the Clan Maclaren are also buried at Balquhidder.

We may return on either side of Loch Earn. Much has been done recently to improve the major road along the northern shore; it gives a better view of Ben Vorlich but nothing extraordinary, as it is a mountain that needs to be climbed or seen at a considerable distance. For those who are not in a hurry and have no caravan to tow, there is much to be said for the southern route in spite of its narrowness and passing-places. Edinchip is the home of the present chief of the Macgregors. Edinample was Glenorchy property, then ruinous, but it is now being restored by a new owner. Ardvorlich has been Stewart for centuries. In 1589 it was the scene of one of the grislier exploits of the Macgregors. The Laird of Ardvorlich's wife was the sister of John Drummond of Drummond Ernoch the king's forester on Glenartney, and the latter had caught some Macgregors poaching and had cut off their ears. In return, the children of the mist killed Drummond. Then, having cut off his head and wrapped it in a plaid, they sought hospitality at Ardvorlich while the laird was away. While his lady was out of the room seeing to their supper, they unwrapped their burden and set it on the table with bread and cheese between its jaws. Not surprisingly it proved too much for the lady's wits.

The Stewarts of Ardvorlich, like the Robertsons, had a healing stone. According to the Old Statistical Account, it was "like a lump of pure white rock crystal, about the size and shape of a large egg, bound with four bands of silver of very antique workmanship. Over a considerable district of the country it is known by the name of Clach Dearg, which means the red stone, arising, probably, from a reddish tinge it appears to have when held up to the light. The water in which the stone has been dipped has been considered a sovereign remedy in all diseases of cattle, and many persons, even from distant parts of the district, are in the habit of resorting to Ardvorlich to procure the water, but, like all similar objects of superstitious reverence, it is now losing its repute" – or so, no doubt, the worthy minister hoped. Ardvorlich was the scene of the gathering of the clans to meet Montrose in April 1645, and is described under the name of Darnlinvarach in Scott's *Legend of Montrose*.

The bloodthirsty story of the Drummond–Fearnoch murder has much in common with one from the eastern end of Loch Earn. There was a small branch of Clan Neish who eked out a lawless existence from their home on a crannog near St Fillans. They had earlier fallen foul of the MacNabs and matters came to a head when in 1612 they managed to intercept the MacNabs' Christmas and New Year supplies on their way from Crieff to Ellanrayne on Loch Tay. All might have been settled, if not amicably, without more than usual bloodshed, had not MacNab's second wife seen it as an opportunity to eliminate the two sons of her husband's first marriage in favour of her own ten. Hoping to involve them in an unequal struggle from which they would not return, she addressed them in words which have gone down in history: "Tonight is the night if only lads were lads!" Inevitably, the dare was accepted, but, to her horror, the two did not go off alone; her own two eldest sons insisted on going too, to take their share in the glory and the revenge. In the long night of midwinter, the four of them, led by the eldest, Iain Min, manhandled their boat over the intervening hills and rowed out to the Neish island home. There they slaughtered all the adults and cut off their heads and returned with them in a sack to their anxious father. "Dread nought" was their cry to him – now part of the clan slogan. Then, when the stepmother emerged, Iain Min, who had guessed her real aim, had his revenge. "What have you got there?" she asked. "Bowls for your bairns to play with", was the reply as Iain undid the sack and rolled out its contents at her feet.

Nowadays, at the eastern end of the loch, there is an outcrop of caravans, hideous to look at but giving great joy to many who, from them, have access to hill and loch – to country unspoilt, and to sailing and water-skiing. With this site and a number of excellent hotels, St Fillans is a popular holiday centre. This St Fillan was earlier than the St Fillan of Strath-fillan and died around A.D. 520, but he too was a healer. Dunfillan Hill with a stone at the top – his seat – and his well at the foot can be reached by a short walk across the golf course. His well was especially frequented on 1st May and 1st August when sufferers walked or were carried three times round the well and then drank from and were bathed in its waters. Sufferers from rheumatism, however, since this was a particularly obstinate malady, had to ascend the hill, sit in the saint's chair, and then be pulled to the bottom of the hill by their legs. Even this was better than the cures prescribed at the saint's other shrine near Tyndrum, where there was another pool to which those suffering from mental disorders had to be taken at night in the very middle of winter. They had to bring up three stones from the depths of the pool, walk three times round three cairns, and put a stone on each. Then they were bound hand and foot, and left for the rest of the night in a ruined chapel. No doubt some were cured by this treatment, as some are cured today by electric convulsion treatment, but Pennant was probably not far wrong, when he said that "death was only too often the angel which released the afflicted".

Just behind Dunfillan is a small ruined chapel, the burial place of the Stewarts of Ardvorlich since 1500, and the hill of Dundurn. The latter is of great interest to archaeologists as being one of the comparatively few Pictish forts which are mentioned in written records. The Iona *Annal* refers to a siege (by the Picts) of the Scottish fort at Dunadd in Argyll in the year A.D.683 and then to a siege (by the Scots) of "Duinduirn" in the same year – what has been called a "home and away match". It has always been thought probable that Dundurn was the fort referred to because its site controls the main east-west route from the heart of Dalriada to the heart of Pictland, and recent excavations lend weight to this view. It is extremely probable that the earlier of two forts on the summit was completed shortly before 683, and the other perhaps a century later. This one might tie in with another mention of

Dundurn in written accounts when, in 889, some time after the unification of the Scottish and Pictish kingdoms by Kenneth MacAlpine, Girg mac Dungall was killed there apparently while suppressing a Pictish rising. Another point of interest was that the timber reinforcement for the stone walls of the earlier fort was secured by nails in the same way as in the fort built by the Picts at Burghead in Morayshire. However at Dundurn there is not a great deal to be seen above ground, and, in any case, it is on private ground; but the view from the road is impressive (*see* plate 15).

Woods and meadows lie to the east until Comrie is reached, another of Perthshire's characteristic small towns. Here, the fort was Roman, built to guard against possible incursions from the highland glens to the west. Comrie is the place with the highest rate of earthquake tremors in Scotland, but these have not so far proved unduly disconcerting, and there are many compensations – the river with its old bridge, the main street, the dignified white church building (no longer the parish church but converted into a youth centre), good hotel accommodation, a Museum of Tartan, a midnight torch procession at Hogmanay, and an excellent cricket ground. This last is the gift of Sir Robert Dundas who learnt his cricket at Glenalmond in the last century and continued to play until he was well into his eighties. He is one of the distinguished legal family of Dundas of Arniston, which produced Pitt's hard-working but ill-starred Treasurer of the Navy, Viscount Melville, Baron Dunira. The latter lived mostly at Dunira after his impeachment and is commemorated by a granite memorial on Dunmore Hill. The house is now a burnt-out ruin.

But the greatest attraction of Comrie is that it is there that the River Ruchill (from Glenartney) and the Lednoch join the Earn. It was by the former that

> The stag at eve had drunk his fill
> When danced the moon on Monan's rill
> And deep his midnight lair had made
> In lone Glenartney's hazel shade

at the opening of *The Lady of the Lake*. Nowadays there is an unsightly army installation near where the Roman fort once was but there is also, at Tullichettle, the hill of sheep, a curious slab over the grave of one, James Riddoch, with a sword and various trade emblems – axe, adze, square, mallet, chisel and plough. Further up the glen, the country becomes beautiful indeed, and utterly unspoilt except in the sad sense that it is so because it was formerly 'cleared' to make way for sheep. So was Glen Lednock, opposite. Its road starts off through a narrow wooded gorge, and is itself narrow with passing places, but parking space is provided for a stop, either to walk up to the Melville memorial for the sake of the view it offers, or to go down to the river bank. A hydro-electric scheme has depleted the flow, and the Devil's Cauldron no longer lives up to its name – but the surroundings are pleasantly peaceful. Further on, the glen opens out again, into wide moorland.

Comrie to Braco is an open moorland road; Comrie to Strowan and Muthill leads past another monument (to Sir David Baird – *see* page 110) and the site of St Ronan's Chapel (his handbell is in the Perth Museum); Comrie to Crieff passes dignified mansions at Lawers and Ochtertyre. Lawers was originally Fordie, and the story was that the laird executed one man on the first of each month lest his right to do so should be questioned. Later it became Campbell property, belonging to a strongly Presbyterian branch of the Glenorchy family. The second Campbell of Lawers was created Earl of Loudon and left the estate to his brother, whose son – according to the Statistical Account –

was appointed to the command of a company of soldiers, and invested with the authority to restrain the freebooters of the surrounding district, or to bring the refractory to justice. In the discharge of his commission he brought a number of the Macgregors in, who were subsequently hanged. This roused against him the vengeful passions of the clan, and they resolved to accomplish his destruction. They accordingly assailed the House of Lawers by night, forced their way to his bedchamber, and were about to put him to death there, even in the presence of his lady. With difficulty they were prevailed on to allow him time to commend himself to God by offering up prayer in the chapel adjoining, before they took his life. On their way thither he employed his time so well, and appealed so successfully to their love of gain, which they were as eager to gratify as their revenge, that they agreed to spare his life on condition of his paying a ransom of 10,000 marks on the following Monday, at a tavern in the neighbourhood. Faithful to his agreement, Lawers proceeded to raise the sum – no inconsiderable amount at that time. The greatest part was collected in halfpence, and carried on horseback to the place appointed. But while he thus fulfilled the letter of his covenant, he also performed more than he had promised, or his captors expected. While the money was being paid, a troop of military surrounded the house, and made the freebooters with their chieftain, Captain Oig Macgregor, prisoners.

Lawers was the scene of one of the earliest recorded 'sporting lets'. In 1749, Sir John Clerk of Penicuik, for his own and his daughter's health, decided that a change of air, diet and occupation, might be beneficial, so he conducted what he called a 'goat whey campaign'. Unfortunately, the goat's whey did not agree with him, and anyway there was a shortage of goats ready for milking. But he went fishing in the Water of Earn, and wrote in his journal that:

> The salmon were very good and the Trouts excellent, all red in flesh, but not many; they were generally between 14 and 18 inches long. I had a fishing rod there, but did little good with it there, for I knew not the right streams, but at last found one above Lawers never wanted salmon, for at one draught we got 4 or 5, tho we had a bad net. . . . There is a third stream under the kirk and boat of Strouan, which is excellent for the rod.

He also visited the church at Comrie, the Innerpeffray Library, the Roman remains at Ardoch, the red deer in Glenartney, and Monzie, Ochteryre and Aberuchil; but for all that, he "wearied very soon, and staid only about 4 weeks".*

Just before reaching Crieff, one can see from the road the eighteenth-century mansion of Ochtertyre, for 500 years the home of a branch of the Tullibardine Murrays, who were holders of a baronetcy so prized that its holder laid down that any of his descendants who should accept a peerage should be thereby disqualified from succeeding to the family estates.

* *Memoirs of Sir J. Clerk of Penicuik,* edited by John M. Gray for Scottish Historical Society, 1892.

These included the castle at Fowlis Easter (*see* page 153) bought in 1667 by the first baronet. The second married a Haldane who spent generously on help for those of his father-in-law's tenants in the Gleneagles neighbourhood who had been so barbarously burnt out of their homes by Mar in 1716. The third baronet with his nineteen children divided their time between Fowlis Easter and the old house at Ochtertyre, which stood rather further up the hill than the existing one and so must have had an even finer view. He is interesting in that his household account book has survived and we are able to know just what was served each day for dinner and supper over a period of three years. There was no lack, right through the year, of beef and mutton or of eggs in the shell which were a standby at supper. In season there was an abundance of game, partridges, woodcock, ptarmigan, wild duck, moor fowl (grouse), geese and hares; the occasional rabbit and plenty of pigeons and, bought in, a variety of sea fish to supplement the salmon and trout. The garden produced the vegetables and the summer fruit to provide something in the way of puddings. A typical winter menu is that for Wednesday, 5th January 1737.

Dinner.	Fish	
	Beef boyld with cabbage pieces	1
	Hares rost	1
	Beefe for servants peices	1
Supper.	Mutton broyld joints	2
	Fowls roast	2
	Fish broyld	
	Woodcocks rost	1

In that week were consumed:

Beefe peices	6
Mutton joints	11
Hares	2
Geese	2
Ducks	4
Capon	2
Fowlls	9
Partridges	5
Woodcock	3
Sheep killed	2

The present house was built by the fifth baronet, not long after Burns had paid an enjoyable visit to the old one. Now of course it is far too large for comfort and it has been, in turn, a successful girls' school and (commercially) a rather less successful small theatre. Recently, it has been sold out of the family.

I have been told (whether truly or not I do not know) that one of the lairds bequeathed to the town of Crieff free water from Loch Turret in perpetuity but that the bequest has gone the way of others, even though of a charitable nature. It is said that a great city coveted the little man's vineyard and secured an Act of Parliament which not only gave them access to the same water supply, which would have harmed nobody but gave them the right to charge a water rate to the citizens of Crieff.

Crieff was the centre of the cattle trade in the first half of the eighteenth century, until Falkirk ousted it around 1770. Black cattle were the one realizable source of wealth in the Highlands and everything depended on getting them to the tryst in good condition. At smaller trysts throughout the north and west, the drovers would assemble the beasts that they were to sell and then lead them by well established routes which gradually converged on Crieff. From the southern Hebrides and Argyll they would come via Tyndrum, Crianlarich and Glen Dochart, or Killin and Glen Lednock. From the north via Drumochter and Coshieville; and from the east via Dunkeld and Amulree. The art was to get the cattle to Crieff as good looking as when their owners had parted with them. They were led, not driven, by stages of about ten miles a day, from one traditional stance to another. These stances were by tradition free, and pasture and water would be available. When Crieff was reached, literally thousands of beasts might be there – and thousands of pounds changed hands – yet there was remarkably little trouble. The policing was the responsibility of the Earl of Perth and was carried out with some pomp; in return, he collected a small toll. It was a cheerful scene:

> The Highland gentlemen were mighty civil, dressed in their slashed waistcoats, a trousing [which is breeches and stocking of one piece of striped stuff] with a plaid for a coat and a blue

bonnet. They have a poinard, knife and fork in one sheath hanging at one side of their belt, their pistol at the other and their snuff mull before, with a great broadsword at their side. Their attendance was very numerous, all in belted plaids, girt, like women's petticoats down to the knee; their thighs and half their leg bare.*

After Crieff, the herds destined for England to be fattened up, crossed the Earn at Dalpatrick ford – hence the surprising place name of Highlandman Loan, and thence travelled via Muthill to Sheriffmuir and Falkirk – or else went due south via Glen Devon; but by the second half of the eighteenth century, enclosures had started to limit the free grazing on the way, and also the amount of land available at Crieff itself; and dues had gone up, so that drovers found it cheaper to press on to Perth and Falkirk. Only a general market remained and a certain amount of horse-trading in Highland ponies. And, since there was little industry except for cottage weaving and kindred crafts, the once prosperous Crieff might well have faded away. Two things saved it. The reputation of the schooling there (see page 20) and the feuing out of plots and the building of small houses used chiefly in the summer months. The town was as long ago as 1790 something of a resort, according to the Old Statistical Account.

By the time of the New Statistical Account, there were fifteen schools charging small fees for a population of 2000 some of whom were certainly too poor to take advantage of them – and a library of 900 volumes, but there was still little in the way of industry. Then came the railway in 1856 and on the crest of a wave of the belief, fostered by Queen Victoria and her doctors, that there was something special in the dry and invigorating air of the Highlands, and in the water of their springs, the remarkable Dr Meikle opened his Crieff Hydropathic Hotel. Forty bedrooms were to let at two guineas a week, including the use of the baths; and it went from strength to strength in spite of the fact that alcohol, tobacco and cards were all taboo. Even today, when it is a large and justly popular hotel with every sort of facility for recreation indoors

* Mackay, *Journey through Scotland* (1723). See also "The Reminiscences Of Dougall MacDougall" recorded by Eric Cregeen and published in the *Journal of Scottish Studies*, Vol. II, 1959, though MacDougall dated from Falkirk days. And Haldane's *The Drove Roads of Scotland*.

and out – dances and a swimming pool and games room, tennis, golf, riding and a private beach on Loch Earn for sailing and water-skiing, there is still no bar. But the modern management (still guided by the same family) is more tolerant than the founder, and to consume one's own alcohol is no longer frowned upon.*

Today, Crieff is plentifully supplied with good hotels and other forms of holiday accommodation. And it maintains its high reputation for schooling, both maintained and independent – the latter being represented by the Morrison's Academy for boys and girls. This was previously grant-aided, but with the withdrawal of the grant felt sure enough of a well-deserved reputation to accept the challenge to go it alone. The situation is better than the emphatically nineteenth-century architecture – indeed architecture is not one of Crieff's outstanding assets. Nor is there much to see in the way of antiquities, except for a very worn market cross under a canopy, and another possibly tenth-century Celtic cross slab. Crieff's attraction lies in the good walking to be had, and the glorious views, notably that from Kate MacNiven's Crag.

* Tolerance has not always been a feature of the town. In a prolonged dispute over patronage in the nineteenth century, one stalwart woman exclaimed "Indeed Sir Patrick, it is no use to urge me further. Mr Macintyre is red-haired and, with my good will, no red-haired man will ever be minister in Crieff!"

V

SOUTH FROM PERTH

As we turn southwards, there is no steady slope away to the Forth-Clyde valley, but a series of ridges. High ground stretches from Glenalmond to Crieff, and, again, along the Gask road from Tibbermuir to Kinkell Bridge; between these ridges there is flat, often flooded land along the Pow Water. Then, to the south is Strathearn proper – a strath being an extensive but broken valley astride the lower reaches of a once mountain stream; a carse, in contrast, is a flatter stretch of rich lowland, as, for instance, the Carse of Gowrie to the east of Perth. Strathearn, in all its beauty, is most fully appreciated from the railway; on the other hand, this view does not do justice to the next ridge, that of the Ochil Hills; they are no mountains but they are shapely and rise to over 1000 feet, and are pierced by famous glens, Glen Farg, Glen Devon and Glen Eagles. In its turn, another stretch of low land succeeds, through which the River Devon winds to join the Forth. The Cleish Hills make one last ridge.

To travel to the south-west, it is best as far as possible to avoid the A9, especially as there are two delightful – and 'different' – unclassified roads, one through Tibbermuir to Madderty with wide views to both north and south, the other largely along the line of a Roman road, for which you leave the A9 at Crossgates. Adjoining their road, the Romans also built a line of signal stations, small enclosures with wooden towers, intervisible from each other. A particularly good example may be seen near Parkneuk Cottage (O.S. 917185) just through a gate into a Forestry plantation. For those who would like to walk a Roman road – or, indeed, just enjoy exercise where the walking is easy – there is an accessible stretch which may be picked up at the turning in the road between Kirkton and Roundlaw (O.S. 960188) and followed westwards to Ardunie. It is completely peaceful and, in May, especially lovely as the mature trees put on their first green, and there are wild flowers everywhere.

On the other side of the road, but not visible from it, is Gask House, home until this century of the Jacobite family of Oliphant since the days when Bruce granted the lands to Sir William to reward his doughty defence of Stirling Castle in 1304. Sir William was buried at Aberdalgie (*see* page 111). His son married a daughter of Bruce and received from his brother-in-law David II, a charter in return for the annual reddendum of a chaplet of white roses at the feast of the Nativity of St John the Baptist. The story was commemorated by a descendant, Mrs E. Maxtone Graham:

The Tribute of Gask

Now ken ye the gift that Gask brought to the King?
   'Tis an offering sae royal, sae perfect, and fair,
   Than jewels of silver so dainty and rare,
   A crown for a maid or a monarch to wear.
The courtier's tribute is but a poor thing,
For what can he offer and what can he bring,
Than the crown of White Roses from Gask to the King?

Now ken ye the service Gask does for the king?
   All for his sake, in the bloom of the year,
   In the gardens of Gask the white blossoms appear,
   The royal White Roses to Scotland so dear.
Then far o'er Strathearn let the praise of them ring,
Let them live once again in the song that we sing,
The crown of White Roses from Gask to the King.

Now ken ye what Gask will yet do for the King?
   In the days that may come, when the roses are dead,
   When the pledge is forgotten, the vows left unsaid:
   What then shall be found for an offering instead?
Oh! then at his feet his heart will he fling.
Truth, Honour, Devotion as tribute will bring
For the crown of White Roses from Gask to the King.

The family was especially to the fore in the late seventeenth and eighteenth centuries. James Oliphant was active in getting an Act passed by the Scottish Parliament to require the local lairds to undertake the redraining of the land to the north of Gask by deepening the Pow – a project originally started by the monks of the Abbey of Inchaffray. He stayed at home in 1715 but sent two sons to fight for the Chevalier. Laurence the elder son married the daughter of the Second Lord Nairne, one of the Jacobite leaders condemned to death after the failure of the rising. Fearing that he might bungle his departure, he wrote a most dignified farewell:

My education has not fitted me for speaking in public and therefor I choose to leave in writing this true account of myself. I was educated and always continued a Protestant of the Church of England. I was honoured with favours from my late gracious Sovereign King James the Seventh; even in his greatest distress my affections never departed from him. I lived a quiet life. I was happy in the best of wives; and we with twelve children and five grandchildren lived in great ease and satisfaction. I found myself (notwithstanding my peaceable behaviour for above twenty years) hunted by the malice of bloody men to be made a close prisoner. Lord Mar appeared, and tho there was no previous concert with me, I joined him, and gave implicit obedience to those he appointed to command me, though I was very quickly sensible of the want of proper Officers for such an undertaking as we were put upon.

The first notice I had at Preston of any intention to surrender was, that a capitulation was agreed to, by which we were made to give up our arms to a most merciful Prince who they did not doubt would pardon us. But after that, we were made an unexampled spectacle to the whole City and having been encouraged to plead guilty (to ye fact only) we found not that mercy.

I forgive all mankind; and if the delusive hopes of life and the importunity of my dear friends have made me say anything before the Lords or in my Petition derogateing from my principles, I beg pardon of God and of all men.

I hope God will support me as he did my grandfather the Earl of Derby who fell a sacrifice for the same cause. That neither Ambition nor Avarice could move me will appear from what was

offered me in a former reign, and my circumstances were easy and
pleasant. God has blessed me with a most tender wife, who is
much dearer to me by her virtues than by the estate she brought
me. I commend to God my dear children who have been so
dutiful to me. And all my noble and kind friends who have with
so much warmth appeared for me at this juncture, I pray God for
them and return them my hearty thanks.

NAIRNE.

Fortunately, he was reprieved twenty-four hours before the
execution was due.

When 1745 came Laurence Oliphant and his son, another
Laurence, were out again, and the twenty-one-year-old heir
acted as A.D.C. to Prince Charles at Prestonpans. The father
was so angry at his tenants when they refused to come out that
he forbade them to cut the corn until his Prince insisted, indeed
cut the first stalks himself. Many relics of the Prince's visit to
Gask survive and are preserved at Ardblair, near Blairgowrie,
where the Oliphants now live. They include a table inscribed:
"Charles Prince of Wales breakfasted at this table in the long
drawing room at Gask 11 September 1745". This resolute
adherence to the Stewart cause drove the two Laurences into
exile, involved Lady Oliphant in much hardship, and brought
about the forfeiture of the above mentioned charter (for a
time) and of the estates, though these were eventually repurchased. Another Laurence, the one who pulled down the
Auld House, was the brother of the Jacobite poetess Lady
Nairne. He replaced it in 1801 with an Adamesque building by
Robert Crichton; it is in private occupation, well screened from
the road.

The road past Gask descends to cross the Earn at the graceful
Kinkell Bridge. Here there was an old church dedicated to St
Bean, overlooking the river, but it has long been ruined.

> Was there e'er such a parish, a parish, a parish?
>   Was there e'er such a parish as Kinkell?
> They've hangit the minister, drooned the precentor,
>   Dang doon the steeple, and drucken the bell.

The minister was the Rev. Richard Duncan who was
hanged in 1683 for the murder of his infant child by a serving

maid, its body being found buried under his hearthstone. After being sentenced by the Earl of Perth in his capacity of Steward of Crieff, he was reprieved, but, so the story goes, the execution was hurried on so that the reprieve should not arrive in time; the precentor was drowned crossing the river on his way to a service; the steeple collapsed; and the bell was sold to the parish of Cockpen, near Edinburgh. To the west is the largely modern Strathallan Castle, with Sir William Roberts' remarkable collection of aircraft. They include a Hurricane, a Lancaster, a Mosquito and many others dating back to 1930. The airfield is the H.Q. of the Scottish Parachute Club.

South past Tullibardine Station, you come on one of those extraordinary treasures that are found in Perthshire stuck right out in the middle of nowhere – Tullibardine Church. In 1445 Sir David Murray founded a Collegiate Church here with a Provost and four Prebends to pray for his soul. On the west wall are his arms and those of his son Sir William Murray and his daughter-in-law, a Colquhoun; otherwise the chapel is plain except for its crow-stepped gables. Beautifully cared for by the Ministry of the Environment, it is still used as a burial vault by the founder's successors, the Earls of Perth. There is a story that Sir William visited his king when he was at Stirling, accompanied by a retinue of seventeen upstanding young men. Since the king had only recently reissued decrees against the maintenance of retinues, his reception was frosty, until he explained that these were his seventeen sons whom he had brought to express their loyalty and devotion.

Just beyond the signal station at Parkneuk is the turning down to the Innerpeffray Library, founded by David Drummond, third Lord Maddertie, in the seventeenth century – probably the first free library in Scotland – and placed in the present building in 1750 by a descendant who was Archbishop of York. It still serves the public but its chief interest lies in its older books: Bacon's *History of King Henry VII*, Major's *History of Great Britain* (1521), Gavin Douglas's *Aeneid*; Coverdale's Bible and a Breeches Bible, Holinshed (1577) and King James VI's *Counterblast to Tobacco* and his verse translation of the *Psalter*. There are also some manuscript notes of the lectures on

Aristotle delivered at St Andrews University from 1663 to 1668, and a pocket Bible belonging to Montrose.

Behind the library is a little low rectangular chapel, built by Lord Maddertie's predecessor, Sir John Drummond, in 1508 to be a Collegiate Church. It is unusual in that it retains its pre-Reformation altar. For long it had only an earth floor and no glazed windows, but it has recently been put into a better state of preservation and, in the process, painted crosses on the walls have come to light. There are also traces of seventeenth-century painting below the laird's loft, a cosy pew which has its own fireplace, and is also well screened from both congregation and minister. Otherwise the plainness of the interior is only relieved by two hatchments. From the graveyard, looking down on a bend in the river, its ideal situation may be appreciated. The substantial remains of Lord Maddertie's small castle lie within private ground and are not open to the public.

The library may also be reached by the more northerly of the two unclassified roads referred to, which leaves the A85 just after Huntingtower. Not only has this even better views, being less wooded, but it passes Madderty and the site of the great abbey of Inchaffray. This was founded on marshy ground which the monks did much to drain – hence its name *Insula messarum*, the Island of the Masses – by Gilbert Earl of Strathearn. Here Gilbert's son, Gilchrist, was buried in 1198 and the measure of his parents' grief was shown by the lavishness of the endowments in the charter of foundation. The abbey received the revenues of five neighbouring churches, and "tithe of the Earl's kain and rents of wheat, meal, malt, cheese and all provisions throughout the year; with tithe of all fish brought into his kitchen, and of the produce of his hunting; with tithe of all the profits of his tribunals of justice and all offerings; with the liberty to its monks of fishing in the Peffray, of fishing and birding over all the Earl's lands, waters and lakes; of taking timber for building and other uses from his woods, and pannage and mast feeding for pigs, as well as bark and firewood, in whatever places and as much as they please".

Its abbots included Maurice who bore the Cross along the lines of the Scottish host before the Battle of Bannockburn.

As John Barbour tells:

> The Scottis men, ful devotly,
> Knelit all don, til God to pray:
> And a schort prayer thair maid thay
> Til God, to help them in that ficht.
>   And quhen the Inglis king had sicht
> Of thaim kneland, he said in hy
> "Yon folks knelis til ask mercy".
> Schir Ingrame said, "Ye say sooth now:
> Thay ask mercy, bot not at yow.
> For their trespass to God thay cry.
> I tell yow a thing sikkerly,
> That yon men will win all or die."

Another abbot was killed fighting at Flodden. Despoiled at the time of the Reformation, its tower survived till the reign of Charles II, and there was still much to see as late as 1870; now there is virtually nothing. Madderty's seventeenth-century church, though, is worth visiting, and the little row of houses at St David's. Here, in 1832, the widow of General Sir David Baird (of Peninsula and Seringapatam fame) created a village as her own personal memorial to him; each inhabitant was to have a cow's grass. Although there are some horrid intruders which surely could have been prevented, the older cottages are charming, each with its little enclosure and its astonishing view to the south over the Ochils.

To get to Muthill, one must go north to Crieff or south to Kinkell Bridge. Best known for its early square church tower, it has also no fewer than ninety-six listed buildings and considerable civic pride, shown in its gaily painted window frames. A recent booklet by Doreen Carraher Manning singles out, among others, a simple three-bay cottage next to Parkview in Willoughby Street – the old Toll House, now Sydbar – Nethercote and the village post office. The 'Willoughby' is after the family of the Earls of Ancaster who came into Drummond Castle and its lands as a result of the forfeiture of the Jacobite Earls of Perth after the Forty-Five. There is a tower-house of 1490 with a Victorian mansion house. Its Italian garden (see plate 18) with its terraces, statues and

formal bedding-out is at its best in late summer, but is outstanding at any time of year, and is opened to the public.

The temptation to omit the A9 altogether is almost ir-
resistible, so awful is its traffic; we can do so with a clear
conscience as far as Aberuthven, because there are two more
profitable ways of reaching it. One is by Aberdalgie, the other
past Kilgraston Convent School for girls, and Strathallan School
with its main building in a former mansion house of Ruthven.
Of the latter's varied achievements, one of the most outstanding has been the series of exhibitions that have been held in
Edinburgh and elsewhere of the school's art. Forgandenny
Church has pre-Reformation foundations and an eighteenth-
century wing, inside an ugly exterior.

Aberdalgie is reached by taking the old road out of Perth, as
far as Bridge of Earn, and turning right at Craigend. Here you
get one of the finest views of Strathearn. It is even more
impressive looking *up* the strath, than looking *across* it from the
hills on either side. There was an old church here, containing
the tomb of Sir William Oliphant who died in 1329. The stone
slab is in shallow relief, somewhat worn, and shows the knight
in armour, surmounted by an intricate carved canopy. The
new church to which it has been moved dates from 1778 and
has been much beautified by the Dewar family. About the time
that the present church was built, the parish had a truly
remarkable schoolmaster, Mr Peddie, who was held to deserve
"all the encouragement that can be given him, few being better
qualified to teach English, arithmetic, book-keeping and the
principles of mathematics; and none more diligent in teaching
them. It will not be improper to add that he has acquired,
without any instruction, the rare art of communicating knowledge to the deaf and dumb".

This is the area of the capital of the old Pictish kingdom of
Fortrenn, and also of Malcolm Canmore's headquarters, but
nothing is left of them except an isolated Celtic cross in a field
to the north of the road, by the farm of Bankhead, Dupplin,
and in the modern church at Forteviot, a handbell and some
fragments of carving, including one showing a Pictish bull
goring a man.

The parish has had a troubled history, at times with no minister, at times with two. And there were perpetual disputes between the ministers and the University of St Andrews, to whom they were indebted for much of their stipend. And some of the ministers were not all that they might have been. The Rev. Edward Richardson who was presented in 1635 and took possession of his four acre glebe by "taking a plough in his own hands and making red earth and sundry furrows", proved to be chiefly interested in hunting; and, what was far worse to the extreme Presbyterians, who got the upper hand in 1649, an Episcopalian and a royalist. He was accused of drinking the king's health and was deposed after a series of unseemly rows in church, when his wife and his servant both shouted down the minister sent to declare the charge vacant. Deposed, he might be – and a successor appointed – but evicted, he would not be, and he managed to hang on in the manse and the glebe for several years. His successor, William Barclay, though called as a Presbyterian, had a long incumbency as an Episcopalian from 1660 until, in 1691, he too was deposed, not for his love of bishops but for his tendency to frequent inns and be the worse for drink. On one occasion, it was alleged, he was unable to stand up when taking a wedding, and, on another, he got himself involved in a drunken brawl with a neighbouring laird. Six years without a minister followed, and, then, when a suitable young man had been found, he died within a year. To end the century, a disastrous call was made to one, Andrew Harlaw who, only two years later, had to be deposed for the grossest immorality.*

Dunning is something of a mixture. Its church is modern and uninteresting, and its burial ground, which could be a pleasant haven as well as a source of interest for its old tomb stones, is poorly kept – and all the town's old houses were swept away by Mar's scorched earth policy in 1716. On the other hand, the eighteenth century was not a bad time to start again and, if you are prepared to explore on foot, there are some attractive little buildings to be found; the Lord Rollo of the day was much more successful in making a place to live in than were those who were responsible for rebuilding Auch-

* *Forteviot. The History of a Strathearn Parish*, Rev. N. Meldrum (1926).

terarder. It was his son, the Master of Rollo in 1773 who was so delighted when at last he was presented with a son, after four daughters, that he exclaimed "Go and ring the old bell until it cracks". He was obeyed all too literally and the bell had to be taken down and recast. Its inscription:

Soli Deo Gloria Joannes Oaderogge me fecit Rotterdam 1681
    Haec ad evangelium
    Hoc ad Christum
    Hic ad coelum
    Vocat peccatores.
This bell calls sinners to the Gospel, it to Christ, and He to Heaven.

A later Lord Rollo gave a fine recreation park to the village in 1946. But the greatest treasure of Dunning is the twelfth-century church tower, Norman, square and solid, dedicated to St Serf, the saint who had a pet lamb. A robber who was suspected of stealing it and eating it, denied the accusation with an oath, taken on the Saint's staff – only to be contradicted by a miraculous "Baa Baa" coming from within him.

West from Dunning, the road leads past a sad stone commemorating the burning of a supposed witch, Maggie Watt, in 1657, and then under the impressive Craigie Rossie and Rossie Law, to the entrance to the former Kincardine Castle – or north to Aberuthven. Kincardine Castle was the chief seat of the family of Montrose in the days of the Great Marquis; and in the churchyard of a little ancient chapel at Aberuthven was their mausoleum. The ruins of the former, and the shambles of the latter, are a sad commentary on the fallen fortunes of the Grahams – gone too from Inchbrakie and Balgowan and Gorthy and so many other of the homes of the lesser branches of the family.

Though the Grahams were so near, and very influential there, Auchterarder itself belonged to the royalist Earls of Perth. Even so, it suffered cruelly at the hands of the Earl of Mar. Just before the Battle of Sheriffmuir, a large part of his army was billeted there, and it was not easy to control a somewhat *ad hoc* collection of soldiers not accustomed to conventional military discipline, who spared neither friend nor foe. Still it would be easier to sympathize with an officer receiving the following letters, if one did not know the enthusiasm with which such officers set about burning every house in the town *after* the battle in order to prevent the Duke of Argyll and the Government forces finding any shelter there.

> Sir: The Earl of Mar ordered me to send you the enclosed, and desires that as far as possible the complaints may be redressed, and expects that you'll allow no such abuses to be committed, and orders you'll take all methods possible to keep the people under command, that our own people may not be oppressed. This, by command above, from, sir, your most humble and obedient servant.
>
> W. Clephane, Adgt.Gen.

Camp at Perth, 8th November, 1715
To His Excellency Lieutenant General Gordon, commanding His Majesty's Forces at Auchterarder.

> My Lord: Last night I had a letter from my niece, Mrs Stirling telling me of the great abuses committed by that part of Your Lordship's Army lying at Gleneagles: upon which I presumed to give Your Lordship the trouble of one, and designed she should deliver it herself: your Lordship's was under her cover: the servant I sent was taken and searched, the letter taken from him; they used the formality to deliver it to her, but withal obliged her to show it them. She being afraid of their jealousy and rage, put the enclosed in the fire, for which she met with very harsh treatment, in so much they would not allow her to give me an answer, nor see my servant. After all they knew not to whom the letter was directed, neither durst she own it was Your Lordship. My servant tells me they have shot a great many black cattle and sheep, plundered their shepherds' and tenants' houses robbed their household servants, broke open the Gleneagles closet, the granaries, and taken what meal they had for their subsistence. In short, poor Mrs Stirling, who certainly wishes them well, was in tears and confined to her room. I wish from my heart that we dont find it in this side of the hill paid home with interest, for as yet they have spared our cattle. I persuade myself, your Lordship knows nothing of this, 'tis so unlike the gentleness and lenity you have shown

hitherto. I am sure Sir John were he present would be very earnest in begging your Lordship's protection for his sister; for God's sake take it into consideration, and put some cheque on these rude people who will certainly bring an odium on our party. In the meantime, my Lord, I humbly beg pardon for the importunity and freedom, wishing your Lordship an entire and sudden sub-version of your enemies, a long and uninterrupted enjoyment of your friends. I am my Lord, your Lordship's humble and most devoted servant,

Ka St Clair

Alva, November 6, 1715.
To the Earl of Mar.*

After 1716, something was done to recompense the villagers who had lost their homes, their all, and a start was made in rebuilding the wide main street, but it was not until after the 1745 when the town was forfeited that some prosperity began to return. The Commissioners of Forfeited Estates started a linen manufactory, built houses and encouraged settlement, though not entirely successfully. Today it would seem, Auch-terarder must rely heavily on its antique shops, serving, no doubt, the large numbers of overseas visitors to Gleneagles Hotel. The golf courses and the dining-rooms of this vast British Railways establishment have the highest reputation and give value for money.

Gleneagles (the glen of the church) nurtured (and still does) the Haldanes, a family which has reached distinction in a number of fields, some of them unexpected. Admiral Lord Duncan of Camperdown was one; Lord Haldane of Cloan was another, and the evangelists, Robert and James Haldane. There may be something in the local air because that remarkable eccentric, the Rev. William Spence came here, after a period as schoolmaster at Abernethy. He had no use for the Episco-palianism of the 1660s and the 1670s, and in 1678 presented to the Presbytery of Auchterarder a protest against the cor-ruptions, doctrinal, liturgical and disciplinary, from which the Church was suffering, and demanded a return to the "gude kirk primitif". Excommunicated, he joined Argyll in Holland. Caught by the authorities, he was brought before the Privy

* Quoted in A. G. Reid, *The Annals of Auchterarder* (Philips, Crieff, 1899).

Council in England who transferred him to Scotland so that he could be tortured till he told all that he knew, first by the 'boot' and, when that failed, by keeping him awake for nine consecutive nights with painful pricks. Finally, resort was had to a newly introduced device from Russia, called the 'thumbkins'. Incredibly he survived all this – and a subsequent death sentence – to be restored in 1690 and serve out his days as parish minister of Fossoway until his death at eighty.

The road south from Gleneagles leads into Glen Devon, one of the most beautiful glens in Scotland, and, for that reason, one to be avoided at the week-end in summer, except on foot in the hills. It leads to the Yetts of Muckart, and Dollar with its Playfair Academy and the ruins of Castle Campbell, but these are beyond our region.

To the west of Gleneagles Hotel, one can again avoid the A9 by taking an unclassified road to Braco and Ardoch.* The seventeenth-century keep of Braco, with later additions, is a private house but its great woods, golden and red and brown in autumn, can be seen from a road which runs north over rather bleak moorland to Comrie. They can also be explored on foot through the courtesy of their owner, and the gardens are open from time to time under the National Gardens Scheme.

Ardoch is entered from just the other side of the bridge at the castle entrance. This Roman fort is vast, and even in its present decayed state incredibly impressive – its inner perimeter is 500 yards and its outer twice that – but some imagination is needed to appreciate to the full its original size and strength. If only the site were a little more cared for, and an information post manned, with diagrams and reconstructions, it would be much easier for the layman to understand.

The north was the most likely direction of attack, and the most dangerous – and here it is nearly 100 yards from the main rampart to the furthest of the successive ditches – so that two intermediate defensive positions were needed; and even on the east side there were six ramparts and five ditches, and an entrance constructed at an angle so as to compel attackers to uncover their vulnerable flank. The last and main rampart stands six to ten feet above the level of the ground inside, and

* There is, however, a Pictish Class I Stone, near Blackford (O.S. 924097) in a field just south of the A9, with a goose with its head turned back carved on it.

17 feet above the bottom of the 20-foot ditch outside – and there was no doubt a considerable stockade on the top of the rampart. The reason for the great width of the defences is thought to have been the need to guard the wooden and thatched buildings inside from being set on fire by red hot missiles, as is known to have happened elsewhere. Plenty of clay sling-bolts were found at Ardoch which could have been intended for this purpose. More recently, Ardoch was the camping ground of Mar's army the night before the Battle of Sheriffmuir.

By November 1715, the Jacobite commander had already missed two good opportunities to attack Argyll with greatly superior forces, or even to by-pass him; and those who criticize Argyll's caution should remember not only his numerical weakness but the fact that his orders were categorical. On 7th October, the Prince of Wales had written to him (in the absence of the King): "All I can say is not to hazard an action without a probable appearance of carrying it through, and rather to shun an engagement, to yield to them the country, than expose the affairs of the King to such ill consequences as would follow from a defeat."

By 10th November when Mar at last bestirred himself to leave Perth, Argyll had received some reinforcements but he had still only some 3000 men, less than half the number of his opponents; on the other hand his army was better organized and better served in the way of intelligence reports than his opponent. Even so, he blundered into the battle almost as ineptly as Mar did. And once the engagement started neither commander could see what was going on. In the event, Argyll's force outflanked the Jacobites on their left, and in this sector, Argyll and his cavalry carried all before them. But, precisely the opposite had happened on the other wing where the Hanoverian forces were swept off the field. Mar was the first to see what the situation was, and it is generally thought that by decisive action at this juncture he could have achieved a victory. But decisive action was not in his make-up, and when Argyll's tired men returned to the battlefield, they were not attacked, and were allowed to withdraw unmolested. Indeed, since Mar also withdrew, Argyll returned to the battlefield next day and was able to collect such arms and equipment as had been abandoned. He could hardly be said to have won the battle but he had won the campaign, because from that day onwards the Jacobite army dwindled away, and, by the time that the Chevalier arrived, it was too late and he never looked like getting south of Perth. If the undulations of the moor prevented the generals from seeing what was going on, the sightseer today has little chance of being able to recreate the comings and goings in his imagination. But the site is worth visiting, if only for the views to the east and to the south over Dunblane. To commemorate the event, the Clan Macrae have erected a cairn where traditionally their men gathered, and half a mile to the north another gathering stone marks Mar's H.Q.

> There's some say that we wan,
> Some say that they wan,
> And some say that nane wan ava, man;
> There's but ae thing, I'm sure,
> That, at Shirramuir,
> A battle there was, that I saw, man.
> And we ran, and they ran,
> And they ran, and we ran,
> And we ran, and they ran awa, man.

The city of Dunblane has a hydro, sought after for conferences, and the Queen Victoria School for the sons of soldiers, sailors and airmen, but otherwise is uninteresting except for the cathedral and its immediate precincts; and even these should be seen before rather than after Dunkeld. The renovation seems rather more obtrusive – or is that a purely personal prejudice? Certainly, Dunblane has an equally fine site overlooking the Allan Water, and a west door finer than anything else of its sort in Scotland. And above the west window, there is the vesica of which Ruskin wrote: "I know not anything so perfect in its simplicity, and so beautiful, as far as it reaches, in all the Gothic with which I am acquainted. ... [The man who built it] was contented to work under Nature's teaching; and instead of putting a merely formal dog-tooth, as everybody else did at the time, he went down to the woody bank of the sweet river beneath the rocks on which he was building, and took up a few of the leaves that lay by it, and he set them in his arch, side by side, for ever."

The oldest part, because it belongs to an older church than the one which we see today, is the Norman tower – four storeys of it built about 1100 and two added later – the whole surmounted by a parapet of 1500 and a small but effective spire. Next comes the Lady Chapel, and then the choir from the thirteenth century. Inside, it is the great height, especially of the fourteenth-century nave, with its tall, deeply recessed pillars that draw the eyes ever upwards. In comparison, the choir is rather dark, but the east window is glorious – narrow pointed lancets crowned with an unusual rose made up of three trefoils. In and around the cathedral, there is much to look at, old and new, but it is the overall feeling of height that one comes away with – that and the memory of the deeply recessed west door which gives the feeling of access to a truly holy shrine.

Historically, the most interesting treasures are a worn Celtic cross carved with animals, a rider, and what has been identified as a wolf, but looks more like a hound; the equally worn effigies of the Fifth Earl of Strathearn and his Countess; and the three blue slabs in the floor of the choir, covering the graves of the three Drummond sisters. Their story was a tragic one. James IV was deeply in love with Margaret, the eldest, and may even have been secretly married to her, when the proposal was advanced that he should marry Margaret Tudor, daughter of the King of England. The three sisters died of poisoning immediately after breakfasting and, at the time, no-one had any doubt that it was not accidental. Certainly, the murderer was not James, who was prostrate with grief and till his death paid for Masses to be said for her soul. It may have been powerful men who were anxious that the advantages of the English alliance should not be lost; or it may have been the relatives of Janet Kennedy, an earlier mistress of James, and the mother of the son whom he created Earl of Moray. There are also the fifteenth-century Miserere seats either side of the communion table, and the Chisholm stalls at the west end, of the same date, deeply carved and among the earliest examples of their kind in Scotland. The cathedral is rich in modern carving too, especially the screen designed by Sir Rowland Anderson; this and Sir Robert Lorimer's woodwork in the choir fit in well, and some of the modern stained glass is very good.

Outside in the precincts, there is the house with crow-stepped gables, built in 1687, to house the books which Bishop Leighton bequeathed for the use of the clergy of the diocese, the Dean's House which now houses the cathedral museum, and the ecumenical Scottish Churches House.

Queen Victoria School was founded in 1906 as a memorial to her and to the men killed in the South African War. It is a boarding-school to give the sons of other ranks in all three services the chance of an education uninterrupted by constant move of station. It has 250 boys from the age of nine and a half upwards, sons of Scottish parents or those serving in Scottish regiments. It is no military academy on the American lines but one like any other inspected by the Scottish Education Department, with a lay headmaster and no special military bias in its curriculum or daily life. Yet, once a year – on Grand Day (prizegiving and parents' day) a parade is mounted such as no school C.C.F. that I have ever seen could approach. With the whole school on parade, from diminutive children to grown men, in kilt and scarlet tunic, they march past in perfect step, to their own pipes and drums, and stand as steady as a rock for the inspection. It is a sight which never fails to move as well as to impress. No pressure is put on the boys subsequently to join the services, but many do.

Still in Perthshire, but beyond the borders of the Tayside Region, is much of interest: Doune Castle* is one of the largest and best preserved, and the Lake of Menteith with Inchmahome Priory†, to mention only two sites. The former was built towards the end of the fourteenth century by the Duke of Albany; its Stewart keepers, the Earls of Moray, in due course became its owners – and remain so. The latter has considerable remains of its thirteenth-century church and cloisters, and the only two examples of late West Highland monumental sculpture outside Argyll – the figures of Walter

* Open April to October.
† Open April to September.

Earl of Menteith and his wife, "which, even in decay, remain one of the most expressive and moving monuments in Scotland", and the low-relief slab of John Drummond from the fourteenth century. Of somewhat different appeal, but exceedingly popular are the Motor Museum at Doune* and the safari wild-life park at Blair Drummond.† Just beyond the Lake of Menteith are the Trossachs, and just south of Doune is Stirling.

There remains a small part of Perthshire which may most conveniently be covered with Kinross. It lies astride the A9 which leaves Perth across the South Inch, where large numbers of French prisoners of war were detained during the Napoleonic Wars. Once a week the prisoners were allowed to appear at their gratings to sell things they had made, some of which can be seen today in the Perth Museum. Margaret Stewart Sandeman's *Life* tells how as a little girl, living in the Watergate, she never missed an opportunity of going with her governess to the weekly sale: "the politeness of the prisoners, and their gratitude for the purchases made, were remembered by her long after the fragile workmanship, dexterously and curiously displayed on boxes, needle books, yard measures, silk-winders made of straw, split and diced, had disappeared from her treasures; for these her sixpences were hoarded. Gentlemen and ladies came for the costly articles such as models of a man-of-war in wood and ivory". A gloomy nineteenth-century prison now stands on the Inch. At Craigend, the last few years have seen the growth of a spaghetti junction which, with the new bridge over the Tay, is intended to divert the very heavy lorries which now shudder down South Street on their way from Glasgow and the south to Dundee and Aberdeen. And soon it will be motorway all the way to Edinburgh; there is only a short stretch in Glenfarg to be completed. To achieve this, an incredible slice has been cut out of Moncreiffe Hill, home of an ancient, if in one way difficult, family. Those who live on the south side of the hill spell their name as above and include Sir Iain Moncreiffe of that Ilk, the head of the family and the Albany Herald. Those

* Open April to October.
† Open Mid-March to October.

who live on the other side of the hill prefer Moncrieff, while
Lord Moncreiff at Tullibole Castle, Kinross, has yet another
spelling. All are descended from a Norman, who took the
name when he received the lands of Moncreiffe and several
members have achieved high legal distinction, and one a certain
reputation for eccentricity. Sir John Moncrieffe of Tipper-
malloch was convinced that he had cures for every ailment
under the sun, such as:

cure for deafness – ants eggs mixed with the juice of an onion,
poured into the ear. Cure for lethargy – the whole skin of a hare
with the ears and nails made into a powder and taken hot
[perhaps the most likely to achieve a cure]. Cure for paralysis –
anoint the parts with an ointment made of earthworms. Cure for
baldness – make a lee of the burnt ashes of doves' dung and wash
the head with it, but the ashes of little frogs will do as well.
Recipe for making the whole face well coloured – apply the liver
of a sheep, fresh and hot.

On the top of Moncreiffe Hill there is a Pictish fort. Little is
now visible of its thick dry-stone walls but the outline of the
ditch is clear enough, and the short ascent is worth it for the
sake of the view alone. At only 700 feet you can see the whole
of Perth laid out before you with the hills of Breadalbane as a
backcloth; to the west, right up Strathearn; southwards to the
Ochils and the Lomonds, north to the Sidlaws, and east out to
sea. Between this hill and the Tay is Elcho Castle. This
extremely well preserved ruin was built in the mid-sixteenth
century when men were beginning to look for comfort and
convenience and not just for security, though a reasonable
degree of the latter was provided by the south-west tower; it
contained the entrance and protected the staircase and was the
only part provided with battlements. The kitchen has the usual
vast fireplaces and with the cellars and storerooms takes up the
ground floor; there is a great hall and a withdrawing-room on
the first floor, with bedrooms above and an abundance of
fireplaces and garderobes. Comfort, with early warning, are the
keynotes throughout. At the top, a parapet gives the necessary
all-round look-out, and an unusual feature over the main door
– a stone six feet long, laid across the angle – provides an

aperture through which missiles could be dropped on any unwelcome guests or cold water be poured on anyone trying to gain access by burning the door down. The castle passed in 1930 from the family of the Earl of Wemyss to the Department of the Environment who care for it and its picturesque setting.

The church of the parish of Rhynd used to be down by the river at Easter Rhynd, where the old burial ground has some interesting inscriptions and stones carved with implements of livelihood such as a ploughshare, and there is one of two smiths at work. A hundred years ago, the church was moved to higher ground in the village and a manse was built which must vie with that at Aberdalgie for having the finest view in the county. To the new church, beautiful inside, have been transferred the pewter flagon and basin of 1716 and two silver cups of 1703, these last bought when the newly Presbyterian parishioners failed to recover the old ones from the formidable Countess of Wemyss who was still living at Elcho and was a resolute Episcopalian. There is also a very old double-locked wooden money chest.

A little book called *The Rhynd and Elcho* by the Rev. James Ballingal quotes a delightful picture of a cottar's cottage in about 1775.

> The cottages were all alike – walls of stone and clay cemented together with chopped straw; roofs thatched with the reeds which grow in great abundance close by at the junction of the Tay and the Earn; the inside divided by box beds into a butt and a ben, and the hallan, a clay partition at the entrance door to exclude the wind.

> The lady goes on to tell of a visit to an old nurse who lived in one of these cottages with a bachelor brother, a weaver.

> To pay a visit to our old nurse was a chief indulgence, and sure of a hearty welcome. On entrance the sound of a weaver's shuttle was heard. The fireplace was at one end of the cottage, and consisted of some neat stones placed near the wall that the smoke might escape through the lum or hole in the roof. A few seats of stone or wood surrounded the fireplace. In one corner stood a cow (for all the cottars had cows), in the other sat a hen with a brood of five chickens nestling under her; yet all so clean

and inoffensive, it had all a look of comfort. Soon a stool covered with a napkin white as snow was set before us, with a cog of nice milk covered with cream, a trencher (or wooden plate) with barley bannocks. A large print of butter, and at times a honeycomb, with large horn cuttys, or spoons, completed the repast, attended by the dear old nurse, for Johnny, the brother, remained at his loom, not wishing to interrupt the young ladies.

Across the Tay, but still in Perthshire, is Abernethy, the seat of one of Scotland's earliest bishoprics. St Bride, the patron saint, is reputed to have supplied sufficient beer to eighteen churches to last them from Maundy Thursday till after Easter – all from one barrel. The little village has been most fortunate in that its pleasant main street has been by-passed in time to preserve it and its treasure, its eleventh-century round tower. Such towers are common in Ireland but this one and its fellow at Brechin are the only two that survive on the mainland of Scotland. Its inside diameter is 8 feet and its walls, 3 feet 6 inches thick, are of well dressed stones, wrought to the cylindrical shape of the tower. Inside, there were six wooden floors, lit by a few narrow Romanesque windows. It lacks the later spire of Brechin and its door is not so high above the ground, but presumably the ground level has risen; originally, access would not have been so easy. Today there is a Pictish stone at its foot, and jougs embedded in its walls.

From Abernethy, we must return to the line of the A90 through Bridge of Earn and Glenfarg. The old bridge of Earn was demolished in 1977 in spite of a campaign to save it, but it had been out of use for many years. Nearly 200 years before, it had been the scene of a remarkable escape. In December 1803 the *Aberdeen Journal* reported as follows:

On Tuesday afternoon, as the mail coach was passing the Bridge of Earn, a horse stood in the way, which the slovenly carter either could not, or would not, quickly remove. The coach struck against the cart with such violence as threw the driver of the coach against the parapet of the bridge, from which he fell inwards just in time to let the wheel of the coach pass over his body. His mournful cries and the jolting of the coach against the side of the bridge, frightened the horses, and they began to gallop

o.f, when the guard by a gallant and sudden effort, sprang over
the top of the coach, seated himself on the box, caught the reins
and checked the horses. The passengers, believing the driver to be
in the agonies of death, wished him to get into the coach. He was,
however, more afraid than hurt, for, to their utter astonishment,
he refused their kind invitation, mounted the box and drove to
Perth.*

If it could be taken out of its present context of heavy
traffic, as soon it will be, when the stretch of M90 from
Edinburgh northwards is joined by that southwards, Glenfarg
would be comparable to Killiecrankie. It is a deep gorge along
the River Farg, thickly wooded with beech; in spring and
again in autumn, its gradation of colours is breathtaking, and
in winter it has the longest icicles imaginable. Queen Victoria
who drove through it on her way to Taymouth in 1842
declared that it was really lovely and her consort considered it
as beautiful as anything in his native Germany. A few years
before, as a boy, Walter Scott had ridden along a slightly
different line, neither the A90 nor what is today known as
Wicks of Baiglie road, but the Wallace Road from Lochelbank
over to West Dron. When he reached a point between Dron
Hill and West Dron Hill, he was so struck by the view over
Perth that he stopped in his tracks:

Childish wonder, indeed, was an ingredient in my delight, for I
was not above fifteen years old; and as this had been the first
occasional excursion which I had been permitted to make on a
pony of my own, I also experienced the glow of independence,
mixed with that degree of anxiety which the most conceited boy
feels when he is first abandoned to his own undirected counsels.
I recollect pulling up the reins without meaning to do so, and
gazing on the scene before me, as if I had been afraid it would
shift like those in a theatre before I could distinctly observe its
parts or convince myself that what I saw was real. Since that
hour, and the period is now more than fifty years past, the
recollection of that inimitable landscape has possessed the strongest influence on my mind, and retained its place as a memorable
thing, when much that was influential on my own fortunes has
fled from my mind.

* Quoted in W. G. Rowntree Bodie, *Some light on the Past Around
Glenrothes*, St Andrews University Press, 1968.

The result was a famous passage of scenic description in the first chapter of *The Fair Maid of Perth.*

This old road is known as the Wallace Road because of the connection which Wallace had with this part of the world; after he had recaptured Perth he defeated the English near Abernethy. Rob Roy, too, was here on a Sunday morning in 1715 on his way to Sheriffmuir and found all the good people at morning service in the little church at Arngask, now a ruin. He divested the congregation of their boots and their Bibles, equipping his men with the first and selling the latter back to their owners by way of acquiring some ready money. At the foot of the Wallace Road is the L-shaped tower-house of Balmanno, restored by Lorimer and in private occupation.

South and south-east from Dunning, two minor roads run through the picturesque Ochil Hills, giving as they ascend and descend panoramic views to north and south. The former leads to the Yetts (or gateway) of Muckhart and the unusual double bridge at Rumbling Bridge; here three fine castles are all lived in – Cleish, Aldie and Tullibole; and, from a much earlier day, there are hill forts at Dunglow and Dummiefaline, the former precipitous on three of its sides. The other road climbs steeply and descends again to Pathstruie and Path of Condie, then up even more steeply and down again, with views over Orwell's eighteenth-century church to Loch Leven.

At Pathstruie, tent preaching lasted until 1862 under the Free Church minister, Rev. Mr M'Queen, a much-loved versatile man who was doctor, vet and lawyer to his flock, as well as, in his own words, "Bishop of the Ochils and Proprietor of the Halfway house between Milnathort and Dunning".

It is about forty years since I first saw Pathstruie. It was a Sacramental Sabbath towards the end of the pleasant month of June. The day was bright and the air mild and balmy. The hills had resumed their vivid mantle of green, the wild flowers were out upon the braes in thousands, and all nature was arrayed in beauty. One could not imagine a more delightful scene. There would be from 1500 to 2000 people assembled at the tent, and, on these occasions, Mr M'Queen was at his best. There was then continuous preaching at the tent from 11 a.m. till 7 at night. ...

In places as far removed as Kinross and Abernethy, it was common for farm servants to bargain, when hiring, for a day at the Fair or at the Paith sacrament.*

Milnathort itself has not much that is old but it is a pleasant quiet place now that the motorway has relieved the pressure of traffic which used to thunder down its long straight street. The exception is Burleigh Castle, formerly the home of the Balfours. Its warm red stone glows on a sunny day and belies its formidable purpose and its horrific past. The square keep dates from about 1500 and had the usual arrangement of kitchen and cellars on the ground floor and the hall on the first, with bedrooms above. The roof has gone and three sides of the courtyard enclosure but the fourth side of the curtain wall is well preserved, as is a rather smaller tower of 1582; this is circular for two storeys, then corbelled out as at Claypotts to form a larger square chamber at the top. It lies half a mile to the east of Milnathort and is in the custody of the Department of the Environment; admission free on application to the key-keeper at the farm opposite. It was visited several times by James VI and has associations with Scott's *Old Mortality*, but is perhaps best known for its connection with a Master of Burleigh at the beginning of the eighteenth century. He had been sent abroad to forget a young lady who was not considered a good enough match for him. On his return, he learnt to his fury that she had married a humble schoolmaster. In cold blood he murdered his rival; arrested and condemned, he managed to escape but he got little joy of his crime, for he lived for years a hunted man. Eventually he was attainted for taking part in the Forty-Five as his father had been for his part in the Fifteen.

Kinross is a county town – small but, then, so is its county. Its centre piece is the seventeenth-century tolbooth repaired by Robert Adam in 1771. It had the county hall and the sheriff court on the first floor with a jailer's flat and a debtor's room above it, and the prison below. The latter was unusual in the liberty that it allowed to its occupants. "On one occasion, when the Prison Inspector called to make his annual visit, he was unable to gain admittance, as the door was locked. The

* From the autobiography of the Rev. James Skinner (Edinburgh, 1893).

jailer, looking out from an upper window, told him that the prisoner (apparently the only one) had gone to Baleave Muir for a walk, taking the key with him and he, the Inspector, would have to wait till he returned."*

Individual in its penal methods, Kinross was equally individual in that its affairs were run for a hundred years by a committee appointed to erect a church steeple. This was in 1741 when they moved the parish church from its old position on the shores of Loch Leven to the High Street; the move may have encouraged the lazy to attend church more regularly but the old site was incomparable and its burial ground most peaceful. It includes the tomb of one of the shadowy figures connected with the Episcopal Church's efforts to maintain the Apostolic Succession in Scotland at the beginning of the eighteenth century, that of Henry Chrystie who had been minister of Kinross from 1676 to 1689. He was consecrated a bishop in 1709 but died soon afterwards, never having had a diocesan charge. Having built its steeple (now vanished), the *ad hoc* committee continued its own existence and served the burgh most efficiently, scavenging the streets, arranging subscription concerts, providing street lighting, at first by cruisie oil lamps in 1793, and then, forty years later, by gas. Kinross House helped to pay for this by holding a musical festival attended by 700 guests as, earlier, it had helped by selling its private fire-engine to the committee. Only in 1864 were the fire-engine and the other municipal services handed over to an elected local authority.

Kinross House is one of the great houses of Scotland and one of its earliest purely Renaissance buildings. Sir William Bruce designed it for himself in 1681. Gracious, symmetrical, light yet dignified, it is perhaps happiest of all in its setting. The west façade is approached by a straight drive between wide green lawns and mature trees. On the far side, the view from the house is over a formal garden to Loch Leven, its castle and the hills beyond – a sight particularly lovely on a summer's evening. This view is partly shared by the general public since a lane runs between the wall at the end of the garden and the lochside, round to the old burial ground, and to a discreet

* Robert S. Young, *About Kinross-shire and its Folk* (1948).

29. Clatchard
Craig hill fort

30. Scotstarvit
Tower

31. Norman
church at Leuchars

32. The town
house at Culross

33. St Andrews
Abbey and St
Rule's Tower

34. Culross

35. Dunfermline Abbey from Pittencrieff gardens

36. Inchcolm Abbey

37.   Dunfermline
Abbey, the nave

38.   Inchcolm
Abbey, the
refectory

39 & 40.   (*Above*) **Burntisland Church** and (*below*) St Monance

41. Outside the Fisheries Museum at Anstruther

42. Crail harbour

gazebo where one can shelter while waiting for the ferry to the Castle Island. The principal entrance to Bruce's magnificent building leads into a pillared hall with a carved oak stairway leading to a double cube saloon. Raeburns and fine furniture set off the interior, which, it is difficult to believe, was once completely derelict. Only in 1902 did Sir Basil Montgomery (a descendant of Thomas Graham who bought the property from the Bruce family) decide to reclaim and preserve. At the same time, he began to recreate the gardens. Today, sheltered with yew hedges and warm stone walls, the beautifully kept lawns show up to best effect the massed roses, the shrubs and herbaceous borders. There are countless corners of special interest but again and again one is drawn back to the artistry of the combination of house and garden and view.*

Loch Leven itself is, by arrangement between its owner and the National Conservancy Council, a nature reserve where fishermen, wild-fowlers and scientists pursue their occupation in harmony. It has always been noted for its pink-fleshed trout and for its geese. As long ago as 1629, Sir Christopher Lowther wrote:

> Lough Leven is four miles square and sixteen miles about. So far the land is good, but here and there many high rocks and hills; in this lough is fish every day gotten for store, none in Britain like, and consider the bigness of it as also for fowl. The general kind of fishes be these – the pikes of which many as big as a man, eels, gelletoughes, chars, perches, camdowes, a kind of trout which have not scales, grey trouts. ... There is a river running out of it they call the Leven eight miles to the sea, and in it is salmons ... there be great store of all kinds of wildfowl, of wild geese there being continually seen 3000 or 4000, and swans many.

Today its trout are still sought after, and, for wildfowl, it is one of the best sites in Europe. Dabbling ducks and diving ducks both find suitable conditions for feeding and nesting; greylag and pink-footed geese and whooper swans winter there together. It is an ideal place for the study not only of birds but of insect and plant life too. Public access is restricted to three areas on the shore, and to Castle Island, but the birds can be seen from the road and from the Royal Society for the

* The gardens – but not the house – are open to the public during the summer.

Protection of Birds' observation post at Vane Farm.

Castle Island may be reached by an absurdly inexpensive ferry service any weekday in summer, and admission is free to the building in which Mary Queen of Scots was imprisoned in 1567. A curtain wall connects two early-fifteenth century towers, one of which had a hall on the first floor and her solar above with an oratory in its east window. Even the most vigorous opponent of Scottish Mariolatry cannot but be moved by the story of her escape, aided by George Douglas, nowhere more movingly told than in the fictionalized account in Scott's *The Abbot*.

On the other principal island in the loch there was a very early Culdee cell dedicated to St Serf but little of this remains, or of the small priory which took its place. On the eastern shore of the loch are a holy well at Portmoak and some standing stones and the H.Q. of the Scottish Gliding Club – which can coexist with a nature reserve more happily than water-skiing could! Above them, on the top of East Lomond are the remains of an early Iron Age hill fort with immense all-round views. Within it was found an interesting slab incised with a Pictish bull.

VI

ANGUS - STRATHMORE

THE road from Perth to Coupar Angus, between the River Isla and the Sidlaw Hills, is not very exciting; to appreciate the width and colour of Strathmore, green in spring and so golden in various shades in summer, one has to climb to one of the tops. From Pole Hill at the southern end, you can see not only the strath but fifty miles to the west to Ben More above Crianlarich or as far out to sea, over Dundee. Dunsinane (with the accent on the second syllable) has a fort on the summit and dubious Shakespearian associations, as also has the highest point, the King's Seat at 1236 feet. For those tied to a car, the A923 south-east from Coupar Angus to Dundee is the next best thing. This road has the additional advantage of taking you to the attractive villages of Kettins, Lundie and Fowlis Easter.

Coupar Angus, in spite of its name, is in Perthshire but the most important part of it was once a rich Cistercian abbey, the lands of which were mainly over the border in Angus; alas, nothing now remains of it but a doorway by the roadside. Its last abbot was Donald Campbell, a son of the second Earl of Argyll, who (so far as he was concerned) had the good fortune to coincide with the beginning of the Reformation. In 1560 he attended the Parliament which abolished the papal supremacy in Scotland, and, in the course of the next two years, set up his five natural sons in estates previously belonging to the abbey – Balgersho, Arthurstone, Denhead, Keithock and Croonan. What was left passed first to the Elphinstones and then to the Ogilvies of Airlie, together with the title of hereditary porter to the abbey.

The church at Kettins dates from the mid-eighteenth century and has a pleasing symmetrical design but, inside, though beautifully maintained, the furnishings are disappointingly Victorian. Its graveyard, however, is full of interest. The Geekie family are represented from 1630 to 1970, and are still in the parish. Another stone is inscribed:

"Here lies ane honest man Patricke Yevlo, husband to Elspit Dwchirs with 5 children, indwellers at the millen of Pette. He and his Forefathers lived two hundred yeirs bygon heir. Departed the 8 of November 1699 of his age 65 yeirs." The stone also commemorates David his son and David's children, and adds a verse:

> Devot and pious towards God
> He was upright to man.
> Most carefull still in his affairs
> But now hes dead and gone
> From time into eternitie
> To ring with Christ in glore
> He is gon befor, follou we must
> Of him wile say no more.

"Here lies ane honest man" – the phrase is common enough in this and other graveyards, but in this case it may have been the more urgent to stress the dead man's integrity in that his relations seem to have been in perpetual trouble with the church authorities. In 1645, Robert Yullo had to pay 6s. 8d for drinking on the Sabbath – and again in 1654 when James Yullo was also at fault. In 1664, Janet Yullo compared before the congregation and professed her repentance and sorrow for her sin of "scolding and swearing, cursing and railing against her neighbour, Catherine Small" and, in 1715, George Yullo, after four years of obduracy, admitted an offence of prenuptial fornication.

Two other treasures are in the graveyard, a Flemish bell dated 1519 and a Pictish stone, early but with the designs already well formed. The bell was lost for many years, hidden in a bog; now it stands outside the west door behind a protective stone screen, with the following inscription: "Maria Troon es minen naem. Meester Hans Popen Reider gaf mi Anno Domini MCCCCCXIX." It presumably came from the abbey of Troon near Antwerp. The Pictish stone was used for many years as a bridge over a nearby burn and so is much worn.

Easier to appreciate but not so easy to find is the proto-Pictish souterrain, two miles further along the A923. This is on private property and surrounded by arable land, but, if permission is given to visit, it may be found by following the wire fence along the west side of the field immediately across the road from Pitcur Castle and farm; it runs beneath a power cable and should be followed as far as the first sparse clump of trees (O.S. 253374). It is large, with a main passage over fifty metres long, but its chief interest lies in the fact that a number of its roofing stones are still in position.

Back on the A94, the next place north of Coupar Angus is Meigle. It is supposed to be the burial place of Arthur's Queen Guinevere; it certainly is that of a more mundane figure – Sir Henry Campbell-Bannerman. His party thought little of him at the time when he became Prime Minister, but, like Mr Attlee, he found unexpected strength and succeeded in an ambitious programme of radical legislation. Meigle is so rich in Pictish remains that it must have been a centre of either government or religion or both. A former school has been converted into a museum to house them and they form a very representative collection. No. 1 is especially worth noticing – a rather simple Latin cross, with a variety of symbols on the reverse, and vigorous horsemen below. Since it has also some very much earlier cup markings underneath it, it may be a prehistoric carved stone, re-worked by the Picts. The cup-markings cannot be seen but there is a cast of them on display. No. 2 is a Greek cross (not so common) with a ring of glory and some beautifully detailed horsemen, their clothing and bridles; on the left of the cross are three climbing figures. No. 3 has an intricate saddle-cloth; No. 4 an elephant and horses on the reverse. There is another elephant on the side of No. 5 (*see* plate 6) Here the stone may have been worked twice over, the incised elephant and the horsemen being older than the cross and its animals which are carved in deep relief. Of the recumbent gravestones, no. 12 is worth noticing for the massive bulls on its side, and 26 for the bears and a curious human swastika.

Two miles south-east of Meigle is Newtyle; two miles east is Eassie. Newtyle, though only a village, had one of the first railways in Scotland, begun in 1826 and completed in 1831. It was an unusual venture.

It left Dundee on an inclined plane half a mile long, with a gradient of 1 in 10 and proceeded through a shoulder of Dundee Law in a tunnel 340 yards long. Altogether there were three inclines where stationary engines drew up the carriages, and two level portions where the carriages were drawn at first by horses, and then by a locomotive. The last incline at Hatton was 1 in 12, reaching an elevation of 544 feet above sea level, from which a descent was made to the valley of Strathmore . . . . On one occasion, a country wife was on her journey for the first time with her basket of eggs for the Dundee market, when a rope of the incline engine broke, and the carriages ran down with increasing momentum until all were turned out; though her eggs were broken smashed, she had no idea that it was an accident, for, when asked afterwards, how she had liked the train, said, "It was a gey gude ride, but it was a rough affputtin."

Two centuries ago, Eassie had a minister of far broader-minded views than most of his contemporaries. Seeing that it was a reevin' day after weeks of muggy weather, he told the people from the pulpit to go and take the corn though it was the Sabbath, as this was an act of necessity and mercy. His stricter brethren must have rejoiced, when not long after, indeed within the week, the roof of his church fell in. It is still roofless, but in the churchyard is a Class II Pictish stone well worth making a detour to visit. On one side the cross with its interwoven pattern has, at the side two seraphim above, and a warrior with shield and spear below, two deer and a hound. On the reverse are further warriors, a double disc with Z symbol, and very fine long-horned cattle.

Inevitably, people go to Glamis principally to see the castle, and surely there is no better money's worth to be had in any stately home. Other places may vie with its wonderful furniture and china, but none with its impressive architecture combined with history enriched with traditions and royal associations. Even the first sight of it stays in the memory;

instead of the rather sombre pile that one expects from black and white photographs – and from its more awful legends – the rich red stone gives a most warm welcome in the sun. But there is more than the castle to see at Glamis – an 8-foot high Pictish cross in the manse garden – another on Hunter's Hill – and the St Orland's Class II stone, two miles to the north-east. And, in 1955, the sixteenth Earl of Strathmore gave a row of nineteenth-century cottages to house the Angus Folk Museum. Its charm is immense, and fully justifies the guide-book's claim that it brings to life "as nothing else could the day to day existence of those who lived and worked in these parts, in the mansions, farms and crofts, cottages and bothies, tinkers' camps and fields, in Angus". Here are the tools that the men used, and the kitchen and household and dairy gear of their wives, the cruisies and cradles and cups and spoons; the children's toys and the men's weapons, including the Deuchar sword wielded at Harlaw in 1411 – and then old. But the special treasures are the work-bench of the Rev. Patrick Bell of Carmylie, who invented the first reaping machine; it was first tried and used in Angus and was the basis of all later devices; the little room arranged as a well-to-do Victorian parlour; and the recreated kitchen with its box-beds, dresser, spinning wheel and range. What makes it specially interesting is that it is not just a random collection of items collected to illustrate a typical kitchen; it was brought entire when a 150-year-old but-and-ben cottage at Craichie was demolished.

The Lyons lived rather differently from cottage folk, even when comforts were few and far between, by modern standards. John Lyon was knighted by Robert II, became his Chamberlain, was given Glamis in 1372 and married the King's daughter four years later. He was killed by a Lindsay of Crawford but the family do not seem to have had quite the same perpetual feuding with the Lindsays that their neighbours, the Ogilvys, had. The Lyons continued to serve their kings, and Sir John's grandson was created Lord Glamis. There was a brief period in the sixteenth century when they fell out of favour at court, owing to the hostility of James V to the

Douglases, into which family the sixth Lord Glamis had married. When he died, his widow was first imprisoned and then burnt as a witch on Castle Hill, Edinburgh, while, during her long imprisonment, the King made free of the castle, often stayed there, and melted down its silver flagons. Restored to favour, her great-grandson became the first Earl of Kinghorne and is the subject of one of the most attractive of the pictures. On one side of a wooden panel is the boy in a mid-sixteenth-century ruff; on the reverse is his secretary, George Boswell, not much older, with a quill behind his ear, and the verses:

> My Lord I am at your command
> As was my father's will
> That I should be ane trew servand
> And yat I will fulfill. Quhat you command me eik
> I shall do my devoir.

The second Earl was a great friend of Montrose but parted company with him when he felt that the Marquis was putting his royalism before his religion. He sacrificed much of his wealth for the Covenant – "coming to his inheritance the wealthiest peer in Scotland, he left it the poorest". Fortunately his son, Patrick, third Earl of Strathmore and Kinghorne, "by prudence and frugality" was able, not only to pay off most of the £400,000 debt, but to beautify the castle and give it some of its greatest treasures such as the plaster ceiling in the drawing-room. I said that the Lyons lived rather more comfortably than the cottagers but Earl Patrick might not have agreed. His childhood had been made most unhappy by his step-father, and, when he came of age and had a home of his own at Castle Lyon (later Castle Huntley) near Dundee, his description of his setting up home might be that of any young couple today:

"Having scrambled together from the deserted castle at Glamis some old potts and pans which were verie useful, and collected some odd furniture" (a bed borrowed from the minister and some chairs and a table that he had had in his student's lodging at the University of St Andrews), he and his sister began to do some decoration with their own hands in order to try to make their lonely habitation more comfortable.

Nor could he afford the equivalent for those days of even a second-hand car: "att that time I was not worth a four footed beast, safe for a little dog that I keeped att and brought with me from St Andrews" and his spoons (only a dozen of them) he had to buy back from his step-father. Even ten years later when, after his marriage, he moved to Glamis, he had "scarce a spare room furnished to lodge a stranger in". Only one floor of the castle had glass in the windows, so the house was extremely cold; it was also inconvenient in that the bedrooms could only be reached by going through the hall "even for the most indecent occasions of drudgerie unavoidable to be seen by all who should happen to be in the room" – and there were rats in the attics. The account which Earl Patrick himself wrote of his gradual improvements has been published by the Scottish History Society and deserves to be read in full, especially, perhaps, his tribute to his wife and children: "I have reason dayly to adore and magnify the name of my God who out of his infinit goodness to me, more than I deserve, and to my family, has blest me with good and virtewous sons and daughters, of good dispositions and frugall and moderat as much as my heart can desire . . . nor can I deny the great advantage I have by their mother who's care has been of her children and to stay at home and guide within the house her part."

In gratitude, he founded four almshouses, possibly where the Folk Museum now is – four lodges for four aged men who had been reduced to want not through their own fault; as well as their lodging they were to receive four bolls of oatmeal and 25 merks Scots money a year, and "a new whyt cloath coat lyned with blew serge once every thrie years". In return, they were "to attend at the church door when we goe there", and one of them was "to attend each day at our Buriall Place whereof a key shall be given to each incomer and a forme of prayer to be read by them by turns by such of them as can read, and if they cannot read, that they learn the same by heart".

It may well have been one of these old men who made a sad prophecy to John, fourth Earl, one day when he was out for a walk with his four sons. "Are not these four pretty boys?" he had asked the old man. "Yes," was the answer, "but they will all be Earls and when the fourth will be Earl, God help the poor." The prophecy came true when the three eldest died without male heirs, and, in the time of the fourth, an intense frost in 1740 was followed by a famine. It was the ninth Earl who married a Bowes heiress from the north of England, and thus added Bowes to the surname and bows to the lion in the coat of arms. His portrait is the most lifelike of the early ones, and the warmest; through her – in the course of time – came the magnificent seventeenth-century fireplace now in the billiard room. The fourteenth Earl had the rare distinction of being a Knight both of the Thistle and the Garter – and was the father of Queen Elizabeth the Queen Mother. The family has made its sacrifices and has had its share of sadnesses, but the castle gave her a happy home in her childhood – and surely it must be the same now for the present generation.

In it, it is hard to single out one room more than another for its interest to the visitor. What is now known as the crypt was originally the great hall of the earliest castle. The drawing-room has Earl Patrick's plaster ceiling with its deep, but never heavy, mouldings and an equally lovely seventeenth-century heraldic fireplace, interesting portraits and lovely furniture. In the room where, by tradition, Malcolm III died – and Mary Queen of Scots slept – there is another splendid ceiling, a plaster overmantel and some blue linen hangings embroidered by Countess Helen in the seventeenth century. In the royal apartments, one of the four-poster beds is that of the first Earl of Kinghorne and has some very old embroidery; the other has some exquisite work by the grandmother of our present Queen. Towards the end of the tour of the castle, you come to the chapel, ornate with unusual paintings by de Wet, and to Duncan's Hall, the oldest room in the place, and finally to the family room; here the exhibition includes a tartan coat and breeches worn by Prince Charles Edward, a bullet-proof vest of Claverhouse, the little phaeton driven by the Queen Mother when she was a child, and many family uniforms, robes, photographs and other treasures.

Outside on the lawns is Earl Patrick's eighty-faced sundial

and a Dutch garden along the east wing of the castle. This is private but the great herbaceous borders and the yew hedges of the Italian garden are open to the public. The fine sweeps all round were laid out by Capability Brown but at the expense of removing seven wrought iron gates which adorned the approach down the main drive.

Between Glamis and Forfar is a Victorian baronial mansion at Kinnettles. This belonged to a former judge in the service of the East India Company, John Inglis Harvey – but only in view of his marriage and "so long as his wife remained above ground". Since the good lady predeceased him, Harvey retained possession of the estate by placing her in a glass case in a mausoleum – above ground. Rochelhill, just to the south of Glamis has what is perhaps the oldest substantial doocot in Scotland. In the days before there was winter feed for the cattle, let alone tins or refrigeration, pigeons provided a most useful addition to the wealthy man's table.

If the Angus Folk Museum provides one foil to the splendours of Glamis, Barrie's birthplace at Kirriemuir is another. Barrie is at something of a discount these days; his biographers have tended to stress his weaknesses, his sentimentality, his inadequacy as a husband, his possessiveness towards the Llewellyn-Davies boys, his exploitation of his mother in *Margaret Ogilvy*, but I do not think that Barrie himself thought of that book as a means of making money; rather as a tribute to the love that he felt he had received at her hands. Yet, was it really love? Was it not really that the whole of the rest of his life was dominated by a pathetic urge to be loved? In his own way, he was immensely kind, most hospitable, yet touchy, moody and lonely. Critics have written him off as just another of the Kailyard school, cloyed with sentiment and all the more damnable in that he was clearly an intelligent man. All this was understandable at the time when George Blake launched his denunciation, and even more understandable in the days of the drama of the kitchen sink and of cruelty. Neither conception would have meant much to Barrie. No. 9 Brechin Road had no kitchen sink, and, though courage certainly did enter the list of the attributes that he admired, cruelty did not. If, at times, he is sugar sweet, there is a place in this world for Benedictine as well as for malt whisky, and because a man can appreciate the former, it does not follow that he is blind to the merits of the latter. And no one has denied that he was a supreme theatrical craftsman; Dearth in *Dear Brutus* not only commands our sympathy more readily than Archie Rice, but will live longer.

Anyway, whether they liked it or not, Barrie painted a lifelike picture of the Auld Licht weavers of Kirriemuir in the early nineteenth century, and, in his early life, saw the changes that came as a result of the industrial revolution. The National Trust for Scotland has done well to preserve the four-roomed cottage in which he was born – he and his six brothers and sisters – three-roomed, really, since the downstairs room held the handloom at which his father earned his living. Some of J.M.B.'s schooling was at the Free-Church school in Kirriemuir, some was further afield under his eldest brother, some at Forfar. The house in which he lived there has been much altered but that to which they returned in Kirriemuir, Strathview, on the Dundee road, is still there, and the little cottage opposite, which housed "The Window in Thrums". In the birthplace the National Trust for Scotland have two of the hair-bottomed chairs which his father carried into the house on the day on which J.M.B. was born, so that the workroom could be converted into a parlour. And, in another room, are the rather grander couch from Barrie's flat in the Adelphi and many other treasures connected with his long career. Outside is still the communal wash-house where, as a child, he staged and acted his first play, and from which he got the idea of the Wendy House in *Peter Pan*.

Once the largest producers of linen in Angus, Kirriemuir is still a prosperous town, with weaving as its chief industry. Its square remains, and some of its narrow wynds. And in a small shelter near the top of the hill cemetery to the north of the town are two Class II and two Class III stones. There are other Pictish and proto-Pictish remains within easy reach, much the most interesting being a souterrain near the little church at Kirkton of Airlie, because its roof slabs are still in position. For this reason, and for the sake of a lovely ten-minute walk, it is well worth seeking it out. From the church, take the road running south-west for about a quarter of a mile, past the Barns of Airlie, to a large pile of stones on the left of the road. Follow the wall alongside the field on the left of the road, into the next field, at the far end of which, turn left along the wall facing you. Here on the top of the ridge is a small hole giving access. You will need a torch. A further good reason for the expedition is that it leads naturally on to the loch of Lintrathen and a drive up Glen Isla or a walk back past the falls of the Reekie Linn. We are now in the Ogilvy country – a family of whom it could be said in 1916 that, with the single exception of Inverquharity, the lands which they had held in the mid-fifteenth century were all still theirs. That castle, long a ruin, has recently been restored and is inhabited again.

Life has not always been easy for the Ogilvys. In the fifteenth century it was a case of perpetual war with the Crawfords, till the Abbot of Aberbrothock – Cardinal Beaton's predecessor – threatened anathema, that "every Lindsay should be poorer than his father and every Ogilvy madder than his mother". Some alleviation came when the third Lord Ogilvy married a Lindsay, but, like many another family they lost an heir at Pinkie. The fifth Lord left a remarkable letter for his grandson, four months before he died:

> When it shall please God that you shall come to the Room that I and your father possessed afore, hold a good and Honest house. Be favourable to your tenants. Place in your Baillerys honest and discreet men to execute justice equally amongst them, give them a good continuance . . . for they say rich tenants make a rich master . . . be helpful to the poor and look ever with pityful eyes upon them. And, seeing nowadays many young scholars give themselves curiously to understand Magick and Necromancy, which are the greatest sins against God that can be, and has been the destruction of both soul and body to many and their houses, I will beseech you, name it not, never let that enter your mind.

The first Earl, born 1586, and his son, suffered grievous depredations through being Episcopalians and loyal supporters of Charles I. Their old enemy, the Marquis of Argyll, secured a commission in 1640 to lay waste their castles of Airlie and Forter, and wrote off to his follower, Campbell of Inverawe: "demolish my Lord Ogilvie's house and, further, see how ye can cast offe the Irone yettis and windows, and take off the rooff, and if ye find it to be langsome, ye shall fire it well, that so it may be destroyed. But ye will not let know that ye have directions from me to fyir it, only ye may say that ye have warrant to demolish it, and that to make short the work ye will fyir it . . . and to bring all the nolt and sheep".

This he did, while the Marquis himself laid waste Airlie Castle. The two events were conjoined, with some poetic licence, in the ballad of "The Bonnie Braes of Airlie". In due course, the Earl got his revenge by leading the cavalry (at the age of fifty-nine) in Montrose's victory over the Covenanters at Kilsyth and by burning down Castle Campbell near Dollar, while his son got his revenge on Inverawe by taking him prisoner at Inverlochy, only to be made a prisoner himself at Philiphaugh. Sentenced to death in St Andrews Castle, he escaped, dressed in his sister's clothes, and lived to the age of ninety-three.

The eleventh Lord Ogilvy followed in their footsteps by joining Charles Edward in 1745. After Culloden, he escaped with one faithful servant, John Thomson, who posed as the master, while Ogilvy acted as his servant. While "making their way over the hill country towards the Ogilvy lands, in the hope of reaching the port of Dundee, they had secured lodgings for the night. The supper was to be porridge and Lord Ogilvy had gone somewhat clumsily about making it. When John saw him throwing in oatmeal by handfuls the prospect of a spoiled supper overcame his discretion, and he anxiously whispered, but unfortunately loud enough to be overhead by those present in the hostelry, "twinkle your little finger, my Lord, twinkle your little finger". John had fairly put his foot in it, thus disclosing his master's identity, with the result that after partaking of the knotted porridge, they had to make a hurried departure. Once in the open, Lord Ogilvy entered into a strict compact that on no account or occasion during their wanderings was he ever to address him otherwise than as Davie. John was not only faithful, he was a man of courage and resource. When Lord Ogilvy was imprisoned at Bergen, John haunted the place of confinement and, when his Lordship made his escape, he was in waiting and joined in his escape to Sweden. Feeling ill after his confinement, Lord Ogilvy found that he could only make the journey with faltering step, and he soon became aware that they were being followed by three men. Unable himself to make much of a defence, the affair looked like resolving itself into a possible contest of three to one. John came to the rescue. He reconnoitred for a position that would yield him some advantage. He was a hill man and knew how to take in the lie of the land. Taking his place in a narrow rocky gorge, he directed his master where to proceed and where to await him; and, drawing his sword, made this stipulation, "Gin I dinna come, ye'll look aifter Nance." John, however, turned up in good time, and with sufficient evidence of having used his sword. On Lord Ogilvy remarking "There is blood on your clothes, John" he received the cool reply, "Och, aye, Davie man, but it's no mine".* Without further adventure, they reached France where Lady Ogilvy joined them, with, one hopes, Nance, because John did not return to Scotland till 1778 when Lord Ogilvy was at last pardoned.

Not the least notable of Ogilvy accomplishments has been to marry ladies of great distinction. The eighth Earl married a Stanley who succeeded in diverting him from the Turf (which had nearly ruined him) to politics and to breeding Aberdeen-Angus cattle. The ninth Countess was lady-in-waiting to Queen Mary (as the present Countess is to Queen Elizabeth II) and the subject of a delightful memoir *Thatched with Gold*. The Hon. Angus Ogilvy is married to H.R.H. Princess Alexandra, while the present Dowager Countess still presides with grace and distinction at Airlie Castle. This has a section of its original high wall and a sixteenth-century gate-house but its most notable features are, perhaps, its siting, superb to resist attack, and its garden. Cortachy Castle, which became the main seat of the family when Airlie was first burnt has three of its fifteenth-century towers but has been added to on several occasions.

* Rev. William Wilson, *A Parish History* (Alex Pettigrew, Coatbridge, 1917).

Both are opened annually under the Scottish Gardens Scheme, and Airlie, sometimes, by prior appointment. A third castle, Forter, up Glen Isla is a ruin but substantial.

Forfar Castle, now no more, was sited to cover the main route north and south through marshy land. Malcolm Canmore used it, and William the Lion. The royal burgh which grew up round the castle became a prosperous market and a centre of domestic industry, especially the making of shoes. These were "of a peculiar kind, called brogues, from the Gaelic word *brog*, literally a shoe. Light and coarse, made of horse leather instead of nolt, they were admirably adapted for travelling among the hills, and were a type of the shoes worn by the old inhabitants of Scotland, which, in more modern times, were denominated *rough rullions*, the brogues differing from these only in having the hair taken off . . .". There is a tradition that, during the summer of 1645, while Drummond of Hawthornden, the historian and poet, was journeying through Scotland, he visited Forfar, and was refused shelter for the night. This want of hospitality is only to be accounted for, we hope, by a fear on the part of the inhabitants that he might communicate to them the plague, which was then raging in many parts of the kingdom. But, be the reason what it may, Drummond found a hearty welcome in the adjoining town of Kirriemuir, and, learning that a feud pended between the inhabitants of those two places, regarding the commonty of Muir Moss, he determined to play off a joke upon the magistrates of Forfar, by addressing a letter to the Provost on the day following. The Estates of Parliament were then sitting at Saint Andrews, and, believing the communication to come from that body, the chief magistrate had the council and the clergymen of the burgh convened, to hear and deliberate upon the contents of the letter. But much to their astonishment and chagrin, this was found only to consist of the following reproachful rhyme upon themselves, in which there is a pointed allusion to the brogue-makers:

The Kirriemuirians and the Forfarians met at Muir Moss,
The Kirriemuirians beat the Forfarians back to the cross;

Sutors ye are an' sutors ye'll be –
Fye upon Forfar, Kirriemuir bears the gree!

Later on, weaving became the main industry, first of wool,
then of coarse linen, then of jute. Even after the decline in the
jute industry, the textile firms have remained the largest
employers, moving into the field of polypropylene production.
But the town prides itself on the extent to which it has been
able to diversify and to keep its unemployment rate lower than
the national average; it has amongst other things, a ladder-
making factory, a canning plant and a shrub nursery. But,
while it is an excellent place to live in, its interest for the visitor
lies more in the surrounding countryside than in the burgh
itself, in spite of the elegance of the eighteenth-century town
and county hall.

One rather ill reputation it had in the past – for the
persecution of witches, especially in Commonwealth times –
poor deluded women who genuinely believed themselves to be
in communication with the powers of Darkness. One confessed
"that about three years the last oate-seed time, she was at a
meeting in the kirkyard of Forfar, and that yr were first there
the devill himselfe in the shape of a black-haired man and a
number of other persons; that they all danced together, and
that the ground under them was fyre flaughten", and another,
"that after dancing awhyle, she and the other women present
went into a house and sat down, the devill being present at the
head of the table; that after making themselves mirrie with alle
and aquavitae, the devill made much of them all, and especially
of Marion Rinde". Nine of them suffered as a result of the
detective activities of an inn-keeper who secured the services of
the "pricker of witches in Tranent" and, for putting the court's
sentence into effect, the "executioner and scourger of the poor"
from Perth.

In the eighteenth century, the self-appointed guardians of
morality confined themselves to the less bloodthirsty harrying
of sabbath-breakers. On one Sunday in 1725, the minister got
his pulpit supplied so that he could go snooping with his elders
during sermon-time. They found "two drinking ale, a third
gathering in his linseed bolls with his coat off and a belt about

him" and a fourth with his family at dinner.

Because of the marshy ground that used to surround Forfar, roads tend to converge there. Of those running east, the A958 leads eventually to Carnoustie but if you take a left turn, just over two miles out, a pleasant drive takes you to Dunnichen. Here there is a replica of a Class I Pictish stone which has been removed to the Dundee Museum to prevent it deteriorating; it has a deeply incised double-disc and Z-rod symbol with mirror and comb below. Here too, by a swamp now drained, was the site of Nechtansmere where, in A.D. 685, the Northumbrian King Ecfrith was defeated by the Picts and slain. The A932 leads to the quaintly named Friockheim (after a German, Freke, with the German suffix being added in the nineteenth century) past Guthrie Castle; it has a three-storey tower house built by Sir David Guthrie in 1468 and its gardens are open in the summer. But it is the B9113 and B9114 which are most rewarding; the former passes Restenneth Priory and the latter Aberlemno.

Restenneth is only a mile from Forfar yet it is remote and peaceful in its setting. When Nechtan, king of the Picts, adopted Christianity he founded a monastery here and it is at least possible that the lowest section (ten feet) of the church tower goes right back to 710 and is the oldest fragment of church architecture in Scotland. Its narrow south door has a round arch cut from a single stone and is certainly very early. The choir is thirteenth-century and the spire fifteenth, the effect of both being greatly enhanced by the way in which the site is maintained by the Department of the Environment.

No less early, and, in their way, as remarkable are the stones at Aberlemno; of the three by the roadside, one is an unshaped Class I stone incised with large symbols, a double circle, a mirror and a serpent; another a Class II wheeled cross with angels below adoring and, on the reverse side a vigorous hunting scene. There is also a large and well preserved cross in the churchyard with, beautifully carved in low relief, a battle scene of warriors both mounted and on foot including a corpse being devoured by a bird of prey. The church itself is not of great beauty but the parish had an interesting period towards the end of the seventeenth century when the minister, Rev. J. Ochterlony, refused to accept the Presbyterian order and withdrew to Flemington Castle (of which he was the proprietor) and continued his Episcopalian ministrations from there.

Flemington is now roofless, and so are the considerable remains of Melgund Castle. The latter was built by Cardinal David Beaton for his mistress, Marion Ogilvy, and combines the comfort suitable for a daughter of the house of Ogilvy with the splendour that Beaton considered necessary for an archbishop. Nettles may contribute to its welcome solitude but one cannot help wishing that it was rather better cared for.

Before going on to Brechin, the narrow steep road over the hill to Finavon is worth taking for the sake of the views and also for the remarkable vitrified fort on the summit. Here, excavation has yielded samples which carbon dating assigns to the sixth century B.C. Even larger and higher are the similar forts, five miles to the north, on the Cathertuns. On the way, Careston Castle is in private occupation but there is an early example of a T-shaped church built specially for Presbyterian worship in 1638 and a motte at Hilton of Fern. The fort on the Brown Cathertun had six ramparts with a massive stone wall on the innermost but it is the White Cathertun which is the more exciting today. Here the larger of the two major defences has been called "the most impressive ruined wall in Britain"; it was originally 40 feet thick. Unrobbed and unexcavated, it may be that this wall remains to quite a height in its original state beneath that part of it which has collapsed. The little road which takes you between the two Cathertuns goes on to cross the West Water and to pass some truly remote settlements on the way to Edzell.

At the beginning of the sixteenth century, the Lindsays built a tower house here; between 1580 and 1604, Sir David Lindsay added a comfortable courtyard mansion, and then a pleasure garden which ranks high among the top twenty of places to visit in Scotland. Defence is provided for in the tower but, as Dr W. Douglas Simpson points out in the handbook, it is overlooked at close range by higher ground and "shelter and an unimpeded sunward outlook rather than defence governed the selection of the site". The risk taken was justified by history. Montrose harried Glenesk in 1645 but a castle could not have prevented that, nor, a century later, could it have held out in the Jacobite interest when it was occupied by the Argyllshire levies. It must always have been a lovely house with ample accommodation, and a great hall well lit by large windows and adorned with hangings and gay paint and a minstrels' gallery. To appreciate them to the full, the garden must be looked at both from above, from the tower, and at ground level, close to. The little box hedges are clipped with infinite care into the Lindsay motto, "*dum spiro spero*", and into the outline of the emblems of France, England, Ireland and Scotland, these last being repeated in stone on the enclosing walls. Roses provide the colour in the centre, and, in the wall recesses, alyssum and lobelia provide the heraldic argent and azure which with gules of the red sandstone were the colours of the Lindsays. All round are carved figures of the planetary deities, the liberal arts (note especially Dialectica) and the cardinal virtues where the excessively plain Prudentia is an admirable foil to the lovely Caritas next her. A summerhouse at one corner, still standing, and a bath-house at the other, completed this lavish design – which, as might be expected, left Sir David as heavily indebted to his contemporaries as we are to him.

Not all Lindsays have been so happily remembered. The third Earl of Crawford suffered excommunication for his ruthless plundering of church lands, and died of wounds received in a conflict between the Lindsays and the Ogilvys as to who should be justiciar of the abbey of Arbroath. He might in fact have carried that day, had not Alexander Seton of Gordon not happened to be staying with Ogilvy of Inverquharity at the time, which meant that, by ancient custom, he must fight for his host so long as food eaten under his roof remained in his stomach. Victory, however, brought little joy to Inverquharity as he too was wounded and then smothered by his own sister who was Crawford's widow. In glee, the Lindsay faction coined the rhyme:

Ugly [Ogilvy] you lived and ugly you die
And now in an ugly place you lie.

The fourth Earl was known as the 'Tiger' or 'Earl Beardie' because of his ferocity and the exuberance of his beard. He, like his father, rebelled against the king in league with the Douglas faction. Defeated in battle at Brechin, he died six months later, some say repentant, but another tradition has it that he sold his soul to the Devil and that he is condemned for ever to play at "the Devil's buiks" in some mysterious hidden chamber in the Castle of Glamis because he refused to give over a game of cards that he was losing one Saturday at midnight.

At least two other heads of the family won an evil name: the sixth Earl was believed to have murdered his own brother, and the eldest son of the eighth Earl was debarred from the succession for parricide as a result of keeping his father in prison till he died, a crime to which he pleaded guilty. Pardoned, he was eventually "sticked by a souter of Dundee for taking a stoup of drink from him". More recently, successive generations have given outstanding service to the country, especially in the spheres of learning and the arts.

Brechin is, at last, by-passed by the A94 and has thus recovered something of the peace which ought to grace a cathedral city. But it was before ever a bishop came that a Culdee settlement raised the great round tower that is Brechin's chief glory. It dates from about A.D. 1000 and its design, notably that of its doorway, is Irish, with figures of the crucifixion above the arch, and clerics on either side, one with the conventional curved pastoral staff, the other with the much older T-shaped cross. Apart from the raising of the earth level round about, and the loss of the internal wooden floors, the tower of red sand-stone blocks still stands as it was built except for the spire which was added in the fourteenth century. By that time, a Romanesque cathedral had come and gone and been replaced by another in the Early Pointed style, and another, square, tower was in course of construction. Sadly, this church was allowed to fall into disrepair and much reconstruction was necessary in 1806 and again a hundred years later. The first was a disaster but the second managed, while incorporating much lovely original work, to produce a harmonious place of worship. The square tower, the nave and the west front with its fifteenth-century window are the best preserved parts; the chancel had virtually to be rebuilt but in it hangs a brass chandelier of 1615, its design markedly conservative and Gothic when compared with the contemporary Renaissance chandelier in Montrose church. Other things of interest are two cross stones, one in the north wall of the chancel showing Northumbrian influence and the other at the west end, Pictish, with David slaying a lion, his staff, his harp and his sheep beside him; there is also a recumbent hog-back, possibly eleventh-century Scandinavian. The Department of the Environment now cares for the round tower and also for the fragments that remain of the thirteenth-century Maison Dieu chapel in the centre of the town.

The town itself has not had a particularly adventurous history, but it stood out against Edward I for twenty days until its lord, Sir Thomas Maule, was killed. Later it became notorious for its beggars who assaulted good men when they got out their purses as they went into church. To remedy this, pewter badges were issued to the deserving and they were allowed to beg through the streets on Thursdays – right up to the Poor Law of 1834. The Maules, now Maule-Ramsays and Earls of Dalhousie, have been here ever since the thirteenth century and have a mansion overlooking the River Southesk. It was designed by a minister and built between 1688 and 1711. A classical façade is flanked by two towers, one old and one new, which blend well with the rest and give the building a more conservative note.

At Brechin we are near the boundary of Angus but one outpost, far to the north, is still within the county. Sixteen miles from Edzell, up the lovely Glenesk, is the ruined castle of the Lindsays at Invermark dating from 1526, and, at Tarfside, a folk museum.

VII

ANGUS – THE COAST

THE LANDS of the Carse of Gowrie must always have been
fertile and good to hold, and it is no surprise to find them
studded with castles. To the south of the road A85 are Pitfour,
Megginch and Huntley Castles; to the north, those of Fingask,
Kinnaird and Fowlis Easter. This road has recently been
realigned to the benefit of all; those in a hurry can reach
Dundee more quickly; those who are more fortunate, can get a
wider view than was formerly possible, up to the Sidlaw Hills
on one hand and over the Tay to the hills of Fife.

At the church door in St Madoes, there is a good Class II
Pictish stone with fabulous beasts alongside the cross on one
side and three cloaked horsemen on the other (protected and
not visible). Pitfour Castle, nearby, is in private ownership, as is
also Megginch but the grounds of the latter are open to the
public at certain times in the summer. The castle itself has
Victorian additions but is basically sixteenth century and has
been lived in for over 300 years by a branch of the Drummond
family, independently minded folk who have followed their
own beliefs regardless of what other Drummonds, or the rest of
the world, might think.

Castle Huntley is impressive at a distance but cannot be seen
near-to as it is a Government institution. Built by the first
Lord Gray in the mid-fifteenth century, it passed to the Lyon
family of Glamis in the seventeenth, and received alterations
and additions at their hands, and was for a time known as
Castle Lyon.

On the other side of the road, there is the sham castellated
mansion of Kinfauns, and then three far more elegant houses at
Inchyra, Glencarse and Glendoick. Glendoick belonged to the

Lord Advocate at the time of the Forty-five but more recently the Cox family have built up here a world-famous collection of rhododendrons. These are open to the public under the Scotland's Gardens Scheme on two advertised days in May.

Fingask Castle has had a chequered career, having been in and out of the Threipland family more than once; they are back there now. Built originally by a Bruce, it passed in 1657 to Patrick Threipland, treasurer and later provost of Perth. He was a royalist, as was his son Sir David who entertained the Old Pretender on 7th January 1716:

> When the King to Fingask cam'
> To se Sir David and his leddy,
> There was a cod's head well dressed in sauce
> Took a hundred pounds to mak' it reddy.

At one time the Threiplands also owned the tall fifteenth-century tower of Kinnaird, when the Kinnairds who had built it – and probably an earlier castle on the same site – moved a few miles down the road to Moncur Castle. When that was burnt down, the seventh Lord Kinnaird planned, and the eighth built, the vast ecclesiastical, Gothic, Rossie Priory, in a part of which their successor still lives. From it, and from the hills above it, are some of the most beautiful views in Scotland. In the old church is another Class II Pictish stone, unusual in that it has a cross on both sides, and on one side the horsemen actually impinge on the cross itself.

Before going on to Dundee, we may notice a number of interesting sites, medieval, Pictish and proto-Pictish, lying within its district but beyond its built-up areas, starting with the restored but exceptional church at Fowlis Easter. Outside it is plain and almost without windows on the north, the near side, but the south door is embellished with swans and dragon-like lions for the families of Gray and Wemyss. The Grays had got the lands of Fowlis in 1377, some 75 years before the present church was put up, and, in expiation for some of their violent deeds, were benefactors to the church and to posterity. The second Lord Gray had been one of those who broke their oaths to safeguard Douglas and helped James II to stab him to death at Stirling; another Lord Gray conspired against James I and another, when Master of Gray, against Mary Queen of Scots, and then against James VI. It was the fourth Lord Gray who was the benefactor by commissioning the fifteenth-century painting on wood, which used to hang over the rood screen but is now on the north wall. In spite of a crowd of some twenty figures surrounding the three crosses, nothing distracts one's attention from the central figure of Christ, emphasized as it is by the long spear piercing His side; there is vigour and character about the living, and equal reality about the dead. One is used to entering some inconspicuous church in a remote village in Italy and finding an unexpected master-piece; in Scotland, a surprise of this sort is almost unique. Another panel, still at the east end of the church, has Christ with ten saints, and a third – damaged – includes the Virgin and Child, and the Entombment. The most surprising thing about the panels is less their remarkable colour and their state of preservation than the fact that they have survived at all; and the same goes for the elaborate aumbry or sacrament house. Orders were constantly given for their destruction at the time of the Reformation but the Gray family seem to have been powerful enough to save what they had given. Only the rood itself and the loft were removed and, even of this, two panels survived and have been incorporated in the wooden screen at the entrance to the nave.

These survivals are by no means all there is to see. There is a stone font carved with scenes which, though worn, can still be identified and are listed in the little guide book, and a perfectly preserved dish of bronze, dated 1487, either for alms or for holding under a child when it was baptized lest any of the water should fall on the ground after it had been blest. Needless to say, with such treasures in it, the church has to be kept locked but the key can be obtained by enquiring in the village. Outside, in the churchyard, there is a rough but very old cross and a coffin slab ornamented with a sword and a hunting horn. Nearby is the seventeenth-century tower (still lived in) of an older castle of the Grays – which passed for a time to the Murrays of Ochtertyre (*see* page 100).

The twelfth Lord Gray married Margaret Blair who brought him the estate of Kinfauns, just east of Perth, and, later, saved his estates for him by a drastic stratagem. As Lord Lieutenant, he had waited on Cumberland at Dundee in 1746 but had been coldly received, and in dudgeon had resolved to join Prince Charles Edward. His wife persuaded him to let her bathe his feet first, after his long day in the saddle, and, in the process, poured boiling water over them so that he was in no state to leave home until all was safely over.

> "I'm brint, I'm brint, how came it this way?
> I fear I'll no ride for mony a day.
> Send aff the men and to Prince Charlie say:
> 'My heart is with him but I'm tied by the tae'."
>
> The wily wife flushed, but the laird didna see
> The smile on her face through the tear in her e'e.
> "Had I kent the gudeman wad hae had siccan pain,
> The kettle, for me, sud hae coupit its lane."

It was the fifteenth Lord Gray who built the Victorian baronial mansion at Kinfauns. Of this, we may say, with an earlier writer (though for rather different reasons) that "the choiceness of its site, the elegance and splendour of its architecture, the character and quality of its paintings and its statuary and the sculpture with which the interior is adorned, do not fall within our scope".

Just north of Fowlis is another medieval church at Auchterhouse, somewhat restored but still in use, and, near it, the original site of St Martin's stone though this has now been removed to the Dundee Museum, to ensure its preservation. Further along the same road is a souterrain which can be reached by a track leading west from the farm in Balgray; though it cannot be entered, it can be well viewed from the fence surrounding it and there is also a sixteenth-century doocot there. On the A929, there are the sparse remains of a fifteenth-century keep in a farmyard at South Powrie and the much more complete Mains Castle in Caird Park with a curtain wall and an unusually high six-storey tower built by the Grahams of Fintry; its restoration is being undertaken as part of the job-creation scheme – that of Powrie by the National Trust of Scotland.

Continuing round the environs of Dundee, the little church of Murroes has been completely rebuilt but its churchyard is full of interest and most picturesquely sited alongside a burn and a still-inhabited miniature castle, its gables crow-stepped and its stairway circular. No longer inhabited, but in extremely good condition, is the four-storeyed tower of Affleck Castle which has a remarkable solar with a beautiful little oratory off it.

With Laws, Carlungie and Ardestie, we return to the prehistoric. The first is quite a low hill but its timber-framed stone fort had a commanding view; it was over 100 yards long and nearly seventy across and its wall was once ten yards thick, immensely strong, but it has been much robbed. According to Duncan Fraser, some 9000 cartloads of stone were removed from the hilltop between 1820 and 1824 – enough to build a wall 4 feet thick, 6 feet high and a mile in length. When this first fort (sixth or seventh century B.C.) began to crumble the proto-Picts built a broch within it, also now much robbed, but of interest in that it is one of the only three known in this part of Scotland, the others being at Hurley Hawkin and Craighill. The souterrains at Carlungie and Ardestie were excavated in 1949–52 by F. T. Wainwright who formed there the theories about their purpose which have been outlined in the Introduction. He showed that the dwellings associated with the underground chambers were huts on the surface, and dated them to the first century A.D. And the huts continued to be occupied as late as the third century, well after the souterrains themselves had been abandoned. Carlungie can be entered and its main entrance and three subsidiary ones fully appreciated; Ardestie is fenced off but is in some ways the more interesting in that it has a drain down the centre of the passage, strengthening the probability that it was used as a byre for cattle and sheep (*see* plate 22).

Following this route, we approach Dundee from the east which is no bad thing because three of its oldest buildings are on that side – two castles and its only surviving gateway from the days when it was a walled town. There is Broughty Castle, so well sited to guard the Firth of Tay that it has been used in successive wars right up to modern times, and so has undergone a great deal of alteration. It is best viewed from a distance across the harbour – or from inside where there are interesting relics, models and photographs of the whaling age. Very different is Claypotts, superb in every way except that – inexplicably – the planners have allowed modern little houses to be built up to within feet of one of Scotland's finest tower houses. Externally it is just as it was built by John Strachan between 1569 and 1588 – a Z-plan tower, unaltered and uncluttered by additions. The round towers at each end enable the walls to be enfiladed, and also provide two extra rooms on each floor; on the top floor they are corbelled out so that they become square and proportionally more roomy. Each tower, looked at individually, is awkward and gives the impression of a change of plan by the builder, but if the castle is looked at as a whole the effect is entirely satisfying. On the ground floor, the kitchen is in the south-west tower and has the usual massive chimney with an oven on one side and a sink on the other. The hall takes up the whole of the area of the central block on the floor above; its fireplace is flanked by two recesses, one to keep the precious salt dry and one to house a wooden cupboard. Opening off the hall, the retiring room in the north-east tower has another cupboard and a garderobe, and a sash window, though this may be a later improvement. Above the hall, the central block has two fireplaces, which suggests that there were probably two rooms which would give fourteen rooms in all. Comfort as well as safety was certainly considered. Its preservation is the more remarkable in that it was never the principal residence of the Grahams who bought it from the Strachans soon after it was completed. When Claverhouse was forfeited in 1689, the lands passed to the ill-starred Douglas family, and then to the daughter of the successful claimant in the Peerage case, and through her to the Earls of Home, who have placed it in the care of the Department of the Environment.

Dundee was once the second, and is still the fourth, city in

Scotland, and as one would expect, from its size and its situation, has had an eventful history. There were settlements here in Neolithic, Bronze Age and proto-Pictish days, but its growth and importance dates from the charter granted by William the Lion. Its nucleus was around Castle Hill with Cowgate Port (still surviving) at its eastern extremity and its western entry near St Mary's tower, which, however, with its church was just outside the walls. Wallace, traditionally, was taught at its grammar school. Edward I captured it and did much damage. Bruce so rated its importance that he made hereditary the post of Constable in the family of the Scrymgeours (or skirmishers) and associated it with that of the standard bearer of Scotland. With its economy based on fishing and trade by sea it grew throughout the Middle Ages, so that by 1482 the parish church of St Mary was no longer considered big enough and was rebuilt. Fortunately not so its tower, four-square and robust, as it needed to be for defence, and above, inside a balustrade, two tiers of lancet windows, and then another balustrade and a rather squat cap. The ascent is worth it for the view, and by a nice gesture is free to old-age-pensioners (though one of them wondered, long before he reached the top, whether this was not a rather ingenious plan of the City Fathers to see that they did not have too many old people to have to look after!). From the Reformation to the Stewart Civil Wars was Dundee's golden age; sea trade prospered and there was also a thriving domestic textile industry in both wool and flax. Then in 1645 the town was taken by Montrose, and again it suffered capture, this time by General Monk, on behalf of Cromwell. On both occasions, even its parish church suffered damage by fire, and on the second its tower was the last strong point held by the defenders. In 1689 it was more fortunate in spite of the fact that the great Dudhope Castle that had been built by the Scrymgeours (to take the place of their original one on Castle Hill) had passed only five years previously to Graham of Claverhouse. So too in 1715, in spite of being royalist, and again in 1745 in spite of being attacked by Lord Ogilvy for having changed its allegiance to support the Hanoverians. Incidentally, the town still has one of only two certain Jacobite flags. The eighteenth century saw the building of a fine town house designed by William Adam but it was some time before real prosperity returned with the coming of the industrial revolution and the railway. Fortunes were made, and often spent on pretentious houses – though not always; among others the Caird family were notable benefactors – but it was a narrow-based prosperity and the town still bears the scars of some of the worst slums of the period. During periodic slumps, there was little food for the factory hands so easily then dismissed. Jute was king for a century but when the demand for that declined and the great depression of the thirties ensued, Dundee was one of the worst hit places in the whole of Britain. Only since the Second World War and the diversification of its industry, and the development of a new industrial estate beyond the Kingsway ring-road, has a measure of its former prosperity returned; more recently still a new life has come to the harbour as a result of North Sea Oil.

Another new turn has been taken by its becoming the seat of one of the new universities. Its College, founded nearly a century ago, was to start with part of St Andrews, but in 1954 took over the medical and legal faculties as Queen's College, and in 1967 achieved full university status with Queen Elizabeth the Queen Mother as its Chancellor. Its new buildings in the very heart of the town are growing up around a peaceful little precinct, and it is also closely associated with one of the largest and best equipped of modern hospitals, further out, at Nine Wells. These new blocks may not always be pleasing near-to, but, seen from a distance, they do give distinction to Dundee's hilly skyline.

But if historically, economically and intellectually, it is a city of great significance, it has not the same wealth of interest as a place to visit. There are certain outstanding things, especially if one includes those already described. It has a splendid situation looking south over the Tay and sheltered from the north, but as in Glasgow the sins of the past still lie heavily on it and there is much abandoned and rotting masonry. But its parks are a tremendous asset, especially

Camperdown Park where within acres of well wooded park-land with facilities for every form of enjoyment there is a great Grecian mansion built by the son of Admiral Duncan, one of Dundee's most distinguished citizens. It houses a museum of golf, and there are plans to add a display of period furniture.

The Admiral himself, son of a provost of the city, went to sea at 15, was captain of a warship by thirty-one, and served with distinction at the Battle of Cape St Vincent. But, as with his contemporary Lord Howe, it was after he was sixty, and anxious to retire, that his greatest services were rendered. The year 1797 was one of the most critical in Britain's history, the only occasion on which a naval mutiny has taken place in time of war, with a hostile army ready to invade. While Howe was recalled to tackle the situation at Spithead, Duncan was in active command of the North Sea fleet based on Yarmouth, with the task of holding off the Dutch fleet which had been commandeered by Napoleon. When his own flagship, *Venerable*, mutinied, he quelled it by moral force, and the love and respect which he had already earned from his men by his efforts on their behalf. When another of his ships, *Adamant*, refused to obey orders, he went aboard unprotected and asked whether any man dare challenge his commands. One man came forward and did so. This time, physical force was added to the moral: sixty-six years old though he was, he picked the man up and held him squirming over the ship's side till the rest of the crew dissolved in laughter and the danger was over.

Sadly, when he had to put to sea to blockade the Dutch, only *Adamant* followed. "I am sorry," he wrote, "that I have lived to see the pride of Britain disgrace the very name of it." It made no matter. Undaunted, he anchored his flagship ostenta-tiously within sight of the enemy, in water shallow enough so that, if his ship were sunk, his flag would still be flying, and made signals to *Adamant*, lying hull-down on the horizon, which ship repeated every signal to any imaginary fleet beyond. For a whole week these two ships thus contained fifteen Dutchmen until, one by one, the Yarmouth ships returned to their loyalty and rejoined him. When, three months later, the Dutch did put to sea with numbers equal to Duncan they had the greater fire-power. Only his indomitable spirit and the determination of the mutineers to redeem their good name, won the day after a three-hour dogfight with heavy casualties on both sides. After the battle, Duncan wrote to his brother-in-law:

Sunday, October the 15th 1797. *Venerable,* getting up to Sheerness

My dear Advocate,

As I am sure no friend will rejoice more at any good fortune that attends me than you will, I write you these few lines to say I hope the action I had with the Dutch, who fought with their usual gallantry, is not exceeded by any in this war. We have suffered much. The returns I have had, and have not had, exceed 191 killed and 565 wounded; from only two Dutch ships, 250 killed and 300 wounded. We were obliged, from being so near the land, to be rather rash in our attack, by which we suffered more. Had we been ten leagues at sea, none would have escaped. Many, I am sure, had surrendered, that got off in the night, being so near shore. We were much galled by their frigates, where we could not act. In short, I feel perfectly satisfied. All was done that could be done. None have any fault to find. I have in my possession three Dutch admirals, an Admiral de Winter, Vice-Admiral Reuter, Rear-Admiral Me Meame. The Admiral is on board with me, and a most agreable man he is. He speaks English well, and seems much pleased with his treatment. I have assured him, and with justice, that nothing could exceed his gallantry. He says nothing hurts him but that he is the first Dutch Admiral ever surrendered. So much the more credit to me! He tells that the troops that were embarked in the summer were 25,000 Dutch, destined for Ireland, but after August that expedition was given up. The Governor in Holland, much against his opinion, insisted on his going to sea, to show they had done so, and he was just going to return when I saw him. I am sure I have every reason to be thankful to Almighty God for his kindness to me on that occasion and all others. I believe the pilot and myself were the only two unhurt on the quarterdeck, and De Winter, who is as tall and big as myself, was the only one on his quarterdeck left alive. After all my fatigue, I am in perfect health and my usual spirits.

Believe me, most faithfully yours,

Adam Duncan

Caird Park is another of Dundee's parks, also on the outskirts, with Victoria Park and Dudhope Park further in, and
the Law with its panorama over the whole city. Dundee is
rightly proud of its parks – and of its museums. And certainly
anyone wanting an introduction to archaeology and prehistory
could not do better than the City Museum in Albert Square. In
quite a small gallery, uncluttered cases round the wall explain
by means of photographs and imaginative reconstructions, as
well as actual finds, the progress of man from Mesolithic times,
through Roman, to Pictish, and models show the methods of
construction of timber-laced forts and souterrains. There are
exceptional carvings of horses (from the Roman legionary
camp at Carpow), and the Picts are represented by the Class I
stone from Dunnichen incised with a Z-rod, 'flower' and
mirror and comb, and a Class II stone from Strathmartine with
horsemen, V-rod and 'elephant' – in both cases there are
replicas at the original site. In the centre of the room are a
long-cist burial from Kinggoodie, Angus, and a short cist from
East Drums near Brechin, and two massive dug-out canoes. In
all cases the printed labels are brief and easy to read and to
understand. There are some beautiful Egyptian things too, and
other galleries are devoted to ecology, geology and natural history – with, upstairs, the Art Gallery containing a wide variety
of Italian and Dutch lesser masters, and an even wider variety
of modern Scottish painters. But, in spite of the catalogue's
modest disclaimer that earlier Scottish painting is rather thinly
covered, some will get most satisfaction from the portraits by
Allan Ramsay and Raeburn. Of the silver, the Fithies communion plate is worth a special look. If that were not enough,
there is a Maritime Museum, just down the road in Barrack
Street, a Golf Museum in Camperdown House, exhibits about
whaling and polar exploration in Broughty Castle, and other
collections in process of development. It is no wonder that
Dundee has a nation-wide reputation not only for pursuing
archaeology and science for their own sake, but also for the
spreading of that knowledge through its services to schools.

One other thing to see – this time not a city museum – is the
150-year-old frigate *Unicorn*, the fourth oldest warship in the

world to be still afloat. It cannot equal the romance of the fully rigged *Victory* at Portsmouth but it is interesting enough in all conscience. And, being less crowded, it is easier as you wander around to absorb the atmosphere and understand the simplicity and the hardness of life afloat during the Napoleonic Wars. In fact, *Unicorn* was not launched quite in time to take part, and by 1824 steam was about to take the place of sail, and iron and steel the place of oak, but that did not prevent this ship having a long period of useful service. After a time as a depot ship, she was commissioned in 1874, as the R.N.R. drill ship at Dundee, a commission which was to last for ninety-five years. Nearly scrapped in 1962, she was saved by the efforts of Captain J. C. L. Anderson, Captain Lord Reith of Stonehaven and others who eventually persuaded Lord Carrington, when he was First Lord of the Admiralty, that she could safely be moved and preserved. Restoration work continues and, one day, it is hoped that she will be fully rigged again.

From Dundee, we take the coast road north through the holiday resorts of Broughty Ferry, Monifieth and Carnoustie which provide good sands for bathing and all outdoor activities; the last has a famous golf course which has hosted more than one open championship. And so, to Arbroath, one of the most attractive of coast towns. Its harbour is backed with green grass and a useful free car-park for the white signal tower which houses a museum of the prehistory, the industrial and the natural history of the surrounding area. Not the least interesting are the pictures and diagrams illustrating the construction of Robert Stevenson's outstanding achievement – the Inchcape or Bell Rock lighthouse.

As one would expect of the home of the 'smokie', that delicately flavoured version of the haddock, Arbroath is well supplied with fish shops, and shopping in the town is made more pleasurable by a pedestrian precinct. Near the middle of the east cemetery are the remains of a souterrain but they are more fragmentary and less interesting than those already described. It is the abbey that one goes to see – a lovely warm red ruin and a place to linger on a sunny day – especially if one can visit it out of season.

William the Lion founded it in 1178 and dedicated it to St Thomas of Canterbury. An English saint might seem a surprising choice at first sight, but William had grown to know and to love Becket during his stay at the court of Henry II. He endowed his project generously and gave to it the custody of the venerated relics of St Columba which were kept in the Monymusk reliquary, the only one of its sort to survive in Scotland; it is now in the National Museum of Antiquities in Edinburgh. And, when he died in 1214 he was buried in the abbey.

The abbot of Aberbrothock was an important person in the realm and Bernard de Linton who took office in 1307 was Chancellor of Scotland, and, as such, drafted the declaration by the great men of the time that they would support Robert the Bruce come what may, so long as he should remain true:

> Yet if he should give up what he has begun, seeking to make us or our kingdom subject to the king of England or to the English, we would strive at once to drive him out as our enemy and subverter of his own right and ours, and we would make some other man who was able to defend us our king; for, as long as a hundred of us remain alive we will never on any conditions be subjected to the lordship of the English. For we fight not for glory nor riches, nor honours, but for freedom alone, which no good man gives up except with his life.

As befitted their importance, Bernard and his successors lived in a large and, for those days, comfortable house, entertained the King, and as lord of the regalia of Arbroath wielded the power of life and death in cases where they had jurisdiction, though normally such power was exercised on their behalf by a lay sheriff from the family of Ogilvy – one of the sources of irritation which led to a feud between them and the Lindsays.

The oldest parts of the abbey remaining are the east end, the south transept and the southern wall of the nave, part of the abbot's house, and the west front. This last is the most archaic in style and the deeply recessed, round-headed arches of the elaborate doorway are very Norman in their decoration. Then, as time went on, and the building went up, the open passage above the doorway received early pointed arcading, and above that again was a large circular window which must have had Decorated tracery, and no doubt beautiful stained glass. Either side of the west front were two towers, complementing the great tower which was raised over the crossing of the nave and the transepts; these, and the cloisters (which have now completely gone) were also in the early Pointed style. The first buildings took fifty-five years in the making; then, a century later, a range was added to the west of the west door to provide rooms for guests, and a lay infirmary and a workshop; under it passed the main gateway to the abbey precincts. Why modern heavy traffic is being allowed slowly to shake it down defeats me. Later again, in the fifteenth century the abbot's house was extended and the sacristy was built for the relics, the silver vessels and other treasures; a room of noble proportions in which one cannot but be affected by the sanctity of the place.

The abbot's house, which was more earthly in its sumptuousness, is now finely restored after many years of neglect during which it was first a factory and then a private dwelling. It may "fairly be said that, although much altered, it is one of the few abbot's houses to survive in Scotland and by far the most extensive and complete". Its contents include two carved wooden panels from the sixteenth century, the tomb chest of Abbot Paniter who built the sacristy, a beautiful fifteenth-century (headless) effigy of a saint, probably Becket, and a quaint stone carving of Death catching up with Old Age, illustrated in plate 26.

Before leaving, it is worth pausing once again to notice the warm hue of the stone of which this great church is built, and to try to recreate in one's mind the immense loftiness of the nave which can most easily be done by looking upwards in the south transept where the walls still reach their original height above a circular window. The Department of the Environment Guide is a wonderful 16p's-worth and helps the effort of imagination needed with a diagrammatic reconstruction, and also a description of the buildings as they were in 1517, just before the Reformation and their decay.

To go back a few hundred years, there is St Vigeans, only a

mile and a half to the north. The church on its little hill is
modern but it incorporates some very ancient stones including
some Pictish ones. Others have been collected into a cottage
museum under the guardianship of the Department of the
Environment (not open on Tuesday, Wednesday or
Thursday). By far the most interesting and the most beautiful
is the Drosten stone; the most interesting because it has, at the
bottom of one of its sides, one of the few inscriptions on such
monuments. This is in runic script and bears three names –
Drosten, Uoret and Forcus – which have tentatively been
connected with three symbols, the double disc and Z-rod, the
crescent and the mirror and comb, and dated to c.850 A.D. It
is the animals on the reverse side that are so beautifully carved
in low relief – a bear, a hind suckling its young, an eagle
preying on a fish, a horned animal like a mountain goat but
possibly meant to be a unicorn, and a man with a crossbow
aiming at a well-tusked boar.

Inland, castles continue to guard fertile fields but these, such
as Collieston, Gardyne and Guthrie are mostly still in private
occupation. At Guthrie, the fifteenth-century family aisle is all
that remains of the old church, but it is kept locked and its
painted ceiling has been moved for safe-keeping to the castle,
which, with its garden, is open under the Scottish Gardens
Scheme and at other times in the summer. Just to the north of
Arbroath, on the coast, is Auchmithie, the Musselcrag of Scott's
The Antiquary – as Arbroath is its Fairport.

Montrose has a long and eventful history. Lower Red
Sandstone deposits at Whanland, near Farnell, yielded fossils of
some of the oldest fishes in the world, including *Ancathodes
Mitchelli*, named after the mid-nineteenth-century revivalist
minister who first discovered it, Hugh Mitchell. And not far
away on Rossie Muir lived Neolithic and Bronze Age folk. On
the island of Inchbrayock – the chapel here was dedicated to St
Brioc, a Welshman – one of the most remarkable of all Pictish
crosses was found. On the reverse, below a huntsman with
hounds pursuing a hind, is a pair of figures which have been
variously interpreted as Cain slaying Abel and as Samson
killing a Philistine with the jawbone of an ass. On the whole

the latter seems the more likely, especially if one of the scenes on the cross side of the slab is Delilah cutting off Samson's hair, based on an illustration from a contemporary manuscript. The stone was moved to the Montrose museum for preservation.

William the Lion had a royal castle here; after sacking by Edward I in 1296 and again by Wallace in the following year, nothing now remains, but there is a contemporary motte at Maryton on which stood the wooden castle of the Norman de Malherbes. The Grahams, with their scallop shells, came to Old Montrose, just west of the basin, by virtue of their fidelity to the Bruce, but it was the Erskines of Dun who were more closely associated with the burgh, not always to its advantage. On one occasion, they seized the North Esk fishings from the citizens, and destroyed and "ete all our corne that grew upone our common lande, and this being done onder cilence of nycht come bodeyn with speris and bovis to youre saide burgh and bostitboure alderman, he beande in his bed, sayande thai suld pul done his houss abuf his hede", and shortly after, "attacked oure fyschars, their wyffiis and servandes gaderynde thair bate to thir lynis ande spuyzeit thaim of their claithis" – such was their complaint, and for a time their almost open war. Later on, one John Erskine (whose father, grandfather and uncle had all fallen at Flodden) became provost of Montrose in spite of a somewhat hectic youth which included murdering a priest – and in church – the very worst sort of sacrilege. Fifteen years later he befriended John Knox and was probably present in 1556 when the latter first celebrated Holy Communion in public, and was certainly moderator of the Assembly of the Reformed Church 1565-9. A hundred years later another provost was John Coutts, great-grandfather of the founder the London Bank of that name.

Meanwhile Montrose's two most famous citizens had spent part of their boyhood days here. Provost Erskine had brought back a schoolmaster, Pierre Marsiliers, from a visit to France on which he represented the burgesses of Scotland at the marriage of Mary Stewart to the French Dauphin. As a result, Andrew Melville was well ahead not only of his contemporaries but also of his teachers when he went up to St

Andrews University with a good knowledge of Greek. Here, too, his nephew James also got part of his schooling, but it was another James whose name will spring most readily to the mind in association with Montrose, that of the great Marquis. Some traditions say that he was actually born in the town in an old but altered and ugly house called Castlested, but Old Montrose is more likely. He certainly often stayed in the town as a boy, and played golf here the evening before he was married to Magdalene Carnegie from Kinnaird Castle; nine days later he sent his servant to St Andrews to get his clubs repaired and to buy six new ones. And it was from here that, on a sadder occasion, he sailed to exile. So too did the Old Chevalier in 1715.

By 1745 the townsmen as well as their neighbouring gentry were strongly Jacobite, largely because the Customs officers were servants of the Hanoverian Government and many burgesses owed their living, and all their comforts, to smuggling. As a result, when an English warship appeared off the harbour, it received no co-operation and proceeded to bombard the town and to sink all the boats except for one into which it loaded the town's few guns. A week of ups and downs followed. Before the English could carry out an attack which they had planned on the Jacobite forces at Brechin under Lord Ogilvy, the latter sent a party under Captain Erskine of Dun, which recaptured the town's guns and trained them on the *Hazard* and compelled its surrender. Further success came with the arrival of a French ship, only to be trumped by a yet larger English ship from the Forth, the *Milford*. Spirits rose again when the *Milford* ran aground. The Frenchmen should have captured it but they had deserted their own ship and missed their chance, and the *Milford* got away. In the upshot, the Jacobites held the town, and the *Hazard*, which they renamed the *Prince Charles* and sent back to France where she picked up a cargo of treasure. There she was given a new captain and an Irish and French crew and the job of carrying £1200 to the Prince. But she was spotted and eventually overhauled. The Captain beached his ship in the Kyle of Tongue, and fought till his crew could take no more, and then carried the treasure ashore. Luck again deserted them but before they had to surrender they had managed to dump most of the treasure in a small loch, where it may be to this day. The disaster for the Prince was twofold: without the money he could not pay his troops, so he had to stand and fight; and he had to do so without the Mackenzies whom he had sent off to get the gold.

With a natural harbour, Montrose has seldom lacked for trade. In the fifteenth century salmon were the chief export – and then, grain and malt. By the eighteenth century she was one of the largest importers of tobacco, and in the nineteenth century of timber and flax. More recently the demand for supply ships to the North Sea oil rigs has helped.

The pride of Montrose's citizens in its past is well exemplified in the delightful writings of that tireless collector of local anecdote, the late Duncan Fraser. It "is the kind of town" he writes "where you expect to see a welcoming archway, boldly lettered 'Antiques Galore'. It has only about 10,000 inhabitants but many a city twenty times its size might envy its many relics of the past." But I am not sure that its worthies have all that to be proud of. Its museum is closed for renovation – well and good, and no doubt something fine will emerge, but surely some temporary home could have been found where the Inchbrayock cross could have been kept on view. In the remoter past, many priceless books have been dispersed from one of the earliest public libraries of Scotland. Of the wonderful chalices wrought by the town's seventeenth-century silversmith, William Lindsay, six nearby parishes still have treasured specimens, but not Montrose. The eighteen wooden panels from the old church, which are one of the most beautiful pieces of Scottish carving of the early sixteenth century have gone to the Museum of Archaeology in Edinburgh. The room in which the Marquis may have been born is an unused basement of the Social Security Office. What remains? A warm welcome for the visitor, certainly, with every sort of recreation from golf and bathing to bird-watching by the basin, or botanizing at the nearby nature reserve of St Cyrus, or collecting semi-precious stones at Elephant Rock. There is a fine broad High Street with some classical frontages and still a few gable-ends left; a handsome town house (1784), a Gillespie Graham church tower,* and, in the environs, Dun House (William Adam the elder, 1710, with ornate internal decoration – now a hotel) and Kinnaird Castle which is open to the public by prior arrangement for parties of at least four. This last is Playfair, 1790, and Bryce, 1845, but is on the site of the home of the Carnegie family for over 500 years. The present owner, the Earl of Southesk married the daughter of the Princess Royal; his heir is the Duke of Fife.

* The church, though Gothic revival, still has the chandelier, or 'hearse', presented in 1623 by Richard Clark, a native of Montrose, who had become an admiral in the Swedish Navy.

VIII

NORTH FIFE

THE KINGDOM of Fife is, in its scenery and in its history, a microcosm of the variety that is Lowland Scotland. There are rolling hills and open plains, and much good agricultural land on both; but there are also patches of scrub, bog and rougher moorland. If the rivers have neither the grandeur nor the salmon of the Tay and the South Esk, they have some lovely stretches; and the Lomonds, it has been said, "attain an almost mountain dignity in the face of their Highland namesake fifty miles away". Overseas trade was once its staple; then coal and textiles, which have left their mark on the countryside; some of the villages are grim enough, but the little fishing burghs more than compensate; and the Kingdom has made a good job of its own 'New Town'. And, for older buildings, Fife has a palace, two cathedrals, the oldest parish church in Scotland and a wealth of castles. For long, the Fifers prided themselves on being a race apart but now, with easy communications to the west, and road and rail bridges to north and south, that is a matter of history.

So far as history is concerned, North Fife is steeped in it. At one end, on Tentsmuir, have been found artifacts of Mesolithic man, dating back to about 6000 B.C., and as old as any in Scotland. At the other end are pre-Roman hill-forts at Castle Law above Abernethy, Clatchard Craig above Newburgh, and Normans Law five miles further to the east. Sited magnificently, they had substantial stone walls which could be strengthened by interlacing with timber, which, in the case of Castle Law, ran horizontally, front to back, as well as longitudinally. When timber-laced walls were set on fire (whether deliberately or by attackers) sufficient heat might be generated for some of the stone to melt and fuse into a conglomerate.

At Clatchard Craig, fast being destroyed by quarrying, the fort is complex, and of at least three periods. On the summit is the smallest and latest enclosure, within which some early Christian finds were made. Around it is another, measuring approximately 300 feet by 200; and around this are still further ramparts in which traces of vitrifaction have been found. Normans Law, at 900 feet above sea level, is the highest of the three and has therefore, if possible, the finest views. A very considerable wall encloses the top of the hill; on the south-west shoulder, another wall encloses the first, plus a further area, in all about 1000 feet by 500, while, within the summit enclosure, there is a third stronghold with walls 12 feet thick. The sequence of building is not certain but it is thought that both pre-Roman and post-Roman work is involved. Almost certainly, such forts were defensive rather than offensive, and would have enclosed rough timber dwellings.

The Romans themselves do not seem to have been particularly active in Fife, but they had a port and camp at Carpow, and, since then, these shores have never been out of the front line of Scottish history. If there are fewer Pictish stones in Fife than in Angus, Pictish place-names abound. From early Christian days there were Culdee settlements at Abernethy and Leuchars. The Abernethy round-tower is probably evidence of Scandinavian pressure. The Normans followed not long after and their monastic zeal bore fruit at Lindores and Balmerino. St Andrews succeeded Dunfermline as the religious capital of Scotland, and, later, became its first university town, and then the centre of the Reformation. Only in the Civil Wars of the seventeenth and eighteenth centuries did North Fife see less than its accustomed share of action – much to its advantage.

Carpow and Abernethy are just in Perthshire and so are dealt with in a previous chapter. Our starting point is the small royal burgh of Newburgh which originally prospered on fishing and the domestic weaving of linen. More recently it has depended on linoleum manufacture in a surprisingly large factory, discreetly hidden below the level of its broad main street, but a question mark now hangs over the future of this plant. There are some pleasant little houses here and a small museum, available by request when the library is open, on Wednesdays and on Saturday mornings; it contains one of the few relics from Lindores Abbey, a carved wooden panel. To the west of the burgh is the 13-foot shaft of a much worn Celtic cross but this is in the grounds of the privately occupied Mugdrum House; and, to the east, beside the A913 (O.S. 262169) and built into the garden wall of a cottage, is a Class I Pictish stone with triple disc and crossbar, and a crescent with V-rod. To the south, up Hill Road, towards Nine Wells, is the base of another cross, traditionally a sanctuary for the Clan Macduff, who could purge themselves by washing in the Nine Wells and giving nine cows in expiation for a killing. There is not much of the cross to see, but half way up the hill road there is a seat from which there is a glorious view back up the Tay and to the hills beyond Perth, with a glimpse of the city itself. An even more extensive view is, of course, obtained from Clatchard Craig, mentioned above.

The truth is that the roads through North Fife, steeped though they are in history, have not all that much to show in hard stone, not even at the once rich Lindores Abbey where were buried Alexander III's elder (and, by then, only surviving) son, and the unhappy Duke of Rothesay. In its heyday the range of abbey buildings must have been well calculated to instil a feeling of religious awe, just as its situation by the river must have been pleasantly peaceful, but little remains now. John Knox and his companions did their work all too well, on their way to Perth in the spring of 1559. "We came to the Abbey of Lindores, distant from St Andrews twelve miles. We reformed them, their altars overthrew we, their idols, vestments of idolatrie and mass-books we burnt in their presence and commanded them to throw away their monkish habits." One substantial Romanesque arch still stands, and the remains of some other walls of red sandstone, but these are marred by an incongruous oil tank in their midst, serving the neighbouring farm. Far more attractive is the remote old church of Abdie where there is nothing to detract from the little chancel with its three lancet windows and the seventeenth-century aisle, burial place of Balfours. Just outside its graveyard is a shelter containing two Pictish carved stones.

From here, fast roads run to Cupar and St Andrews, and to Newport and the Tay road bridge, but greatly preferable is an unclassified route which hugs the shore of the Firth of Tay, past the fourteenth-century stronghold of the Earls of Rothes, Ballinbreich, and the shell of a little chapel at Flisk. Eventually you reach some more fragmentary monastic remains at Balmerino. Alexander II's widow founded it for Cistercians in 1225, bringing monks from Melrose. It belongs now to the National Trust for Scotland but it has not yet been possible to make the fabric safe enough to admit the public; for all that, one can see something of the cloisters, and of the fifteenth-century chapter house from outside the fence. Another rather different Trust property at Balmerino is a range of houses built by the present Earl of Dundee, hereditary standard bearer of Scotland, in memory of his brother, killed at Anzio.

Neither Wormit, terminus of the railway bridge, nor Newport at the end of the 1966 road bridge, are in themselves exciting, but the bridges are over two miles long and both in their day revolutionized transport in eastern Scotland. At Tayport, the church tower is seventeenth-century and there are some old fishermen's cottages and a plaque commemorating General Ulysses Grant's visit on his way to see the first Tay bridge, so disastrously blown down in 1879 while a train was passing over it. With Tentsmuir, we reach the eastern extremity of North Fife, and it behoves the visitor to invest in a slim pamphlet called *What to see in East Fife* published by the Standing Council of East Fife Preservation Societies. The Tayport Society has laid out two walks through the forest which take in the bird sanctuary at the Morton Lochs. The first inhabitants of this sandy deposit (which was only gradually being built up when they were there) have already been mentioned at the beginning of the chapter. Another almost equally shadowy people were the 'Chancey Fowk,' a much later community of shipwrecked Scandinavian sailors who eked out what living they could, by what means they could, but were seldom seen by law-abiding citizens.

The flatness of the land, all round, made it inevitable that the Royal Air Force should cast loving eyes on it, and they have been here since 1920, taking over an earlier, pre-war experimental flying station of the Royal Engineers. Now there is a vast complex supporting the fastest, most sophisticated, and noisiest, planes of Strike Command. Another giant to move in has been the Guard Bridge Paper Company. Guardbridge itself is named after the old five-arch bridge over the Gair, originally cobbled and only wide enough for one carriage to pass over it at a time; only chaises were allowed – carts had to ford when the tide permitted.*

The Paper Company recently celebrated its centenary by publishing a *History* describing how, after some fluctuations in fortune, it became one of the first British mills to brand papers, a process which necessitated accurate quality control, an efficient laboratory and sophisticated control equipment. Since then, its production has doubled, and mergers have followed, so that Culter Guardbridge Holdings now includes servicing the oil industry, transport, electrostatic copying and micro-filming, and has a local pay roll of 360.

But it is neither the paper mill nor the air station (except on open days) that people go to Leuchars to see but the tiny parish church, something out of this world, in more senses than one. Its chancel and apse are pure Norman, with a double arcade and blind walls – glass was not to be thought of at that date – and for the chancel, a semi-circular arch enriched with a damier pattern and chevron work. All is 700 years old "the second finest fragment of Norman in the British Isles" according to one authority. Probably built by Saier de Quincey, a crusader, and the son of a crusader, it was consecrated in 1244. Many years later, it had for its minister Alexander Henderson, moderator of the momentous Glasgow Assembly of 1638, his face noted as being "yellow from the fever contracted in the marshes of Leuchars". By then, the secular lairds were the Bruces who built the fine house of Earlshall; of them, Sir William is commemorated in the church, having survived Flodden and died at the great age of ninety-eight:

* *See* W. Rowntree Bodie, *Some Light on the Past Around Glenrothes.* The same book preserves the delightful advertisement of a coach which would leave the Grassmarket Edinburgh "every Tuesday, God willing, but on Saturday, whether or no".

Heir lyis of all piete
Ane lantern brycht
Schir Villyam Bruce of Erleshal Knycht.

Also commemorated is his great-grandson's wife, in 1635, as "charitable to the poor and profitable to that house". Less happily remembered is her son who was the commander of the party of dragoons which killed Richard Cameron and eight other Covenanters at Airds Moss and struck off his head and hands for display in Edinburgh and elsewhere. In the nineteenth century, Earlshall fell into disrepair but was nobly restored by Lorimer – one of his first commissions. The seventeenth-century tempera painting on the ceiling of the great gallery, with its 218 panels of heraldic devices, is remarkable indeed.

From Leuchars it is only a step to St Andrews, but we must first explore an alternative route from the Bein Inn in Glen Farg by the A912. through Strathmiglo, Auchtermuchty, Falkland and Cupar. Almost immediately, on your left, you pass Balvaird Castle. Its site is impressive enough with wide views all round, yet it is somewhat strangely placed; there are better viewpoints on several of the neighbouring hills and one at least of them must have water available, where Balvaird Farm now stands. The fifteenth-century keep is built of red stone, L-shaped with its staircase in the inner angle. Originally it belonged to the Barclay family but when their male line died out, it passed through a daughter, to Sir Andrew Murray in 1507. A later Andrew was the minister of Abide whom Charles I created Lord Balvaird – to annoy the Presbyterians for whom he was too moderate in his views – and who also inherited the Stormont title. From him descends the present Earl of Mansfield to whom the castle still belongs.

At Gateside this road joins the A91 to Strathmiglo, the older houses of which, and the tolbooth, have been saved by being just off the modern main road. This tower is typical of those which the Fife burghs vied with each other in building in the eighteenth century with their squat spires and balustrades round them. That at Auchtermuchty is rather more elegant but has unfortunately been spoilt by Victorian windows cut into the main part of the Tolbooth. On the other hand, Auchtermuchty has much the finer church and a number of most attractive gables on the old houses round it. Once noted for its roofs thatched with rushes from the banks of the Tay, it has few of them left and little chance of these surviving since the last local reed thatcher died in 1972. Its inhabitants, hand-loom weavers in the old days, always tended to be independent-minded, from the seventeenth-century minister who had to be "gravely rebuiked for being ane frequent hunter with dogs, ane player at cards, and a runner of horses on courses", to the radicals of the 1860s.

The tolbooths and the cottages of Strathmiglo and Auchtermuchty may be something in the way of collectors' pieces for the architectural specialist, but Falkland is for everyone. Only its situation is against it, too near to the Lomonds and overshadowed. Otherwise it is amongst the most rewarding villages in the whole of Scotland, and it deserves a great deal more than a cursory look when one is exhausted by a tour of the palace, or made drowsy by the insidious charms of its lovely gardens. It has its showpieces – a town house, of course, with an 1805 spire; the Covenanter Richard Cameron's birthplace near the fountain; a thatched house opposite the palace with the inscription over the door: "Al praise to God and thanks to the most excellent Monarche of Great Britane of whose Princelie liberalitie this is my portione Deo Laus Esto fidus adest merces Nicoll Moncrief 1610"; the next door house (now an inn) not to be outdone, with "1607 God saif ye King of Grit Britain France and Ireland our soveran for of his liberality this house did I edify". These are in the crowded hub of the place but less than a hundred yards in each direction old corners may be found, often set in scraps of green, and quite unspoilt. And where it has been necessary to restore, this has been beautifully done with the inspiration of, and sometimes the help of, the National Trust for Scotland. Brunton Street is just one of those worth seeking out, and Sharp's Close, off it, still with its cobbles and the Mill Wynd.

The palace was built by successive Scottish kings to provide a more comfortable – and a grander – home alongside an earlier castle. Of the latter (which was levelled by the English in 1377 – rebuilt – and then, after the death of the Duke of Rothesay at the hands of his uncle Albany, allowed to decay) only the foundations of a great round-tower survive. Nothing is left, either, of the great hall and the other buildings which once formed the north range of the palace courtyard. Most of what we can still see was built by James IV and embellished by James V. Both loved the place and the hunting and the hawking which it provided, as did Mary Queen of Scots and the last king to live there, James VI. Its only formidable part is its gateway with its round flanking towers and its pit dungeon. For the rest, though the windows may be heavily barred, they are designed for light rather than defence. The most splendid part is the south range (*see* plate 28) and especially its inner face, essentially Renaissance both in conception and detail. Its buttress columns and its medallions are similar to French work of the same date and it has been called "the best of tributes to the Auld Alliance". In it, was – is – the royal chapel which retains more of the original decoration than any other part; the carved wooden screen at the entrance is original, its hand-turned pillars, each different, and part of the royal pew; and its tapestries are of the period. The ceiling has traces of the work ordered by Charles I when he visted Scotland in 1633 and ordered repairs to the chapel. At that time it was used for his Anglican services but the family of its keeper being Roman Catholic it has now been restored to the religion of its original royal builders.

The east range is roofless but scarcely less impressive. Here were the gorgeously coloured apartments of the king – his guard hall, presence chamber and privy dining-room, more convenient than the draughty great hall, and more private. Behind these were two galleries on either side of a cross house, added to provide a more comfortable royal bedchamber. The third Marquess of Bute and his grandson, the present keeper, have restored this wing and have recreated a bedchamber decorated as James V's would have been with crowns, monograms and coats of arms in bright heraldic colours, and a four-poster bed with gold hangings as the centre piece. Here, though not in this actual bed which is sixteenth century, one can imagine the disillusioned James V, only thirty, turning his face to the wall and dying of despair at the news that his queen had given birth to a girl and not to the male heir that he so desired. Sir David Lindsay of the Mount brought the news and was one of the few persons present when he died. "The deil gang wi' it. It will end as it began. It cam' wi' a lass, and will gang wi' a lass." Lindsay's own farewell to Falkland was:

> Fare weill Faulkland, the forteress of Fyfe,
>   Thy polite park under the Lowmound law,
> Sum tyme in thee I led ane lustie lyfe
>   The fallow dier to see them raike in row.

There was hawking too, and the King's lion to look at, and a performing seal, and a royal tennis court which can still be played in and is only rivalled for age by that at Hampton Court. Finally there is the garden, a long stretch of lawn, flanked with beds of iris and lupin and climbing roses, *ceanothus*, viburnum and *weigelia* – one of the most delightful places to linger in in the whole of Scotland (*see* plate 27).

Falkland to Cupar takes you in the shadow of East Lomond where there is an Iron Age fort on the summit, past Pitlessie – not much here now to remind one of David Wilkie's rustic Pitlessie Fair (in the National Gallery of Scotland) – to the church at Cults. Here Wilkie's father was minister, and the artist is said to have found all the types he included in the crowded scene. But it may well have been in an earlier building because his father, during his thirty-eight year incumbency, got a new church erected, spacious and dignified; it retains some of its old box pews and a number of memorials to various of his descendants.

The other road, from Auchtermuchty to Cupar, passes Collessie, Melville House and Monimail Church. At Collessie there are the remains of a large cairn in which were found bones from a cremation and a riveted dagger, gold-mounted, now in Edinburgh in the National Museum of Antiquities; and 300 yards north-east of the farmhouse of Newton of Collessie there is a standing stone 9 feet high. Melville House was built between 1695 and 1705 for the Earl of Melville to the square, symmetrical, wholly pleasing design of James Smith. Its panelled rooms were once beautifully furnished, and the mansion set in a magnificent formal garden, but for many years now it has ceased to be in private occupation, and the furniture and flower beds are gone; but a new use has been found for it which will at least preserve the main fabric; twenty or more boys live there as part of a joint venture of the Social Work Department and the Education Authority. What is left of Monimail Palace – an episcopal residence of the Beatons – stands in the grounds, and Monimail Church just outside. It is not structurally distinguished but, admirably, it is kept unlocked so that one can see the Adam ceiling, well lit by large clear windows.

Cupar is interesting, historically, as the place where Sir David Lindsay of the Mount's satirical play *Ane plesant Satyre of the Thrie Estaitis* was performed on Castle Hill in 1552 in the open air. French prisoners of war built an indoor theatre on the site, 250 years later, which in its turn was incorporated into the Castlehill school. And this in its turn was incorporated into another of Cupar's distinctions, the Bell-Baxter High School founded by Dr Bell who made a name for himself by the advocacy of the use of pupil teachers in schools.

Cupar's streets are broad and its shops are good as befits a town that was once the seat of the Thanes of Fife and a thriving market – and then the County Town – but once you stray behind the main frontages, you may find yourself in little old wynds among picturesque old houses with crow-stepped gables, especially around the parish church. The church is gone save for the strong early-fifteenth-century tower and for three arcades preserved in the wall of the modern building; the former was hardly improved by the addition, in the seventeenth century, of a spire with an unusual gallery round it, half-way up; it throws the structure out of proportion. In the graveyard, a stone declares, on one side, that here lies interred the heads of Laurence Hay and Andrew Pitulloch who suffered martyrdom as Covenanters in 1681 and one of the hands of David Hackston who was "cruelly murdered" in Edinburgh, 30th July 1680 (for his part in the killing of Archbishop Sharp); and on the reverse:

> Our persecutors filled with rage
> Their brutish fury to assuage
> Took heads and hands of martyrs off
> That they might be the people's scoff.
> They Hackston's body cut asunder
> And set it up a world's wonder
> In several places to proclaim
> These monsters gloried in their shame.

Just behind is a new Roman Catholic church of circular design with a central altar, not very beautiful outside, but quite lovely in its simplicity within. Why is it possible for it to remain open without any sign of vandalism while the parish church has to be kept closed? Back in the centre of the town where Crossgate meets Bonnygate ('gate' from the Scandinavian, meaning 'street') stands the mercat cross with its marred unicorn. It was restored to the town in 1897 after a long sojourn on Wemyss Hill.

Sir David Lindsay of the Mount (1486–1555) lived a mile or so to the north, successor as Fife's poet to Robert Henryson of Dunfermline. He carried James V as a child on his back, and was faithful to the last.

> How, as ane chapman bears his pack,
> I bore thy Grace upon my back
> And sumtymes, stridlings on my neck,
> Dansand with mony bend and beck.
> The first syllabis that thou did mute
> Was PA, DA LYN. Upon the lute
> Then playit I twenty springs, perqueir,
> Whilk wes gret piete for the hear.

He was a writer of great versatility, a master of rhyme and rhythm; telling a story well, as in "Squire Meldrum"; a satirist without being bitter and a reformer without being a bore, as in "Kittei's Confession"; and, above all, an entertainer in the rollicking rudery of *The Thrie Estaitis*, in which he adds dramatic sense and an ability to draw character in the round.

As near Cupar to the south is the sixteenth-century Scots-

tarvit Tower, L-shaped, plain, strong and tall with five storeys
and an attic, a parapet on corbels and a small conical cap over
the staircase. It is sited so as to give a tremendous view all
round. Here in the seventeenth century lived Sir John Scot,
author of "The Staggering State Of Scots Statesmen". Disap-
pointed himself of influence as a statesman, he devoted himself
to scholarship and hospitality. He founded a Chair of Latin at
St Andrews and endowed scholarships at Glasgow University,
and he enlisted the help and draughtsmanship of Timothy
Pont for the production of the sixth volume of Blaeu's *Atlas*.
The castle is in the care of the Department of Environment and
is open to the public. So is the neighbouring National Trust
property, Hill of Tarvit, a Lorimer house with lovely gardens.

Ceres has a long history and some interesting things. Its
annual games on the last Saturday in June still commemorate
the husbands and sons who went to Bannockburn and were
fortunate enough to return; and the Fife Folk Museum preserves past ways. A quaint figure of a former provost is dated
1578. The single-span Bishop's Bridge (named for the murdered Sharp) and the weigh-house are both over 300 years old,
as are a number of the old houses. In the modern church is a
medieval tomb of a knight in plate armour, and in the
graveyard, the vault of the Lindsay family. The Classical 1765
masonic lodge of St John has been restored as a private
residence. A walk along the nature trail by the Craighall Den
passes a recently restored lime-kiln.

More remarkable still, for the beauty of its scenery, is the
walk through the gorge of the Dura Den, past its waterfall –
and more famous too, for in the gorge was found a unique
collection of fossilized fish, some of the oldest in the country.
From here a three-arched ancient bridge crosses the River Eden
to David II's ruined castle and the old church of Dairsie. In
truth, the latter is not very beautiful, nor in very good
condition, but it is most unusual in that it was built after the
Reformation for Episcopalian worship – by Archbishop Spot-
tiswood in 1621. It is also a very early specimen of Gothic
revival, but the Decorated tracery of the windows is clumsy.
The best thing is its octagonal tower. Should Dairsie be

approached by the main road and not through the Den, an unsignposted minor road must be taken to the south, just before reaching the village.

After Edinburgh, St Andrews must be the best, most visited place in Scotland – attracting alike the student and the golfer, the historian, the lover of architecture and the holiday-maker. That such an out-of-the-way place, however beautiful, should come to have such importance is due as much to chance and superstition as to anything else. Iona, Dunkeld, Dunfermline, each in turn seemed likely to become the headquarters of the Church of Scotland, while Kirrimond, as the place was then called, remained an insignificant Culdee cell. Then, at some time in the eighth century, to this small community were brought some relics believed to be those of St Andrew. As one of the first two apostles, Andrew was much more of an attraction than Kentigern or Ninian or even Columba, but it would have surprised Kenneth MacAlpine and Malcolm Canmore to know the extent to which their saints were so completely supplanted by a foreigner. Indeed it is slightly ironical that the modern Scottish Nationalists should have adopted so readily an emblem based on such an essentially Catholic symbol as the cross of St Andrew. Anyway, in 908, the seat of the only Scottish bishop was transferred from Abernethy to St Andrews, and in due course Queen Margaret's emphasis on episcopacy increased his influence. But the real growth in the city's importance really dates from the reign of David I. He it was who most likely built the square tower of St Regulus (so like that of Wharram-le-Street in Yorkshire) to house the saint's relics – though some prefer a date fifty years earlier than 1126 – and then a quire for it. Certainly he founded an Augustinian monastery with some monks from Scone under their Yorkshire prior, and planned for them the much larger church which was to become the cathedral. The importance and wealth of the monastery can be gauged from its size and the extent of the wall surrounding its precincts; that of the bishop from the remains of the castle which was his palace and his fort. A third great church – for the parishioners – dedicated to the Holy Trinity was added in 1410.

In medieval times, it was as natural that learning should follow the Cross as that, in the nineteenth century, trade should follow the flag. Round about 1410 a group of scholars from Paris began teaching in the city, and Bishop Wardlaw granted them a charter of incorporation – that bishop who was so hospitable that his steward asked him, in desperation, at least to name his guests; to whom the bishop replied that the first two were Fife and Angus. Pope Benedict XIII added six Bulls, declaring that

> considering also the peace and quietness which flourish in the said city of St Andrews and its neighbourhood, its abundant supply of victuals the number of its hospices and other conveniences for students, which it is known to possess, we are led to hope that this city, which the divine bounty has enriched with so many gifts, may become the fountain of science, and may produce many men distinguished for knowledge and virtue.*

Of course, both bishop and pope looked to the university to uphold the orthodoxy of Rome and to forestall heresy rather than to encourage free enquiry and the pursuit of knowledge wherever that pursuit might lead. Lawrence of Lindores, the first head of the Pedagogy, was an Inquisitor and John Fogo, Professor of Theology, secured the burning of a Hussite. More widely remembered than Wardlaw was his successor, Bishop Kennedy, founder in 1450 of the College of St Salvator (the Holy Saviour) for the training of priests. Boys came in their early teens for a four-year course, more like that of a secondary school than a modern university degree course. Regents visited the students each evening to ensure that they were studying, and there were strict rules (enforced by public flogging) about what the undergraduate might wear, and where, and even when, he might walk abroad.

St Leonard's College followed in 1512, though at first it was more of an appendage to the priory than a college in its own right. Its students had to proceed in a crocodile, two and two, to their weekly half-day's play on the Links – from which recreation ground they were later displaced by the wealthier boys from St Salvator's, with whom they tended to fall out.

* Quoted in Douglas Young, *St Andrews, Town and Gown, Royal and Ancient.*

Neither set was supposed to play football which, by and large, they preferred to the officially approved martial exercise of archery. Finally, in 1537, came St Mary's, intended to be a bulwark for Catholic theological orthodoxy but destined in the long run to be the centre of Presbyterian ministry. Whatever the intentions of the founders, and however conservative the bishops – later archbishops – such as James Beaton and his nephew and successor, Cardinal David – it was inevitable that the introduction of Greek into the curriculum, and the comparison of the Greek text of the New Testament with the Latin of the Vulgate, should lead in Scotland, as elsewhere, to the questioning of papal dogma. Nor did the secular lives, and open disregard for their vows of celibacy, of prelates such as the Beatons earn respect for the doctrines they enforced. Finally, when a character as saintly and as well-connected as George Wishart was burned in St Andrews, it was too much. A group of desperate men, including two Leslies and Kirkcaldy of the Grange, managed to gain entrance to the Castle where Beaton "had been busy at his accounts with Mistress Marion Ogilvy that night who was espied to depart from him by the privy postern that morning; and therefore quietness after the rules of physic, and a morning sleep, was necessary for my Lord".

Pitifully he pleaded for his life but he got no more mercy than he had shown to others.

> The said John Leslie strook him first anes or twice, and so did Peter Carmichael of Balmaddie. But James Melvin, a man of nature most gentill and most modest, perceaving them to be boyth in cholore, withdrew them, and said this work and judgement of God, altho' it be secreit, it aught to be done with greater gravitie, and, presenting to him the point of the sweard, said, "Repent thee of thy former wicked life, but especiallie of the shedding of the blood of that notable instrument of God, Maister George Wishart, which, altho' the flame of fyre consume before men yitt it cryes a vengence upon thee, and we from God are sent to revenge it ... ". And so he stroke him twyse or thryse throwgh with a slog sword; and so he fell, never a word out of his mouth but "I am a preast! I am a preast! fy! fy! all is gone."

The body was hung over the castle wall, for all to see.

These things we write merrily [adds Knox, and] because the
weather was hot (for it was May as ye have heard) and his funeral
could not be suddenly prepared, it was thought best, to keep him
from stinking, to give him salt enough, a cope of lead, and a nook
in the bottom of the Sea-Tower (a place where many of God's
children had been imprisoned before) to await what exequies his
bretheren the bishops would prepare for him.

The upshot was a siege of the Protestant extremists in the
castle where, in due course, they were joined by Knox himself,
who, though he approved of the murder, did not approve of all
that the defenders did. In the intervals when the investment
was not close, they had a way of issuing from the walls to
plunder the surrounding countryside, killing and burning, and
using "their bodies in lechery with fair women, serving their
appetite as they thought good". An elaborate mine was tunnel-
led towards the castle walls, to be met with a counter-mine,
both of which survive and can be followed to this day, but the
defenders managed to hold out until French help was enlisted.
Twenty French galleys were sent under command of Leon
Strozzi, the lay prior of Capua, a Florentine. He had guns
which, by a considerable feat, he managed to get up to the
roofs of the cathedral church and St Salvator's. A six-hour
bombardment made such gaps in the walls that, before Strozzi
could launch the assault which he had planned with slaves
from his galleys whom he had promised to free if it was
successful, Kirkcaldy of the Grange was sent to ask for terms.
Knox says that Strozzi agreed to spare the lives of the defenders
and transport them to France where they would be free to
enter the service of the King of France, or, if they did not wish
to, to go to any country other than Scotland. This is disputed.
At any rate, on arrival in France, the gentry were imprisoned
in various castles, and the lesser folk such as Knox were made
slaves in the galleys.

Knox, in his *History of the Reformation in Scotland*, tells
little of his sufferings in the galleys, except for two incidents
which he considered of significance – one of defiance and one
of faith.

Those men in the galleys were threatened with torments if they would not give reverence to the Mass (for at certain times the Mass was said in the galley, or else heard upon the shore, in the presence of the forsars); but they could never make the poorest of that company give reverence to that idol. Yea, when upon the Saturday at night, they sang their Salve Regina, the whole Scotsmen put on their hats, their hoods, or such other thing as they had to cover their heads; and when that others were compelled to kiss a painted brod, (which they called "Nostre Dame") they were not pressed after once [when] a glorious painted Lady was brought in to be kissed and amongst others was presented to one of the Scottishmen then chained. He gently said, "Trouble me not; such an idol is accursed; and therefore I will not touch it". The Patron and the Arguesyn, with two officers having the chief charge of all such matters, said "Thou shalt handle it"; and so they violently thrust it to his face, and put it between his hands; who seeing the extremity, took the idol, and advisedly looking about him, he cast it into the river, and said, "Let our Lady now save herself: she is light enough; let her learn to swim". After which was no Scottishman urged with that idolatry.

And:

Master James [Balfour] and John Knox being in one galley ... would oftentimes ask him "If he thought that they would ever be delivered?" Whose answer was ever, from the day that they entered into the galleys, "That God would deliver them from that bondage, to his glory, even in this life". And lying betwixt Dundee and St Andrews, the second time that the galleys returned to Scotland, the said John being so extremely sick that few hoped his life, the said Master James willed him to look to the land, and asked if he knew it? Who answered, "Yes I know it well; for I see the steeple of that place, where God first in public opened my mouth to his glory, and I am fully persuaded, however weak I may now appear that I shall not depart this life, till that my tongue shall glorify his godly name in the same place."

The castle which had been battered into submission was rebuilt by the Cardinal's successor, Bishop Hamilton, another worldly and carnally inclined ecclesiastic of near-royal blood, but though Queen Mary liked the town, castle and cathedral had

had their day. With the coming of the Reformation, both were neglected and in due course fell down. Mary came as a holidaymaker in the 1560s to get away from the affairs of state that she found so troublesome and, when the English ambassador tried to deliver a message from his Queen, she told him "I sent for you to be merry, and to see how like a bourgeois wife I live with my little troop; and you will interrupt our pastime with your great and grave matters. You see neither cloth of state, nor such appearance that you think that there is a Queen here." But being the woman that she was, she could not entirely escape troubles. It was at St Andrews that her slightly crazy admirer Chastelard was executed after forcing his way into her room when she was staying down the coast at Burntisland.

The sixteenth and seventeenth centuries were a time of intellectual distinction too. In 1563 John Napier of Merchiston graduated at the university – the inventor of logarithms and much else including a pumping machine – and in 1668 James Gregory who made the first reflecting telescope was Professor of Mathematics. But it was Andrew Melville, between the two, who left the most abiding mark on the history of Scotland by his share in composing the Second Book of Discipline. Under him, new life was breathed into the university and its influence extended by attracting students from abroad, especially French and Dutch. Most – especially the native Scotsmen – were poor, as for instance Melville's nephew James, but the rich came too; the great Marquises of Argyll and of Montrose were alumni, and both won the coveted silver medal for archery. And there were lesser gentry in plenty, often accompanied by their own private tutors.

Such, in the eighteenth century, were the twin sons of John Mackenzie of Delvine (Inchtuthil), an advocate. Previously they had, from the age of eight, been boarded out to receive their first lessons in writing, arithmetic and Latin from a tutor, James Morrice. Then, at twelve, they were sent to join an older brother at the university. But he, being none too industrious himself, found it impossible to make them attend to their studies and so Morrice was again engaged and sent to supervise all three, and to report regularly on their progress. His letters make fascinating reading, describing, as they do, in detail, the books they were prescribed and the way in which they were taught and examined, the extreme cold of the lecture rooms and the chapel, and even the date at which they were first allowed to powder their hair (which was when they ceased to be Bejants); even the number of their golf clubs, viz: "ane play club, ane scraper and ane tin-faced club". As far back as 1691, their father had referred to St Andrews as "the Metropolis of golf" and he allowed the boys to play twice a week.

At first, Morrice found them tractable enough, but then difficulties arose over their food:

Dec 20 1712

Much Honoured,

The late misunderstanding between your Ho. and me obliges me to give a more particular accompt of your sons as to their diet and other particulars. Ken and Th get a chopin of good fresh milk and as much pottage as they can sup for their breakfast and Alexr [the elder brother] has eggs and fresh butter ... and for their dinner they get sometimes broth of boiled beef, and sometimes of boiled mutton with some of either of these roasted, and sometimes a pock pudding instead of broth; they got not fish beyond twice at dinner: and for supper either boiled milk and bread or rice for all; when Kilcowie and Alexr get not eggs in the morning they readily have them at night and a little cheese; and sometimes a collop but then the twins do not take it and are sure to have bread and milk to their supper. If Sir there be aught in this diet wrong, let me know of it and it shall be mended. Kilcowie [he was another boy in the same household] – who is truly a Gentleman of a sweet and pleasant humour – eats broth and boiled meat with pleasure and prefers our oatcakes to wheat bread. But Alexr cares not much for any kind of broth and seldom tastes any of the boiled flesh, and his example begins to influence the twins to follow it, who could formerly have made a dinner of broth and boiled meat with abundance of pleasure at your house, but if your will be to have it otherwise, it shall be followed. My Authority with the twins is not gone, tho I have observed them sometimes since I came hither behave with that disregard to me

quhich they would not have ventured on before and I would not
have let slip without chastisement, had not their aunt told me that
my former humour was degenerate into a barbarous inhumanity
towards them; however I threatened both to whip them and give
you an accompt of it, which so terrified them that they promised
not to be guilty thereof again . . . .
>   I am
>   Much honoured
>   Your faithful, very affectionate and most humble
>   servant, Ja Morrice

And a few week later, this was followed up by another letter:

On Tuesday we had stewed Veal and roasted beef for dinner and
a little of the stewed veal being set before K and Th they would
not eat it which when I observed I told them they would get no
more for their meal unless they first eat up what was on their
plate whereat they began to weep and told me they came not
hither to fast .˙. . but a little after dinner when they began to think
on what they had said, they promised not to be guilty of the like
again and entreated me not to write to you.

For all that Morrice was far from unkindly, and constantly
urged the boys' mother to relax her rule that they should not
wear two pairs of stockings even when the Fife winter was at
its coldest, and begged, when this was refused, that Thomas
(who suffered from chilblains) should at least be provided with
thicker stockings.

Initially the Reformation had benefited learning at St
Andrews but the temporary triumph of Presbyterianism during
the Civil Wars, and its total triumph on the arrival of William
of Orange, led to loss of income, of students, of distinction even
among the professors. This and the end of the archbishopric led
to a similar decline in the fortunes of the town. Its population
fell from 14,000 to 2,000 and grass grew in the streets; there
were barely a hundred students in the university. Such was the
position when Dr Johnson paid his famous visit. Cathedral and
castle had been plundered for building stone, and:

The university within a few years consisted of three colleges
but is now reduced to two; the College of St Leonard being lately

dissolved by sale of its buildings and the appropriation of its revenues to the professors of the two others. The chapel of the alienated college is yet standing, a fabric not inelegant of external structure; but I was always by some civil excuse prevented from entering it. A decent attempt as I was since told, has been made to convert it into a greenhouse by planting its area with shrubs. This new method of gardening is not successful; the plants do not hitherto prosper. To what use it will next be put I have no pleasure in conjecturing. It is something that its present state is at least not ostentatiously displayed. Where there is yet shame there may in time be virtue.

And he added: "The kindness of the professors did not contribute to abate the uneasy remembrance of a university declining, a college alienated, and a church profaned and hastening to the ground."

It was during this recession in its fortunes, that golf came to the rescue of the town. It had always been a popular pastime on the links, at least since the fifteenth century when Parliament had tried to prevent it interfering with the more important business of compulsory weapon-training. In 1458 it was decreed that "wapinschawings be haldin be the lords and baronys spirituale and temporale four tymis in the Zeir. And that the fut ball and the golf be utterly cryit doune and nocht usyt". But James IV certainly played, and James VI, and lesser folk appear in the kirk session minutes as guilty of playing golf on the Sabbath. By the time of Montrose, there were differentiated clubs such as "play clubs, Bonker clubs and irone clubs" but the game was still no more standardized than is a modern paperchase. You played where you wished, in what direction you wished, for as many 'holes' as you wished. And, although in the course of time, St Andrews was accepted as the H.Q. of the game, and its eighteen holes accepted as the norm, its club when first founded in 1754 adopted rules already in use at Leith. Originally the Society of St Andrews Golfers, it became the 'Royal and Ancient' under the patronage of William IV (of England – III of Scotland). Allan Robertson, Tom Morris and his son Tommy, were in succession greenkeepers and created the Old Course, that narrow strip of green of which

Bobbie Jones wrote: "If I had ever been sat down in one place and told I was to play there and nowhere else for the rest of my life, I should have chosen the Old Course at St Andrews."

To it have been added the New Course, the Eden Course and the Jubilee Course. Anyone can play on them. You do not have to be a member of the Royal and Ancient which is a private club, with premises not open to the general public. But it is the ruling body in golf where laws affecting the game are drafted, and its championship committee is responsible for running the British open and other major tournaments.

The renaissance of the university came slowly during the nineteenth century with a visitation, an Act of Parliament and much hard work by some distinguished men such as Brewster, Tulloch and Forbes – and then an extension (later to be reversed) to Dundee. It was in the forefront in the admission of women students. It was richly helped with gifts from Andrew Carnegie and Edward Hark- ness. It is (once again) able to provide an exceptionally large proportion of residential places. It has had to share in the crash programme of expansion, but it takes pride in the fact that, with less than 3000 undergraduates, it is still an intimate community. And it would claim to be not only the oldest but the most 'universal' of the Scottish universities.

A tour of the city should start with an early morning spent peacefully within the precincts of the cathedral, before others arrive. Attention is focused on the square, solidly built tower of St Rule, lit only by slits in the lower storeys and by round-headed two-light windows near the top. Adjoining it is the tall quire, but a sanctuary which stood to the east, and a rather later nave to the west, are gone – as is the spire which added grace to the tower. Further east, just outside the precincts stood the church of St Mary of the Rocks which may have had a round tower like those of Brechin and Abernethy. Probably the site of the original Culdee settlement, it was certainly their home when their Augustinian rivals were established in the great cathedral. The twelfth-century remains are very sparse but they are worth visiting for the sake of the site overlooking harbour and pier.

Just how much has been lost by the utter decay of the cathedral, one can realize simply by standing within its walls. It was great in size – the longest in Britain after Norwich – and elaborate in detail with the evolution of style to be expected in a long period of building. The east end is the earliest and most magnificent survival, with its line of three Romanesque windows; originally two further rows stood above but these were replaced later by a much larger Decorated window. Little else remains of the quire (finished by 1238) but the south wall of the nave, and part of the south transept, still stand, the latter showing the transition from round-headed to early pointed arches. The entrance to the chapter-house is fine, and the four-bay defended gateway, the Pends, dating from the fourteenth century, but, for the rest, it is a matter of imagination to reconstruct from the excavated foundations the size and the majesty of the cloisters and the other monastic buildings. The little guide-book is essential, as is a visit to the museum. This contains a thirteenth-century carved head of Christ, some fragments of Bishop Wardlaw's tomb with remarkable detail of his vestments, and many early free-standing crosses showing the historical connection between St Andrews and Northumbria from the eighth to the tenth centuries. But the most beautiful – and the rarest treasure – is the Pictish sarcophagus with its spirited and lifelike carving of animals and men including David rending the jaws of the lion.

Next in historical importance, and only a few yards to the north on the cliffs stands the bishop's castle – a pentagonal enclosure, protected by a ditch where nature had not already rendered the site impregnable before the coming of gunpowder. The earliest stone work and the notorious 'bottle dungeon' date from the thirteenth century but most of what can be seen today is what Archbishop Hamilton built to repair the damage caused by the long siege which followed Cardinal Beaton's murder. His fore-tower and the wing adjoining it which includes his entrance gateway (originally balanced by a similar wing on the other side of the fore-tower) are Renaissance in feeling and in detail. In the sea-tower as Knox said, "many of God's children were imprisoned". Most interesting of all are the subterranean tunnels, the one dug by the besiegers from outside through the solid rock in the hope of reaching the castle walls and placing a mine underneath them, the other dug by the defenders to cut off the attackers tunnel and to prevent this. Marvellously the defenders succeeded and their breakthrough can still be seen; photographs and a diagram in the inexpensive Department of Environment guide make clear this complicated operation. All the effort was however to no avail as the cannon mounted on the towers of the cathedral and St Salvator's achieved such a battering that the defenders could no longer hold out.

From the castle, the sea-road, the Scores, takes you past university buildings and places where, in bygone days, witches were burnt or drowned, and where young men practised their archery, to the links, the Royal and Ancient Club House and the four golf courses. Thence Golf Street leads back into the High Street, one of the three wide medieval ways which so impressively converge on the cathedral. Half way along is the College of the Holy Saviour – St Salvator's – founded by Bishop Kennedy in 1450 to be a seminary for the training of priests in theology and the arts and a Collegiate Church for the daily celebration of the Mass. His foundation has changed out of all recognition and most of the old building has gone but the beautiful chapel remains. Roof and window tracery have been renewed, and Catholic altars and statues have been swept away, but enough remains to preserve the medieval atmosphere. The south wall facing on to the street is as it was, though with modern glass; the north wall has no windows because, originally, a two-storey cloister adjoined it. In an apse is the tomb of the founder; it is much damaged but the carving is intricate, as is that of an aumbry nearby. At the west end is a simpler but most effective incised tomb of an ecclesiastic in his vestments. Other treasures are three valuable medieval maces, one of French craftsmanship dated 1461, and those of the faculties of Arts and Canon Law (not usually on display), and the sixteenth-century carved wooden pulpit which was brought from Holy Trinity. Seen from the street, the tower and the adjoining house are both impressive; the former contains the

Founder's 'Kate Kennedy' bell and also one moved from St Leonard's when the two colleges were joined.

Of the three great streets converging on to the cathedral, Market Street is perhaps the least interesting but it was once the hub of the town; it still houses many good shops, and, with South Street, the annual Lammas Fair in the second week in August; and its narrow eastern end has some old dwellings, refurbished and lived in. South Street, on the other hand, is full of them and those that are mentioned are but a few of those which can be discovered by leisurely exploration – and to find them for oneself is far more satisfying than being directed to them. For those in a hurry, Nos.19, 42 and 141 are outstanding, and there are similar houses in South Castle Street. South Court, at number 42, leads through a little garden to the Byre Theatre. Outside staircases and little stretches of cobbles and crow-stepped gables are common.

At the cathedral end of South Street, near the Pends, was St Leonard's College where now a famous girls' school of that name flourishes. It includes an irregular old house traditionally that used by Queen Mary in 1564, open to the public from 3-4 p.m. on Thursdays. Behind it is the restored chapel of St Leonard. A church has certainly stood here since the twelfth century and some of the masonry that survives is Romanesque but it is likely that there was extensive rebuilding at some time, and the windows are in the square-headed Perpendicular style. The interior was also remodelled at the time of the Reformation, and again after a fire in 1702. From 1761 the building was out of use until a careful renovation was funded by Sir David Russell and the Pilgrim Trust, and supervised by the architect Ian G. Lindsay. The result is an intimate little place of private devotion which can also be used for services for a limited number. Its simplicity is Presbyterian, but its medieval atmosphere has been recovered by the erection of a screen (now holding an organ instead of a rood) between nave and quire, and by the collegiate arrangement of the seating and the focusing of attention on the east end. The modern wood work including the pulpit is graceful and the plastered walls give light. In the quire are two aumbries, three sixteenth-century tombstones in the floor, covered to preserve them, and, on the north wall, an elaborate monument to Robert Stewart, Earl of March who died in 1586. No attempt was made to replace the tower which had stood to the west of the nave. This is a lovely quiet corner of St Andrews.

The third college, that of St Mary's, was the refounding by Archbishop James Beaton in 1538 of the old Pedagogy established by the Faculty of Arts a hundred years before. Physics, medicine and law were to be studied as well as theology and arts, but over the years St Mary's has become the home of the Divinity faculty. Its earliest surviving buildings are those of Archbishop Hamilton dating from 1554 who, though intensely conservative in his religious opinions, did work to bring new life to the university. On one side of its shady court is the old library, contributed to by James VI and inaugurated by Archbishop Gledstanes in 1612, completed in 1643. The lower floor has been repanelled, but the upper has the original fluted pillars supporting a gallery. Here James Gregory carried out many of his astronomical observations and the line which he used may be seen in the floor, and the bracket for his telescope. Adjoining it is the panelled senate room, in the building where Parliament met in 1645.

On the other side of South Street is the very large town kirk, dedicated in 1410 to the Holy Trinity. There had been an earlier church with the same dedication within the monastery precincts. Its nave and east window are most impressive, and it has some good modern glass, but its most interesting feature, perhaps, is the elaborate late-seventeenth-century memorial of Dutch workmanship to Archbishop Sharp, depicting his assassination.

At one time, both the Greyfriars and the Blackfriars had churches but of these only a fragment of the latter survives dating from the sixteenth century; its vaulted north apse shows how elaborately beautiful the complete building must have been. Behind it is Madras College, another of Dr Bell's great bequests to the kingdom of his birth; alongside it and contrasting with its grandeur, are the little houses in the cobbled Rose Lane. Finally we may take our leave of St Andrews through the West Port, "ane cumlie and Perfite Pend", as Martine described it – very old but reconstructed in 1589 and again 1843. Here, at one of the only two town gateways surviving in Scotland, the students' Rector is still welcomed with a ceremonial address in Latin.

IX

SOUTH FIFE

The Scottish coal belt runs from South Ayrshire, through the central region, into Fife, and it was in Fife that it was first exploited. The monks of Dunfermline Abbey had servants winning coal for them as early as the thirteenth century. By the sixteenth there were a number of lay lairds developing mines on their lands, usually in connection with salt pans, and burghs such as Culross, Wemyss and Methil were all exporting both coal and salt. It was at Culross that Sir George Bruce took James VI along a mine under the sea which emerged on a caisson; surrounded by water and always ready to suspect a plot against his life, he shouted out "Treason" and was not easily reassured. So unpleasant was the work involved that, in order to obtain a sufficient labour force, a number of Acts were passed by the Privy Council (on which the Fife lairds were well represented) which reduced to serfdom all those who worked in mines or salt pans. They were not technically slaves, in that they received wages, but, once they had accepted employment, they could not leave it. The miner "became a piece of mining equipment that could be bought or sold and inherited by his master, with the sole proviso that he might not be separated from the works at which he started his bondage".* Furthermore, in practice, the serfdom extended to the whole family; the miner's wife was needed to carry to the surface the coal that he hewed; and his children were solemnly bound at the time of their christenings to follow the calling of their parents in return for an 'arles' – a payment to their father from his master. Thus a child's work underground would often start as early as the age of six or seven, and, at a time when serfdom had long vanished in England, it was rife in Scotland. There

* T. C. Smout, *History of the Scottish People.*

was not even a Habeas Corpus Act to protect the miners.

In the growing humanitarianism of the late eighteenth century, such a state of affairs could not continue indefinitely. Indeed the famous Mansfield Judgement of 1772 which declared that no man could be a slave on English soil might have been anticipated in Scotland in 1770 when the Fife colliers collected money to challenge the detention of a negro slave who had been brought to the country, but, owing to the death of the slave-owner, the case was not decided. It may have been just as well; the Court of Session of those days might not have been as far-seeing as Lord Mansfield – or as the Earl of Dundonald who ended two of the worst abuses in his Culross mines in 1793 – underground work by women, and payment by truck. Even when an Act of Parliament abolished serfdom in the same year, these two abuses (and child labour) continued in many other places with the result that mining families too often went on living in squalor; the wives had no time to clean their houses or to cook food or to care for their children and "no man wanted to marry a collier's daughter, so little did they know of domestic duty. So degraded did they become," declared Hugh Miller, "that they were marked by a peculiar type of mouth, that I learnt to distinguish them from all other females of the country. It was wide open, thick-lipped, projecting equal above and below, and exactly resembled that which we find in prints of savages at their lowest and most brutal state, in such narratives of our modern voyagers as, for instance, the narrative of Captain Fitzroy's Second Voyage of the *Beagle*." So much looked down on were they by their neighbours that, in parts of Fife there was opposition to their being buried in consecrated ground.

The nineteenth century saw a greatly increased demand for coal and by 1914 one in every ten of Fife's working population was engaged in mining; but improvements in pay and working conditions and housing came only slowly, leaving a long legacy of bitterness which was increased by the failure of the General Strike, and by the depression of the thirties. The next decade and the nationalization of the industry brought great hopes to the region. "The Lanarkshire coalfields were by

now in a serious decline and it was expected that their output
would continue to decline as the seams then being worked
were exhausted. This permanent fall in output had to be made
good as quickly as possible by expansion elsewhere, and this
expansion would take place mainly in the coal-fields of Fife . . .
it was estimated that 6500 additional miners would be needed
. . . a doubling of the mining population."

Furthermore, a report published in 1944 had recommended
that "miners should wherever possible be housed away from
the collieries and should have the advantage of living in a
mixed community side by side with members of other trades
and occupations". Some of the new miners were to be housed
in Kirkcaldy, but, for the rest, an entirely new town was to
come into existence – Glenrothes. In the event, unexpected
geological difficulties were encountered and the Rothes pit had
to be abandoned, but not the new town nor the determination
to increase Fife's output. Instead, recourse is being had to the
deep, limestone coal which lies under the Firth of Forth from
Seafield near Kirkcaldy and Valleyfield near Culross, and, in
the very west of the region where Solsgirth, Castlehill and
Bogside are linked together to the Longannet mine where coal
comes to the surface and serves the new 2400-megawatt
electricity generating station. At Westfield there is an opencast
mining, and at Dysart, the Francis pit (the oldest now working), there are plans to join up with Seafield and the important
Michael colliery reserves.

Away to the west, and at the very edge of the region, is
Kincardine-on-Forth. It has a seventeenth-century mercat
cross decorated with the arms of the Earl of Kincardine, and a
number of old houses, one with an inscription above its
doorway:

> God is my lyf, my land and rent
> His promise is my evident
> LAT THEM SAY.

Here, too, are the Police College at Tulliallan Castle (H.Q. of
the Polish General Sikorski during the war) and the ruins of an
older castle at Blackadder, near the golf course on the minor
road to Alloa. Some 600 years old, it is unusual in that the

vaulted hall is on the ground floor. Off it was a pit-cell and, in 1619, five men were tried for the incarceration there of a man "in the pitt of Tulliallane, quhair throw want of intertenement, he famischet and deit of hunger". Back in the town, and a little way north of the existing parish church, is an older church of 1675, Classical in style. It has both round-headed and square windows, and a round-headed west door beneath a very elegant tower and bell chamber. It stands in peaceful surroundings only marred by four towering blocks of flats. It is true that the district is already weighted with the vast Longannet power station on this side of the Forth, and Grangemouth on the other, but these are distant and active; the flats, though inhabited, look dead.

From Kincardine the main road speeds on to Dunfermline sparing Culross the 'new town' of which is Scotland's treasure house of sixteenth-century burgh architecture.* There is so much to see, and it is all so compact, that one can spend hours here happily on a sunny day. Coming from Kincardine one passes first Dunimarle Castle, now a convalescent home for miners and a museum (closed at the time of writing), and below it on the sea-shore the site of the saltpans associated with Sir George Bruce's coal pits, and the old boat shed of Balgownie House. But that way, one is in the centre of the burgh before one is ready for it; far better is to come in from the north and to capture the feeling of the past by visiting first the church and the ruins of the monastic buildings, and then walking down Tanhouse Brae. Malcolm Earl of Fife founded a Cistercian house here in 1217 and parts of the church date from that time, in particular the porch. This with its Romanesque doorway is formed by the east and west walls of the *pulpitum* and the rood screen which divided the monk's quire from the lay people's nave; of the latter, only a part of the south wall remains. Only one other church in Scotland, that of Inchcolm, still has both *pulpitum* and rood. Above the porch rises a strong square tower built by Abbot Masoun at the beginning of the sixteenth century. Inside, of interest are the seventeenth-century wooden pulpit and its canopy, two carved stone figures on the Argyll tomb in the north transept, and the Bruce aisle

* It is no coincidence that George Scott-Moncrieff in his *The Stones of Scotland* has more illustrations of Culross than of any other place - even Edinburgh!

beyond. Sir George's magnificent tomb monument has alabaster figures of his three sons and five daughters; these are stylized and almost identical but the larger, life-sized ones of Sir George and his wife are deeply moving; they might indeed be lying together in death. There is also in this aisle a tablet which reads:

Near this spot is deposited the HEART of
   Edward Lord Bruce of Kinloss
Who was slain in a duel fought in the year 1613
With Sir Edward Sackville (afterewards Bart) of Dorset
   Near Bergen-op-Zoom in Holland
To which both combattants had repaired
The one from England, the other from Paris
For the determined purpose of deciding their feud by the sword

and, for the story, the reader is referred to Lord Clarendon's *History*. Not a great deal survives of the other monastic buildings except one vaulted chamber and some useful drains, but the massiveness of the walls, the lawns and border so beautifully kept, and the stupendous view over the Forth, tempt one to linger. The adjoining Renaissance mansion was built by Sir George's elder brother, father of the first Earl of Elgin; it is in private occupation and not open to the public. For some time it was the property of the Cochranes of Ochiltree, and then of the Prestons of Valleyfield, the two families who succeeded the Bruces as the entrepreneurs of Culross – but it is now back in Bruce hands again.

This is not the place for a guided tour of Culross. The National Trust for Scotland, which has done so much to preserve, and where necessary restore, the old houses with their crow-stepped gables and their pantiled roofs, has prepared both a brief walkabout and a fuller guide. It is the general impression of the place that is its chief charm – its cobbled causeways with their higher stepping stones in the centre on which the well-to-do could keep their feet dry, and the little gardens and the many inscriptions. Over Snuff Cottage, at the top of Tanhouse Brae, is, "Wha wad ha' thocht it", the first line of a couplet which, completed, runs, "Noses wad ha' bocht it?" and over another, in Greek characters: "God provides and will provide." But, if it is the atmosphere which is the most important, there are a number of buildings which are notable in their own right. Bishop Leighton's house and the Study are around 1600, and the town house 1626 with a clock tower of 1783. This is open to the public, as is, at stated times, the outlook room of the Study and a large panelled room on the first floor, the contents of which illustrate three centuries of domestic life in Culross; the remainder of the house is the home of the resident National Trust representative in the town. Greatest of all is the Palace which is well worth the time needed for the conducted tour. It was built for himself by Sir George Bruce between 1597 and 1611. After being long a ruin, its old windows have been lovingly restored, as they were originally, with glass only in the top half, and the bottom half, wooden shutters; some of the rooms are panelled, others have sixteenth-century tempera paintings from which the dirt of ages has been carefully cleaned. Bought by the National Trust for Scotland in 1932 (their very first property), it and its terraced gardens are now cared for by the Department of the Environment.

From Culross, one road runs north-east along the coal belt to Dunfermline, Cowdenbeath and Glenrothes, another along the coast, past Limekilns, where the Ship Inn was the starting point of *Kidnapped,* and the naval base at Rosyth, to Inver-keithing.

Dunfermline is, by a few thousands, the largest town in Fife. There was early a church and a royal castle here, but it was Queen Margaret's love for the place that started its real importance – that cosmopolitan saint who did so much to shape the religious and the aristocratic complexion of Scotland for generations, and even its speech. The subsequent prosperity of the town was based on coal and on the manufacture of linen. As far back as 1291 the monks had a grant "to the religious men, the abbot and convent of Dunfermline a coal pit in the land of Pittencrieff, wherever they may wish, excluding the arable land, that they may get a sufficiency for their own use but not to sell". But the limitation was not effective. Later, linen had its ups and downs and has since given place to

man-made fibres. And a very important new source of employment was the creation of the naval base at Rosyth. More
than most places, it has been subject to fluctuations of prosperity. After bad times in the eighteenth, and then again in the
nineteenth, centuries, and between the two world wars, the
Third Statistical Report could claim that it had low unemployment and negligible juvenile delinquency. Today with a
dramatic decline in the number employed in coal-mining, and
with the nation-wide difficulty which school-leavers have in
finding jobs, things are not quite so easy, but the unemployment rate remains better' than the national average. New
industry associated with North Sea Oil and the petro-chemical
industry in particular have helped.

One thing that no economic depression has ever been able to
take from it is the beauty of its situation. The millionaire
Andrew Carnegie who was born in an attic of a small house at
the corner of Moodie Street and Priory Lane, to very poor
parents, later wrote: "Fortunate in my ancestors, I was supremely so in my birthplace. Where one is born is very
important . . . Ruskin observes that every bright boy in
Edinburgh is influenced by the site of the castle. So is the child
of Dunfermline by its noble abbey, the Westminster of
Scotland" – and by Pittencrieff Glen, which he later gave to the
town to make one of the best of public parks: "It always meant
paradise to the child of Dunfermline. It certainly did to me.
When I heard of paradise, I translated the word into Pittencrieff Glen, believing it to be as near to paradise as anything I
could think of. Happy were we if, through an open lodge gate,
or over a wall or under the iron grille over the burn, now and
then we caught a glimpse inside."

The abbey dominates all. Beneath the church that we see
today – the work of Margaret's son, David I that "sair saint for
the crown" – are the foundations of two earlier buildings, a
small Culdee church and that of Malcolm Canmore of around
1074, in which he and Margaret were buried. She had been
married at Dunfermline, her children were born there, and
though she died in Edinburgh, she was brought back to rest
there, as were six later Scottish kings. The great Norman nave

was based on Durham, and its massive pillars and severe round arches, ornamented only with plain zigzag, give the impression of strength rather than beauty. But there is beauty to be found, once your eyes have attuned themselves to the dim light, especially in the arcading round the walls. Otherwise, all the colour and the carvings that would have filled this vast empty shell were swept away at the Reformation. On the floor, the outlines of the older churches are indicated by a brass strip, and five gridded openings can be illuminated to show traces of the actual masonry. In place of the original choir which had fallen into decay, a dignified Gothic building in the Perpendicular style was put up in the early nineteenth century to serve as the parish church. At the junction, stands Bruce's tomb. From the outside, the church is best viewed from a distance, where the west front is better appreciated and the later buttresses are less obtrusive - ideally from the gardens of Pittencrieff Park.

As interesting, and even more beautiful, are the ruins of the Benedictine monastery, built in the thirteenth century, burnt by Edward I in 1303, and rebuilt in the fourteenth century. The earliest part is the frater range which would have originally been joined to the church by the other two sides of the cloisters; it is later in style than the church and, naturally, more elaborate in decoration, especially in its great west window. The remains of the pulpit may be seen, from which the monks heard suitable readings at mealtimes. To the east, lay their dormitory and reredorter; to the west, a great gate-house, and beyond that the kitchen. West again lay the guest accommodation, on a lavish scale, to accommodate, when need be, the Court. It was here that the King made the decision so disastrous to Sir Patrick Spens:

The Sailing

The king sits in Dunfermline town
    Drinking the blude-red wine;
"O where will I get a skeely skipper
    To sail this new ship o' mine?"

O up and spake an eldern knight,
    Sat at the king's right knee;

"Sir Patrick Spens is the best sailor
  That ever sailed the sea."

Our king has written a braid letter,
  And sealed it with his hand,
And sent it to Sir Patrick Spens,
  Was walking on the strand.

"To Noroway, to Noroway,
  To Noroway o'er the faem;
The king's daughter o' Noroway,
  'Tis thou must bring her hame."

The first word that Sir Patrick read
  So loud, loud laughed he;
The neist word that Sir Patrick read
  The tear blinded his e'e.

"O wha is this has done this deed
  And told the king o' me,
To send us out, at this time o' year,
  To sail upon the sea?

Be it wind, be it weet, be it hail, be it sleet,
  Our ship must sail the faem;
The king's daughter o' Noroway,
  'Tis we must bring her hame."

They hoysed their sails on Monenday morn
  With a' the speed they may;
They hae landed in Noroway
  Upon a Wodensday.

The Return

"Mak ready, mak ready, my merry men a';
  Our good ship sails the morn."
"Now ever alack, my master dear,
  I fear a deadly storm."

"I saw the new moon late yestreen
  Wi' the old moon in her arm;
And if we gang to sea, master,
  I fear we'll come to harm."

They hadna' sailed a league, a league,
  A league but barely three,
When the lift grew dark, and the wind blew loud,
  And gurly grew the sea.

The ankers brake, and the topmast lap,
  It was sic a deadly storm:
And the waves cam owre the broken ship
  Till a' her sides were torn.

"Go fetch a web o' the silken cloth,
  Another o' the twine,
And wap them into our ship's side,
  And let nae the sea come in."

They fetched a web o' the silken cloth,
  Another o' the twine,
And they wapp'd them round that good ship's side
  But still the sea came in

O laith, laith were our gude Scots lords
  To wet their cork-heeled shoon;
But lang or a' the play was play'd
  They wet their hats aboon.

And mony was the feather bed
  That flatter'd on the faem;
And mony was the gude lord's son
  That never mair cam hame.

O lang, lang may the ladies sit,
  Wi' their fans in their hand,
Before they see Sir Patrick Spens
  Come sailing to the strand!

And lang, lang may the maidens sit
  With their gowd kames in their hair,
A-waiting for their ain dear loves!
  For them they'll see nae mair.

Half-owre, half-owre to Aberdour,
  Tis fifty fathoms deep;
And there lies gude Sir Patrick Spens,
  Wi' the Scots lords at his feet!

This royal use of the abbey buildings was regularized after the Reformation, when James VI enlarged them and gave them to his queen as her palace. Carnegie's benefactions included not only Pittencrieff Park but £10 million to the Scottish universities, half to help students who could not (in 1901) afford their fees, and half for new buildings and to help research – further gifts to provide libraries, before local authorities stepped into this field, and to provide swimming baths and playing fields, to encourage music and subsidize adult education – and, not least, a special trust for his own home town. He was a pioneer in many directions.

Two other of Dunfermline's sons deserve mention, an ingenious mechanic and a pioneer of Scottish poetry. The former was James Blake. By feigning dumbness as a workman, he mastered the intricacies of the damask loom of a factory at Drumsheugh and then constructed one of his own in the abbey Pends in 1718. This and the subsequent introduction of power looms did much to bring back prosperity to the town.

Dunfermline's poet – and schoolmaster in the later fifteenth century – was Robert Henryson, author of some engaging animal fables after the Chaucerian manner; of a sequel to "Troylus and Criseyde"; the "Bludy Sark"; and, perhaps most delightful of all, the dialogue between Robene and Makyne. Robene is a laggard shepherd whom Makene would woo:

> Robene sat on gud grene hill,
> Keepand a flock of fe;
> Mirry Makene said him till,
> "Robene, thou rew on me;
> I haif thee luvit lowd and still,
> Thir yeiris two or thre;
> My dule is dern bot gif thow dill,
> Dowtless but dreid I de."
>
> Robene ansuerit "By the Rude
> Nathing of lufe I know . . .".

and, though Makene instructs him, he is too slow in response, too concerned with his sheep, and so, when at last he is aroused, Makene's answer is:

"The man that will not quhen he may
Sall haif not quhen he wald"

And when Robene further urges

"Makene the nicht is soft and dry
The wedder is warme and fair,
And the grene woid rycht neir us by
To walk attour all quhair.
There may no langlour us espy
That is to lufe contrair;
Thairin, Makene, bath ye and I
Unsene we ma repair."

the answer is

"Robene, with the I will nocht deill;
Adeu, for thus we mett."

Makyne went hame blyth anneuche,
Attour the holttis hair.
Robene murnit, and Malkyne lewche
Scho sang, he sichit sair.

Robert Henryson is remembered in William Dunbar's
"Lament for the Makars", one of the most moving of all the
poems of his age – his lament for those of his poet friends who
have already died, his remembrance that he must be the next to
go, stressed in the tolling Latin refrain:

Lament for the Makars

I that in heill was and gladness
Am trublit now with great sickness
And feblit with infirmitie;
Timor mortis conturbat me.

Our pleasance here is all vainglorie,
This fals world is but transitorie,
The flesh is bruckle, the Feynd is slee;
Timor mortis conturbat me . . . .

Unto the death gois all Estatis,
Princis, Prelatis, and Potestatis,
Baith rich and poor of all degree;
    Timor mortis conturbat me.

He takis the knichtis in to the field
Enarmit under helm and scheild;
Victor he is at all mellie;
    Timor mortis conturbat me.

That strong unmerciful tyrand
Takis on the motheris breast sowkand,
That babe full of benignitie;
    Timor mortis conturbat me.

He takis the campion in the stour,
The captain closit in the tour,
The lady in bour full of bewtie;
    Timor mortis conturbat me.

He spairis no lord for his piscence,
Na clerk for his intelligence;
His awful straik may no man flee;
    Timor mortis conturbat me . . . .

In Dunfermline he has tane Broun
With Maister Robert Henrysoun;
Sir John the Ross embrast has he;
    Timor mortis conturbat me.

And he has now tane, last of a,
Good gentil Stobo and Quintin Shaw,
Of Quhom all wichtis hes pitie
    Timor mortis conturbat me.

Good Maister Walter Kennedy
In point of Death lies verilie;
Great ruth it were that so suld be;
    Timor mortis conturbat me.

Sen he has all my brether tane,
He will naught let me live alane;
Of force I man his next prey be;
    Timor mortis conturbat me.

Since for the Death remeid is none,
Best is that we for Death dispone
After our death that we may live;
Timor mortis conturbat me.

After more than fifty years, the first time I heard that poem
remains with me as vividly as ever – hearing Bernard Fergusson
speak it to an audience of 200, not one of whom could
understand much more than the Latin refrain, and holding
them spellbound. If Fife cannot claim Dunbar as a born son, he
must have spent many days and nights here when the Court
was at Dunfermline or at Falkland where he very likely wrote
"The Thistle and the Rose" for the marriage of James IV to
Margaret Tudor.

We may speed on through Cowdenbeath and Lochgelly to
Glenrothes. That this 'new town' did not prove a costly failure
was a remarkable achievement on the part of the planners.
Their objective in 1950 had been a town of 32,000 to serve the
needs of the Rothes colliery; twenty-five years later, in spite of
the sealing off of the pit, the target has been reached and a
self-supporting and diversified community has been built up,
with 10,000 houses and 14,000 jobs. Its Development Corpora-
tion can confidently claim that its shopping and recreational
facilities are second to none in the new towns, and that access
to the surrounding countryside, and even further afield, is as
easy now as it once was difficult. Its spacious Balbirnie Park
includes a remarkable show of rhododendrons, a re-erected
stone circle and a craft centre. At its eastern entrance is the
worn Stob Cross which of old marked the bounds of another
sanctuary, and Markinch has a church tower dating from the
twelfth century and the grave of General David Leslie who
died nearby in Balgonie Castle. For this is Leslie country.

The family came from Leslie in Aberdeenshire in the fourteenth century and the Earldom of Rothes dates from the
fifteenth. The seventh Earl (and the only Duke of Rothes) is
the best known, a staunch royalist who was rewarded at the
Restoration by being made Lord President of the Scottish
Privy Council, and later Lord Treasurer. His enemies condemned him as "mad for drunkenness for, as he drank, all his

friends died, though it scarce appeared that he was ever
disordered, and, after the greatest excesses, an hour or two of
sleep carried all off so entirely that no sign of them remained",
and also as a harrier of the Covenanters. But, in fact, he does
not seem to have been himself a cruel man and he used to
allow his duchess to shield persecuted clergy, and even gave her
warning on occasion. "My Lady," he would say, "my hawks
maun be abroad the morn, ye had better look after your
blackbirds." When he died, a funeral of tremendous pomp
went far to ruin the family. His successor – he had no son – is
credited with the introduction of the turnip to Fife. They had
a castle on the Firth of Tay at Ballinbreich and a splendid
mansion at Leslie; the latter suffered by fire in the eighteenth
century but a gracious central block survives and is now a
Church of Scotland Eventide Home.

Another branch of the family, the Earls of Leven, are
descended from "the little old, crooked soldier", Alexander
Leslie, who learnt his trade fighting for Gustavus Adolphus and
returned to his homeland to command the Scottish army
against Charles I in the Bishops' Wars. He was no genius as a
tactician, but he was experienced and a good organizer and had
the gift of managing men, including the "notoriously difficult
Scots Lords, of whom he had a dozen or so as colonels under
him". Later, he fought at Marston Moor with yet another
Swedish-trained member of the family, David, as his major-
general commanding the Scottish cavalry. In due course, David
made the greater name for himself, defeating Montrose at
Philiphaugh and Colkitto at Dunaverty. But his greatest
triumph came in 1650 when he completely outmanoeuvred
Cromwell before the Battle of Dunbar and was only robbed of
the rewards by the interference of the fanatical ministers
accompanying his army. Taken prisoner the next year at
Worcester, he spent nine years in the Tower of London until
the Restoration.

From Leslie, with its modern replacement to the 'kirk on
the green', there is a pretty drive westwards between the
Lomonds and Loch Leven past the holy well at Scotlandwell to
Milnathort, but we must return to Inverkeithing to take the

road along the coast.

During the last war, a subaltern in the Argylls led his platoon into action in Burma with the slogan "Another for Hector". He was recalling the Battle of Inverkeithing, when the Chief of the Clan Maclean was in imminent danger. One of his men, "seeing his chief was in danger, sprang between him and his foes but was soon cut down. Immediately another Maclean, calling out 'Fear eile airson Eachainn' (another for Hector), assumed the same post of danger, and was likewise slain. Another and another followed with the same self-sacrificing cry and the same result, until eight brave clansmen had unselfishly and gloriously yielded up their lives, trying to shield their heroic chief" who was, in spite of all, killed not long after. Such stories are common enough in all clan histories but most relate to the dim and misty past of legend embroidered in song and verse. What makes this story different is that it relates to Sunday, 20th July 1651 when Cromwell's General Lambert defeated the royalists, and of Hector's 800 only about thirty-five returned to their homes.

Nowadays Inverkeithing is a centre for paper-making and ship-breaking but, at that time, it was a port, chiefly exporting coal, but with some fishing and ship-building. Earlier still it had been a favourite resort of Queen Arabella, wife to Robert III. When she wished to get away from Dunfermline and perhaps from "the worst of kings and the most unfortunate of men", she used to seek peace in the house of the Greyfriars here, of which the *hospitium* may still be seen, basically fourteenth century but often tinkered with. Its ground floor maintains the hospitable tradition by providing a club for senior citizens, while the hall on the first floor contains a museum designed to perpetuate the little royal burgh that was swallowed up in a region in 1975 – an Authority which, believe it or not, finds itself unable to maintain in print (even for sale) the museum catalogue with its excellent brief account of Inverkeithing's history. At the back of the *hospitium*, where the main monastic buildings formerly stood, a peaceful little garden has been made. Other things of note in the town include the church tower, though the clock and the spire are modern; they are wholly inoffensive but do distract somewhat from the strength of the rest; inside is a medieval font with beautifully carved coats of arms. Across the street is Fordell's Lodging, town house of the enlightened coal-owner, Sir John Henderson, mentioned above. Where the broad High Street narrows into Bank Street is another old house with an inscription dated 1617, "Except the Lord Build the Hous they labour in vain that build it". Rosebery House in King Street is even older and belonged in turn to the Earls of Dundee, of Lauderdale and of Rosebery. To complete the number of interesting things in this little place, there are the mercat cross gaily painted in heraldic colours and the 1770 tolbooth with its outside staircase and octagonal tower.

We are now embarked on that string of royal burghs along the coast which James VI called the fringe of gold, and of which Andrew Fairservice said "There's the kingdom of Fife, frae Borrowstownness to the East Nuik, its just like a great combined city – sae mony royal burghs yoked on end to end, like ropes of ingans, with their hie-streets, and their booths, nae doubt, and their craemes, and houses of stane and lime and forestairs". Aberdour is the next, just beyond Dalgety Bay (currently threatened by a petro-chemical development), where there is a thirteenth-century chapel of St Bridget down by the seashore, and Donibristle House where the Bonnie Earl of Murray was murdered by Huntley in 1592. Not many places of the size of Aberdour can boast of two such well-known ballads as that of Sir Patrick Spens and:

> Ye Highlands and ye Lowlands,
>   O where have ye been?
> They have slain the Earl of Murray
>   And have laid him on the green.
>
> Now woe be to thee, Huntley!
>   And wherefore did ye sae!
> I bade you bring him with you,
>   But forbade you him to slay.
>
> He was a braw callant,
>   And he rid at the ring;
> And the bonny Earl of Murray,
>   O he might have been a king!

He was a braw callant,
  And he played at the ball;
And the bonny Earl of Murray
  Was the flower among them all!

He was a braw callant,
  And he played at the glove;
And the bonny Earl of Murray,
  O he was the Queen's love!

O long will his lady
  Look o'er the Castle Doune,
Ere she see the Earl of Murray
  Come sounding through the town!

The remains of Aberdour Castle are extensive and, like all those cared for by the Department of the Environment, greatly enhanced by their well-tended surroundings. The lower courses of the main tower are built of the small cubical blocks characteristic of the thirteenth century (as is the north wall and chancel of the little church). This tower may have collapsed at some time; at any rate it was rebuilt in the fifteenth century either for this reason or to give greater space and comfort, and added to in the sixteenth, from which time the central range also dates. Finally Earl William Morton (who died in 1648) added the eastern range, the whole first floor of which formed a picture gallery. The castle is approached through a square walled garden, flanked by herbaceous borders, while, to the south, the old terraced gardens are being recreated with considerable labour; they lead to a doocot shaped like a bee-hive. The official guide-book includes not only the story of the Douglas owners and a detailed description of the buildings, but includes an interesting inventory of the furniture for 1647 (which included a billiard table) and another of 1675, and a list of the trees bought for the garden in 1691.

Down a rose-lined walk is the church which was restored and taken back into use in 1926. The modern stained glass makes it dark, but no darker, of course, than it would originally have been. Much of the nave, the chancel arch, and some of the windows are original – a very good example of

Scottish Romanesque architecture.

From Aberdour used to run a ferry to the island of Inchcolm but for the time being no one can be found to adventure the rewarding trip. The earliest shrine here is, by somewhat dubious tradition, that of the hermit who in 1123 gave shelter to Alexander I when he was "constraint be violent tempest to remain three days" on the island, in gratitude for which the king founded an Augustinian house. Its church still retains both *pulpitum* and rood, and in its chancel was discovered the finest example of thirteenth-century wall painting left in Scotland – a procession of priests carrying censers and a holy water sprinkler. Another unusual feature is the cloister which runs under the buildings flanking the central open space instead of projecting from them under a lean-to roof, as is more usual. Plates 36 and 38 show the inside of the refectory and a general view which gives some idea of how extensive are the remains.

Three miles on is Burntisland which, with its well-constructed harbour, was once a prosperous centre for trade and fishing – and, later, for shale oil and quarried stone, ship-building and the conversion of bauxite into alumina. It was at its fine tower house, recently saved from dereliction by Robert Hurd and partners, that Queen Mary was staying when her French admirer Chastelard committed the final indiscretion which led to his summary execution. The other notable and beautiful building is the first church in Scotland built specifically for Protestant worship. It is square and has the pulpit in the middle with an aisle and gallery all round. Outside, a dignified substantial stair leads to the 'sailors' loft', while inside, the magistrates' canopied pew and the seats for the various guilds are gaily painted with the appropriate symbols. Nine years after it was completed in 1592, James VI convoked a meeting of the Assembly here, while he was at Falkland, at which was first suggested the new translation of the Bible which became 'King James's Version'. Nearby, in Somerville Street are some seventeenth-century houses – and some others!

Kinghorn is small, but yet another royal burgh. It is interesting historically as the place where Alexander II's horse stumbled and killed him; Balwearie, two miles to the north, is the site of the castle of Sir Michael Scott, the thirteenth-century wizard, but the ruins visible today are later, probably fifteenth-century. At Pettycur is a caravan camp, looking down to the splendid sands below and over Inchkeith to the Lothians.

Kirkcaldy, with 50,000 inhabitants, is as different as could be from the smaller royal burghs, but, in spite of its size, remains a friendly place. Unhappy as its history has often been, it is intensely proud of its past and the many famous men it has bred. It has been looted often – by the Danes in 847 and 1035, by the French in 1559 and by the Jacobites in 1715. General David Leslie was an elder of the church at Dysart. Robert Adam was born here and so was Adam Smith, who returned to the haunts of his youth to write *The Wealth of Nations.* Carlyle taught for a while at the grammar school and John Ritchie, the founder of the *Scotsman,* studied there. John Buchan is said to have got the idea for *The Thirty-Nine Steps* from those at Pathhead where his father was the Free Church minister. Cromwell stayed here after his defeat of the Covenanters had made 200 widows in the town, but, for most people, it is 'the lang toun', the town of the Links Market each spring along the sea-front (the largest in Europe), and the home of linoleum. Other forms of floor-covering are made there now, and furniture on a large scale, and there is support work for the North Sea Oil Industry and a vast National Coal Board installation at Seafield. But it was linoleum that made the town famous when the Nairn family turned it from an economy based on cotton and flax to one which by impregnating jute with linseed oil converted it into a cheap and easily washed floor covering – with only one disadvantage; the process of manufacture gave off a smell which became an uncomfortable joke. That smell, in its turn, gave birth to one of the most delightful of all poems of childhood; it recaptures the ecstatic excitement of the irrepressibly talkative little boy as he travels from Edinburgh by train for his holiday:

> "Whit wey does the engine say toot-toot?
> Is it feart to gang in the tunnel?
> Whit wey is the furnace no pit oot
> When the rain gangs doon the funnel?

What'll I hae for my tea the nicht?
A herrin', or maybe a haddie?
Has Grandma gotten electric licht?
Is the next stop Kirkcaddy?

There's a hoodie-craw on yon turnip-raw!
An' seagulls sax or seeven.
I'll no fa' oot o' the windae, Maw,
It's sneckit, as sure as I'm leevin'.
We're into the tunnel – we're a' in the dark!
But dinna be frichtit, Daddy,
We'll sune be coming to Beveridge Park,
An' the next stop's Kirkcaddy.

Is yon the mune I see in the sky?
It's awfu' wee and curly,
See, there's a coo an' cauf ootbye,
An' a lassie pooin' a hurly!
He's chackit the tickets an' gi'en them back,
Sae gie me ma ain yin, Daddy:
Lift doon the bag frae the luggage rack,
For the next stop's Kirkcaddy.

There's a gey wheen boats at the harbour mou',
An' eh! dae ye see the cruisers?
The cinnamon drop I was sookin' the noo
Has tummelt an' stuck tae ma troosers.
I'll sune be ringing ma Gran'ma's bell.
She'll cry, 'Come ben, ma laddie!'
For I ken masel' by the queer-like smell
That the next stop's Kirkcaddy."

Indeed the railway is as good a way to approach Kirkcaldy
as any, and the station an excellent point from which to start a
tour of the town. Outside are the colourful war memorial
gardens, and two museums: the industrial (which is only open
in the afternoons) and the main one which is full of interest.
There is a varied and too-little-visited collection of paintings in
the art gallery and many things of historical note downstairs,
including a plaster cast of the unique picture of men rowing a
Pictish boat, from the caves at Wemyss. From the museums it
is no great walk, past the imposing town hall, gay with flowers

outside and in, down to the esplanade. Here, in Sailors' Walk, a corner of old houses has been saved and given new life by the National Trust for Scotland. Now they are white and harled again, as they should be against the weather, but one sigh may perhaps be permitted for the ruggedness of the old stones beneath. The Customs House has a painted ceiling. Not least of the pleasures of Kirkcaldy is the extensive Ravenscraig Park and, in it, the two round keeps of the castle, joined by a high curtain wall. Started by James II in 1460 and completed by his widow, it is interesting as being the first British castle to be designed for defence by artillery. Its construction on such a sheer rock is an astonishing feat.

There is more industrial urban development ahead at Coaltown of Wemyss and Methil, but two gems off the main road must not be missed, Dysart and West Wemyss – the former most successfully reclaimed, the latter, one hopes, waiting to be, before it is too late. Dysart's High Street has a tolbooth, part sixteenth, part eighteenth century and a number of old houses whose charms are greatly enhanced by the various shades of colour with which they are washed. Down by the sea at Pan Ha' (Haugh not Hall as on the O.S. map) have been restored for occupation some really lovely cottages that had become derelict. The thirteenth-century church with its rather later tower is roofless but it is still sometimes used for services; inside is a garden most lovingly tended – open to the public on Sundays, 2-5 p.m. or by prior appointment.

West Wemyss once had six fairs a year and a weekly market but now its houses and even its tolbooth have a dejected air about them. East Wemyss has the considerable remains of MacDuff's castle and caves which were inhabited from Bronze Age times right up to the seventeenth century when one of them housed a workshop making glass. The *Scots Magazine* of November 1977 carried an interesting account of them by A. C. McKerracher with drawings and photographs of their carvings which show both Pictish and Scandinavian influences, and an amusing story of a visit to the caves by James IV:

> The Court Cave is named after the medieval Baillie Courts at which landowners dispensed their own justice and summoned

people to attend inside the cave by ringing a bell suspended from the roof. It also received its name from the visits of James IV who often came here incognito in his role of the Gudeman of Ballangeich. Once he stumbled upon a band of gypsies who were inhabiting the cave, and was nearly killed when a quarrel broke out among the Romanies. One of the gipsies had been in love with Mary Sibbald, daughter of a local landowner, and she had left home to live with him. She was falsely accused of stealing by a jealous gipsy woman and was sentenced to be flogged. The shock was too much for Mary who died of a broken heart.

On the occasion of the King's visit, the real thief, one Jean Lindsay, was being accused by several of the tribe, and her kin folk drew swords to protect her. A fearful fight was about to break out when the ghostly figure of a woman made its appearance, and all fled in terror. James made his way to the nearby castle and told the Baron Baillie what had happened. The Baron confessed that he too had been haunted since the morning of Jean Sibbald's trial.

The ghost continued to haunt the cave until the real thief confessed her guilt, and even yet it makes occasional appearances in the grounds of MacDuff's castle, and in the cave. An old woman who died in 1909 maintained that as a child she had seen the apparition of a fully dressed woman looking out of the east tower of MacDuff's castle, to which there is no access.

In recent years a visitor took a flashlight photograph of the interior of the cave which appeared to be completely empty, but when the film was developed it showed the figure of a seated woman.

Buckhaven and Methil are industrial, fishing having given way to coal. Coal in its turn declined but there seemed hope when Redpath Dorman Long got an order to produce a steel oil rig platform jacket for the North Sea; sadly the boom in employment was temporary and a hiccup followed. One more order has been won, in June 1978, by a new consortium but the long term future is likely to have to depend on something else. Leven, adjoining Methil, has wide sands and a famous shell house of greater ingenuity than beauty; and there are well-known golf-courses here and at Lundin Links. Inland, at the privately owned Durie House, a doocot of unusual octagonal shape, with 15,000 nesting boxes, has recently been restored.

From the troubles of the present to those of the year 1701 when John Selcraige elder and his wife and his sons Alexander, Andrew and John younger were all cited to appear before the kirk session of Largo. On November 25th, being examined:

> What was the cause of the tumult that was in his house, he said he knew not but that Andrew Selcraige having brought in a can of salt water of which his brother Andrew did drink through mistake and he laughing at him for it his brother Alex came and beat him, upon which he runs out of the house and called his brother John ... [who] as he came in at the door he did see his brother Alex at the other end of the house casting off his coat and coming towards him where upon his father did get betwixt them but knew not what he did other ways his head being borne down by his brother Alex but afterwards being liberated by his wife did make his escape ... she did follow her husband and coming into the house she found Alex Selcraige gripping both her father and her husband and she labouring to loose Alexander's hands from her husband's head and breast her husband fled out of doors and she followed him and called back again "you fals loun will you murder your father and my husband both", whereupon he followed her to the door but whether he beat her or not she was in so great confusion she cannot distinctly tell but ever since she has had a sore pain in her head.

When the Session met again on 29th November:

> after prayer Alexander Selcraige scandalous for contention and disagreeing with his brother was called and compeared and being questioned he confessed to the tumult and beating his brother Andrew twice with a staff he confessed also that he challenged his elder brother John to a combate as he called it of drynieffels then he said he would not care to do it even now, which he did afterwards refuse and regrate, whereupon the Session did appoint him to compear before the pulpit agst to-morrow and to be rebuked in face of the congregation for his scandalous carriage, and on the next day, he was so rebuked and promised amendment in the strength of the Lord and so was dismissed.

This Alexander Selcraige (or Selkirk to use the more usual

spelling) who was so quarrelsome, went off to sea in a
privateer, and again got into a quarrel, this time with his
captain, with the result that he was marooned on a desert
island in the Pacific, 400 miles from the nearest land. Here he
lived for four years, entirely alone, until he was taken off by
another ship and brought home. In due course, he met and told
his story to Daniel Defoe and was immortalized as Robinson
Crusoe. A statue has been erected on the site of the house in
Lower Largo where he was born but the house has been
replaced long ago. The sea was the natural place to turn to for
a livelihood in the Largo of those days, as is reflected in John
Ewen's song:

The Boatie Rows

O weel may the boatie row, And better may she speed;
And weel may the boatie row, That wins the bairns' bread.
The boatie rows, The boatie rows, The boatie rows indeed.
And happy be the lot of a', That wish the boatie speed.
I cuist my line in Largo bay, And fishes I caught nine,
There's three to boil, and three to fry, And three to bait the line.
The boatie rows, The boatie rows, The boatie rows indeed;
And happy be the lot of a', That wish the boatie speed.

When Jamie vow'd he would be mine, And wan frae me my
    heart,
O muckle lighter grew my creel. He swore we'd never part.
The boatie rows, The boatie rows. The boatie rows fu' weel
And muckle lighter is the lade When love bears up the creel.
My curtch [cap] I put upon my head; And dress'd mysel' fu'
    braw
I trow my heart was dowf [sad] and wae, When Jamie gaed
    awa'.
But weel may the boatie row, And lucky be her part:
And lightsome be the lassie's care, That yield's an honest heart.

When Sawnie, Jock and Janetie, Are up and gotten lear[ning]
They'll help to gar the boatie row: And lighten a' our care
The boatie rows, The boatie rows, The boatie rows fu' weel.
And lightsome be her heart that bears The murlain and the creel.

And when wi' age we're worn down, And hirplin' round the
  door
They'll row to keep us dry and warm, As we did them before;
Then, weel may the boatie row, That wins the bairns' bread
And happy be the lot of a' That wish the boatie speed.

Upper Largo too had a famous sea-going son, Sir Andrew
Wood, Admiral to James III and James IV, and twice victor
over the English ships of Henry VII. Only one circular tower
remains of the castle that he built, and little of the canal (the
oldest in Scotland) that he made his English prisoners dig from
it to the church so he could be rowed in state each Sunday to
hear Mass. And as little remains of a later mansion designed by
Robert Adam for the Durham family; but the eighteenth-
century manse still stands. By it, the old church is remarkable,
less perhaps for its architecture or the beautiful way in
which it has been kept – or even for the Pictish carved stone at
its gates – than for its quietness, its atmosphere of devotion, its
sense of on-going worship through the ages. It is *of* the village
and yet a sanctum behind its encircling wall, which was put
up, as the stone of 1657 records, by John Wood when he
returned to the place of his birth after an absence of fifty-five
years.

One other son of Largo is worth mention, Mr John Lamont,
for the diary that he kept of this part of the world during the
ups and downs of the years 1649–1671. In it national events
such as the first and second coronations of Charles II rub
shoulders with stories of strange illnesses and fires and freaks of
weather:

> 1652, Nou, and Decemb. – The wheat, after it was sowen, did
> spring againe in severall places in the shyre of Fyfe, betuixt 9 and
> 12 dayes; about this tyme also, the greatest pairt of all the tries,
> whither fruit tries or other tries, begane to bud againe. The
> whine generallie did blome, and some brome also, in some places.
> The veilet also hed its floure; the fege trie young feggs; the crawes
> also, in some places, begane to gather sticks to their old nests;
> strawberries leaues blomed the first of Jan. 1653.
>
> 1653, Feb. – Ther was an hermophrodite hanged att
> Edenbroughe: it was because of uncleanesse; for the report went

that he had lyen with seuereal mens wives in Edenbroughe. (He was both man and woman, (a thing not ordinair in this kingdome); his custome was always to go in a woman's habit).

He tells of difficulties with an unsatisfactory schoolmaster who had to be cast off

for profainlie taking the name of the diuill in his mouth twyse, especiallie upon the last Sabath the communion was giuen in Largo, viz. May 29, 1653; for ordinary tippling and drinking, and not praying alwayes euening and morning, in the schole, but sometimes onlie; as also because mutch giuen to mockeing and taunting

and of a murder:

1662, Jun. 16. – In the afternoone at Kirkekaldie, one George Griue, maltman ther, was killed by the shot of a pistoll, by his owne sonne, for the son fyred upon his father deliberatly and one sett purpose, while his father was turning the malt kill, and shot him throw the head; he took a stone in his bannet and brake all his feace, and afterewards smote him with the said stone on the breast diuers tymes. After the fact, he came from the place, and began a simeing repentance, crying out, and saying that his father and he had discorded, (ther was disagricment amonge them before, for it is reported that his father had layen in adultery this 17 or 19 yeire bypast with diuers persons; for his custome was to drinke mutch of the day tyme abroad and to be absent from his owne howse att night). Some dayes after he was put to deathe att Kirkekaldie, and his body put up on a gibett at Kirkekaldie, aboue the towne. (Some say, that before his death, he confessed that he had lyen with his father's cowe.)

Other extracts, and a detailed account of the building, can be found in *Largo Kirk* by Douglas Lister and the late James Gillies, on sale in the church.

The best way to Earlsferry and Elie is the walk along the shore; failing that, take the A921 through Colinsburgh since it passes through the village of Kilconquhar, a conservation area, and to a fine viewpoint just east of that village, looking back over the loch.

Elie is now the Rye and the Frinton of Scotland, combining

a good golf-course with a sandy seashore for children and safe sailing. The tourist office even adds the chance of finding rubies there but most people will consider themselves extremely lucky if they manage to find (and recognize) a garnet. Facing south it is really an ideal place for a holiday, with good walking all round. Kincraig Point, an extinct volcano, with its wild flowers and caves and a farmhouse of 1680, makes an excellent object- ive, or, in the other direction, St Monans; the cliffs on the way have special interest for geologists. In Elie itself, the church is basically seventeenth century and so is the large house in South Street, known as the 'Castle'. Most attractive of all are the fishermen's cottages which can be best seen from the granary at the far end of the mole which shelters the harbour.

The castles at Ardross and St Monans are ruined but the latter's church is the most attractive of all those along this stretch of coast. It lies at the western extremity of the little port, on cliffs above the sea, so that nothing obstructs the view of the (not quite) square tower and octagonal stone spire. Founded by David II, the church passed to the Dominican Friars and, not being intended for parochial use by the laity, never had a nave. Especially notable are the vaulted stone roof with its heraldic shields, the Decorated tracery of the windows, the *Sedilia* and the *Piscina* at the east end – and the fact that, unlike so many of the churches, it is kept open and is therefore easy of access. Fishing has not died out here, and a boat with the somewhat surprising name of *Fidelitas* was up on the slip- way being painted in the spring of 1978. As elsewhere in Fife the National Trust for Scotland has been active here and it is worth seeking out a narrow wynd named the Cribbs. Newark Castle has a circular doocot and was once the home of General David Leslie.

Pittenweem also has a still busy fishing harbour – a difficult one to enter but spacious and protected in its inner reach, and backed by well-proportioned cottages and one or two larger seventeenth-century houses as at 18 East Shore Road and The Gyles. Kellie Lodging in the High Street is a century older. Unlike that of St Monans, the church is kept locked but its strong tower with its windows half glazed, half shuttered, as at the palace, Culross, and its stone spire can be admired from the outside. Behind it, protected by a high wall, the remains of the priory buildings make an impressive private house. This (inevitably) royal burgh is a peaceful and pleasant place today, but its history was too often murky, as in its persecution of witches – as late as 1705 Janet Cornfoot was pressed to her death – and in the lawlessness of its smugglers. It was a robbery from James Stark, a Customs collector here, that led to the Porteous Riots, described in Scott's *Heart of Midlothian*. A baker, Andrew Wilson, had had his smuggled goods confiscated and he and another man called Robertson tried to steal them back. Betrayed by an accomplice, they were imprisoned in the Tolbooth in Edinburgh to await their execution. On their last Sunday, Wilson created a disturbance in church and enabled his fellow prisoner to escape, thus earning the sympathy of the populace. A certain Captain Porteous was given the thankless task of keeping order on the day that Wilson was to be hanged; a bad choice because he lost his nerve when the crowd turned nasty and ordered his troops to fire, killing six. He, in his turn, was sentenced to death, but, when it seemed possible that he would be reprieved, he was abducted from his prison and lynched, with the result that the Scottish judges suffered the humiliation of being summoned to appear at the bar of the House of Commons in London, and a large fine was imposed on Edinburgh because no one would identify the culprits.

Further picturesque harbours await us at Anstruther and Crail but, lest the visual memories of all should be merged in a conglomerate that is none of them, a diversion inland is to be recommended – to Balcaskie House and its gardens if it is one of the days when it is open to the public, or to Kellie Castle which, though still lived in, is, as a National Trust property, open every afternoon in the summer except Monday and Tuesday. Balcaskie was an early seventeenth-century house which Sir William Bruce bought and extended for himself before he embarked on Kinross House. As at the latter he gave great attention to the approach to the house, to the view from it, and to the garden on its terraces. For many years it has been the home of the Anstruthers.

Kellie Castle consists of two fourteenth-century towers, austere and functional, joined by a more decorative sixteenth-century range, the whole making a thoroughly satisfying composition, unspoilt by later alterations or additions. Its exposure to north and east winds must be trying at times, but compensated for by a wonderful view over the Firth of Forth to the Isle of May and North Berwick. A high stone wall protects a garden of lawns and borders. Inside the castle, the appeal is less of the period of the castle builders (with the exception of the unusual shape of the ceilings and some lovely plaster work) than of the personal taste of the present occupants, sculptor Hew Lorimer and his wife. Just over a hundred years ago, his grandfather saved the castle from the dereliction into which it was falling by renting it from the Earl of Mar and Kellie whose family had succeeded the Oliphants as owners. He was a Professor of Law but two of his sons (as well as his grandson) achieved distinction as artists; Sir Robert Lorimer designed the Thistle Chapel in St Giles and the Scottish National War Memorial in Edinburgh Castle, and did much restoration as well as original work throughout Scotland; an older brother who succeeded his father as tenant of the castle was a painter whose "Ordination of the Elders" hangs in the National Gallery of Scotland. It is a marvellous piece of character creation, though it was painted in the castle and not in church, and the minister was really a sheriff, and only one of the six solemn-looking elders a member of a kirk session. A self-portrait is in the castle.

Impressive as the old building is, what makes a visit so supremely satisfying is its contents; in every room there is something beautiful and interesting, often contemporary, often of native origin but not necessarily; it may be of any date or country, anything that has taken the fancy and justified the taste of the owner – or rather the occupier since his home has now been given to the nation by means of the National Trust for Scotland.

The royal burghs of Anstruther Wester and Anstruther Easter, with Cellar dyke and Kilrenny, are contiguous. The churches of the first two and the last have old towers, and

Anstruther Easter one of the finest of Reformation manses still in use as a manse. James Melville built it in 1590, in ten months, at a cost of £2300; not only the heritors but the burgesses contributed, out of respect for their minister. It is however not very easy to find – or to see – being behind a high wall, at the end of School Green, down Burial Brae. John Dunbar in his *Historic Architecture of Scotland* tells how "Melville himself bent all his considerable energies to the task in hand and closely supervised the day-to-day progress of the building operations, afterwards reflecting, in sentiments that have been echoed by builders of all generations, that the house 'wald neuer haiff bein perfyted giff the bountifull hand of my God haid nocht maid me to tak the wark in hand myselff.' "

Anstruther has the Scottish Fisheries museum (*see* plate 41) and its neighbour Cellardyke has good examples of little houses with crow-stepped gables, pantiled roofs and foresteps, features which tell of the constant traffic between the Fife burghs and the low countries. From Anstruther, a visit may be made to the bird sanctuary on the Isle of May, five miles off shore.

Last of the golden tassels on the fringe of Fife is Crail, perhaps the most photographed and painted of them all – and with good reason. It was also in some ways the most distinguished in that its provost was Rear Admiral of the Forth. Full of interest as is the harbour with its unusual construction, its little boats and its restored Customs House, it is the admirably planned Marketgate and Nethergate that are of most interest. Marketgate, wide and tree-lined, has one of the best tolbooths – early sixteenth century with a tower of Dutch type. It has a fish weather-vane, a notable coat of arms and an attractive cottage next door. Most of the houses in the street are worth study, especially one dated 1686. The mercat cross (though not as old as its pedestal) still has its unicorn and the burgh – till 1952 – still had its bellman. The thirteenth-century church no longer has the tracery of its windows but its tower and spire still stand, and the pillars of the nave. Plain glass and light woodwork do something to compensate for what has been lost. Some interesting monuments in the churchyard, especially the Lumsden tomb in the north-west corner, an eleventh-century cross in the Victoria Gardens, and a Pictish carved stone, complete the antiquities of the town itself, but there are caves to be explored, and the rocks at the East Neuk of Fife, before we are back at St Andrews.

And St Andrews is the right place from which to take leave of the two regions of Strathtay and Fife, portrayed herein, their most famous city and the most international. We opened this book with the refusal of the Kingdom of Fife to be absorbed in Tayside but, on the very day that these closing words are written, comes an announcement that after all a forced marriage is to take place – if only a very partial one. The two regions are to be conjoined for the purpose of electing a representative for the Parliament of the European Economic Community. Southern Pictland has been recreated – and the Auld Alliance – and the close economic and cultural connection between this part of Scotland and the Low Country – one hopes, to their mutual advantage. But whether we shall be represented in the European Parliament by those who, locally, support Willie Hamilton, or those who support Nicholas Fairbairn, or those who support G. D. Crawford, is anybody's guess. We are a mixed lot, hereabouts.

FURTHER READING

The Statistical Account of Scotland, 1793.

The New Statistical Account of Scotland, 1845.

The Third Statistical Account of Scotland, 1964.

Department of the Environment Guides to various buildings in their care, especially those for Aberdour, Claypotts, Edzell, and Huntingtower Castles and the Cathedrals of Dunkeld and St Andrews.

Scotland's Gardens, annual guide to gardens open under the Scottish Gardens Scheme.

National Trust for Scotland Handbooks, especially those to Culross and Ben Lawers.

Atholl, ninth and tenth Dukes of, *Guide to Blair Castle.*

Cant, R. G., *Guides to St Leonards and St Salvator's Chapels.* 1955. 1971. St Andrews University.

——, *Historic Buildings of Angus.* 1975. Angus Historical Buildings Society.

Cockburn, J. Hutchison, *Guide to Dunblane Cathedral.* 1972. Society of Friends of Dunblane Cathedral.

Cowan, S., *The Ancient Capital of Scotland.* 1904. Simpkin, Marshall, Hamilton Kent & Co.

Cruden, S., *The Early Christian and Pictish Monuments of Scotland, with a guide to the Meigle and St Vigeans collections.* 1978. H.M.S.O.

Dunbar, J., *The Historical Architecture of Scotland.* 1966. Batsford.

East Fife Preservation Society, *What to see in East Fife.*

Elphinstone, Lady, *Guide to Glamis Castle.*

Feachem, R., *Guide to Prehistoric Scotland.* 1963. Batsford.

Fraser, D., *Discovering East Scotland*. Montrose Standard Press.

——, *Highland Perthsire*. 1969. Montrose Standard Press.

Gillies, W., *In Famed Breadalbane*. 1938. Munro Press.

Henderson, I., *The Picts*. Thames & Hudson.

Lindsay, J., *Kirkcaldy Past and Present*. 1975. Kirkcaldy Town Council.

Linklater, E. and A., *History of the Black Watch*. 1977. Barnie and Jenkins.

Lister, Rev. D., *Largo Kirk*. 1968.

MacGregor, A. R., *Short Excursion Guide to the Geology of Fife and Angus*. 1968. Blackwood for St Andrews University.

Mackie, E., *An Archaeological Guide to Scotland*. 1975. Faber and Faber.

Moncreiffe, Sir I., *Guide to the Royal Palace of Scone*.

——, and Crichton Stuart, Lord N., *Guide to the Royal Palace of Falkland*.

Old Blairgowrie – Tours, History, Memories, Tales, Anon.

Robertson, J. P., *St Andrews*. 1973. Citizen Office, St Andrews.

Scott, Sir Walter, *The Antiquary*.

——, *The Fair Maid of Perth*

——, *The Heart of Midlothian*.

——, *The Legend of Montrose*.

——, *The Monastery* and its sequel *The Abbot*.

Simpson, W. Douglas, *The Highlands of Scotland*. 1969. Robert Hale.

——, *History of St John's Kirk, Perth*. 1958. Friends of St John's Kirk.

Soutar, W., *Poems in Scots and English* ed. W. R. Aitken (Scottish Academic Press.)

Stewart, Alexander, *A Highland Parish* (about Glen Lyon). 1928. Alex Maclean.

Stewart, Alexandra, *The Glen That Was*. 1975. Club Leabhar.

Thoms, B. D., *Illustrated Guide to Brechin Cathedral*. 1975.

Tranter, N., *The Fortified House in Scotland*, Vols 2 and 4. 1966. Oliver and Boyd.

——, *The Queen's Scotland*. Hodder and Stoughton.

Walker, F., *Brief Introduction to the Geology of Tayside*. 1961. Dundee Museum and Art Gallery.

Wilson, Rev. W., *A Parish History* (Airlie). 1917. Alex Pettigrew.

Young, R. S., *About Kinross and its Folk*. 1978. Milne, Tannahill and Methuen.

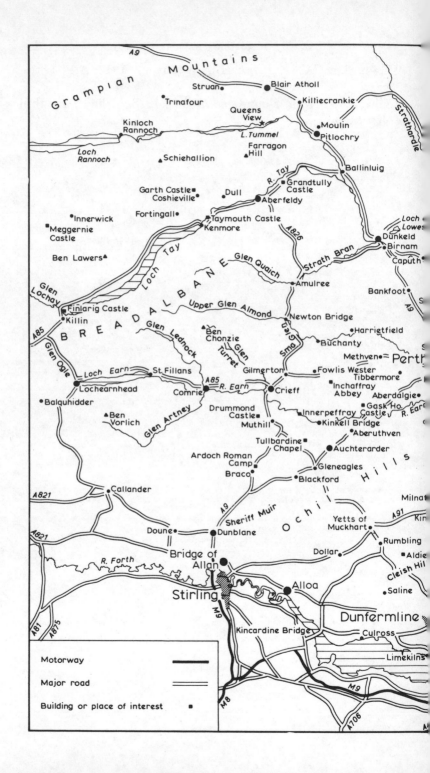

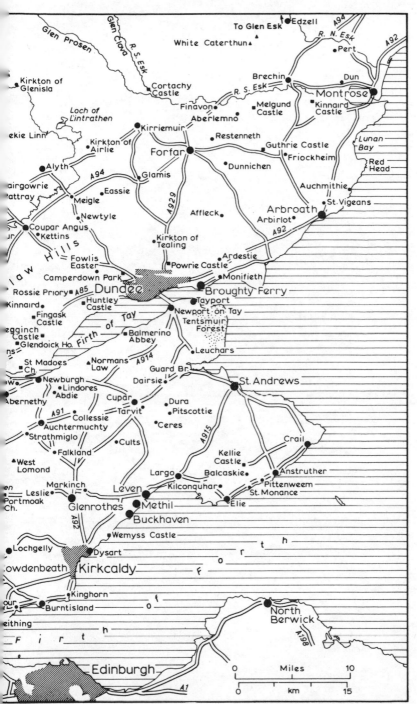

Based with permission on the Ordnance Survey. Crown Copyright Reserved.

INDEX

Plate numbers in bold type

Abdie, 172
Abercairny, 63, 82
Aberdalgie, 105, 111
Aberdeen-Angus, cattle, 22
Aberdour, 213
Aberfeldy, 23, 65, 66, **10**
Aberlemno, 15, 146
Abernethy, 17, 124
Aberuthven, 113
Agricola, 14
Airlie, 18, 140
Alexander I, 87, 215
Alexander II, 32, 215
Alexander III, 32, 172
Alyth, 55
Amulree, 65, 86, 101
Anstruther, 22, 226, **41**
Arbroath, 18, 162, **24, 25, 26**
Ardestie, 14, 155, **22**
Ardoch, 14, 116
Ardvorlich, 94
Arngask, 126
Atholl, Dukes of, *see* MURRAYS
Auchmithie, 165
Auchnafree, 66
Auchterarder, 113
Auchterhouse, 154
Auchtermuchty, 175

Baird, Sir David, 110
Balcaskie, 225
Balfours, 61, 127
Balgray, 154
Balmerino, 173
Balquhidder, 93
Barrie, Sir James, 139
Barry Hill, 14, 55

Beaton, Cardinal David, 147, 184
Beaton, Archbishop James, 184, 195
Bell, Andrew, 22, 179, 195
Bell, Arthur, 38
Bell-Baxter High School, 22, 179
Ben Chonzie, 66, 86
Ben Lawers, 78, 90, **14**
Ben Vorlich, 78, 94
Black Watch, 23*ff*, 66
Blair Atholl, 60, 62, **8**
Blair Drummond, 121
Blairgowrie, 52*ff*
Bowes-Lyon, family of, *see* LYON
Braco, 116
Breadalbane, 65*ff*
Brechin, 149, 150, **21**
Bridge of Earn, 124
Bruce, Sir George, 197, 200, 201, 202
Bruce, Sir William, 22, 128, 225
Buchanty Spout, 85
Burntisland, 215, **39**

Caird, 158
Caird Park, 161
Cameron, Richard, 28, 175, 176
Cameron, Seargeant Mor, 76
Cameronians, 27
Campbell, Duncan (schoolmaster and
    author), 71
Campbells,
    of Argyll, 18, 49, 58, 117, 131, 142,
        187, 200
    of Breadalbane, 20, 68, 83, 86*ff*, 91
    of Glenlyon, 68
    of Glenorchy, *see* BREADALBANE
    of Inverawe, 24, 141

235

Campbells of Lawers, 98
  of Monzie, 84
Camperdown Park, 159
Carlungie, 14, 155
Carnegie, Andrew, 191, 203, 207
Carnegies, 167, 169
Carnoustie, 162
Carpow, 14, 161, 171
Carse of Gowrie, 151
Castles,
  Affleck, 155
  Airlie, 142, 143
  Aldie, 126
  Ardblair, 49, 54, 107
  Ballinbreich, 173, 211
  Balloch, see TAYMOUTH
  Balmanno, 126
  Balvaird, 175
  Blackadder, see TULLIALLAN
  Blair, 49, 60, 62ff, 8
  Braco, 116
  Broughty, 156
  Burleigh, 127
  Careston, 147
  Claypotts, 156, 23
  Cleish, 126
  Cortachy, 143
  Dairsie, 181
  Dochart, 87, 93
  Doune, 120
  Drummond, 110, 18
  Dudhope, 157
  Edinample, 87, 94
  Edzell, 147ff, 20
  Elcho, 18, 122
  Falkland, 18, 177, 27, 28
  Fingask, 151, 152
  Finlarig, 70, 91
  Flemington, 147
  Forter, 142
  Fowlis Easter, 153
  Garth, 74
  Glamis, 134ff, 149, 17
  Grandtully, 66
  Guthrie, 146, 165
  Huntingtower, 77
  Huntley, 136, 151
  Invermark, 150
  Inverquharity, 141
  Kellie, 225, 226
  Kilchurn, 87
  Kinnaird (Angus), 167, 169
  Kinnaird Priory (Perthshire), 152
  Loch Leven, 130
  Mains, 154
  Meggernie, 68
  Megginch, 151
  Melgund, 147
  Menzies, 67
  Methven, 77
  Murroes, 155
  Newton (Blairgowrie), 49, 54
  Powrie, 154
  Ravenscraig, 218
  Ruthven, see HUNTINGTOWER
  St Andrews, 185, 192
  Scotstarvit, 181, 30
  Taymouth, 70, 87
  Tulliallan, 199
  Tullibole, 126
Cathedrals, see BRECHIN; DUNBLANE;
  DUNFERMLINE; ST ANDREWS
Cathertons, 14, 147
Ceres, 181
Charles I, 45, 49, 175, 177
Charles II, 49, 60, 222
Charles, Edward, Prince, 55, 67, 107,
  138
Clans, Battle of, 34
Clatchard Craig, 14, 170, 29
Cleish Hills, 104
Clerk of Penicuik, Sir John, 99
Coal, 18, 22, 197
Comrie, 97
Coupar Angus, 131
Coutts, John, 166
Covenanters, 60, 79, 175, 179, 211
Craighall of Rattray, 53
Crail, 227, 42
Crawford, Earls of, see LINDSAYS
Creag nan Callich, 14
Crieff, 20, 84, 101
Croftmoraig, 14, 90, 12
Crusoe, Robinson (Andrew Selcraige),
  220-21
Culross, 200ff, 32, 34
Cultoquhey, 38
Cupar, 22, 179

Dairsie, 181
David I, 182, 203
David II, 224
Dewar, First Lord, 39, 46
Dickson of Kilbucho, Colonel, 25
Droving, 101, 102*n*
Drummonds, 18, 48, 52, 87, 94, 101, 108, 110, 113, 119, 152
Drummond-Moray, 82
Dull, 17, 19, 68
Dummiefaline fort, 126
Dunbar, William, 208*ff*
Dunblane, 17, 118
Duncan, Admiral Lord, 115, 159
Dundas, Sir Robert, 97
Dundee, 17, 18, 22, 155*ff*
Dundee Museum, 14, 154, 161
Dundurn, 15, 96, **15**
Dunfallandy, 59
Dunfermline, 17, 18, 20, 197, 202*ff*, **35, 37**
Dunglow fort, 126
Dunkeld, 17, 48, 57, 101, **7**
Dunnichen, 146
Dunning, 112, 113
Dunsinane, 14, 131
Dura Den, 181
Dysart, 218

Earlshall (Leuchars), 175
Eassie, 15, 134
Edward I, 43, 150, 157, 166, 204
Edzell, 147, **20**
Elcho, 18
Elie, 223
Ericht, River, 53, 56
Erskines, 166*ff*

Falkland, 18, 175*ff*
Fearnan, 71
Fendoch, 85
Fergusson, Bernard, (Lord Ballantrae), 27, 210
Fergusson of Baledmund, 59
Fife and Forfar Yeomanry, 27
Finavon fort, 147
Fincastle, 59
Finlarig, 87

Folk Museums,
    Angus (Glamis), 135
    Fife (Ceres), 181
    Tarfside, 150
Forfar, 144
Forteviot, 17, 39, 111
Fortingall, 68, 69
Fowlis Easter, 152*ff*
Fowlis Wester, 81
Friockheim, 146

Gardens, 22
    Abercairny, 83
    Balcaskie, 225
    Branklyn, 41
    Drummond Castle, 110, **18**
    Edzell Castle, 148, **20**
    Falkland Palace, **27**
    Glamis Castle, 139
    Glendoick, 151
    Guthrie Castle, 146
    Keillour, 81
    Kinross, 129
Gask, 20, 105
General Accident Company, 39*ff*
Glamis, 134*ff*, **17**
Glas, Rev. John, 38
Gleneagles, 115
Glenrothes, 199, 210
Glens,
    Almond, 65, 86
    Artney, 97
    Devon, 102, 104, 116
    Dochart, 93, 101
    Eagles, 104, 115
    Esk, 148
    Farg, 104, 125, 175
    Isla, 141
    Lednock, 98, 101
    Lyon, 68*ff*
    Ogle, 93
    Quaich, 86
    Tilt, 48
Gow, Neil, 57
Gowrie, Carse of, 151*ff*
Gowrie, Conspiracy of, 35
Graham of Claverhouse, John (Viscount Dundee), 60, 138, 156, 157

Graham, James (Marquis of Montrose), 18, 45, 77, 95, 109, 113, 136, 148, 157, 167, 187
Graham, Thomas (Lord Lynedoch), 28, 81
Grahams,
of Balgowan, 28, 81, 83
of Fintry, 154
of Inchbraikie, 83, 113
Grandtully, 66
Grays, 151*ff*
Guardbridge, 174
Guthrie, 165

Haldanes, 87, 115
Harrietfield, 85
Harris, William, 22
Hazard, H.M.S., 167
Henryson, Robert, 207*ff*
Highlandman Loan, 102
Hill of Tarvit, 181

Inchaffray Abbey, 109
Inchcolm Abbey, 18, 215, **36, 38**
Inchtuthil, 14, 56
Innerpeffray, 108
Innerwick, 69, 90
Inverkeithing, 18, 211, 212

James I, 31, 32, 34, 46, 49, 153
James II, 152, 218
James IV, 49, 79, 119, 177, 190, 210, 218
James V, 63, 64, 135, 177, 180
James VI, 18, 34, 46, 63, 127, 153, 177, 190, 195, 197
James VII, 60, 106
James Edward, Prince, 152, 167

Keillor, 22
Keillour, 81
Kenmore, 65, 90
Kenneth MacAlpine, 17, 32, 49
Kettins, 131
Killiecrankie, 18, 60, **9**
Killin, 93, 101, **16**
Kincardine-on-Forth, 199
Kinclaven, 48, 56
Kinell, 91
Kinettles, 139

Kinfauns, 151, 154
Kinghorn, 215
Kinghorne and Strathmore, Earls of, *see* LYON
Kinkell, 107
Kinnaird, 152
Kinross, 127*ff*
Kirkcaldy, 18, 216, 217
Kirriemuir, 139, **19**
Knox, John, 18, 43, 172, 185

Largo, 220
Lawers, 98
Laws fort, 155
Leslies, 184, 210, 224
Leuchars, 174, **31**
Lindores, 172
Lindsay of the Mount, Sir David, 178-180
Lindsays, 135, 141, 147*ff*, 163, 178, 181
Lintrathen, 141
Lochs,
Earn, 77, 94
Freuchie, 65
Leven, 127*ff*
of Lowes, 48, 57
Rannoch, 48, 76, **11**
Tay, 65, 77, 86, **13**
Tummel, 48
Logiealmond, 85
Lomonds, 122, 130, 178
Longannet, 199, 200
Luncarty, 37, 56
Lyon, Bowes-Lyon, family of, 35, 135*ff*, 151

MacGregor of Glenstae, Gregor, 69
MacGregors, 24, 87, 92, 93, 94, 98, 126
Mackay, General, 60
Maclaren, Ian, *see* WATSON, REV. JOHN
Maclarens, 93
Macleans, 61, 212
MacNabs, 87, 91*ff*, 95
Madderty, 109
Madras Academy (St Andrews), 22
Malcolm Canmore, 17, 111, 144, 203
Mansfield, Earls of 50, and *see* MURRAYS
Mar, Earl of, 112, 113, 117
Margaret, Queen, 17, 182, 202

Margaret Tudor (wife of James IV), 79, 119
Markinch, 17, 210
Marshall, Thomas Hay, 38
Mary Stewart, Queen of Scots, 63, 64, 130, 153, 177, 187, 194, 215
Maule-Ramseys (Earls of Dalhousie), 150
Maules, 150
Maxtones of Cultoquhey, 83, 105
Meigle, 133
Meiklour, 48, 52
Melville, Andrew, 19, 166, 187
Melville, James, 19, 167, 187, 227
Melville, Viscount, 97
Melville House, 178
Menzies, 67, 68, 87
Mercers, family of, 36, 52
Methil, 219
Methven, 18, 28, 77
Milnathort, 127
Milton Eonan, 90
Moncrieffe, family of, 121, 122
Moncrieffe Hill, 121, 122
Moness, Falls of, 48, 66
Monimail, 179
Montrose, 18, 19, 165ff
Montrose, Marquis of, see GRAHAM, JAMES
Morgan, John, 22
Morton Farm (Tentsmuir), 13, 173
Moulin, 59
Munro of Fowlis, Sir Robert, 23
Murrays, 18, 27, 48, 50, 57, 62ff, 81, 83, 99, 175, 224
Murroes, 155
Muthil, 17, 102, 110

Nairne, Lady, 55, 107
Nairne, Lord, 106
National Trust for Scotland, 41, 57, 81, 90, 139, 155, 173, 176, 181, 201, 202, 217, 226
Nechtan, King of the Picts, 146
Nechtansmere, 146
Neishes, 95
Newburgh, 171
Newton Brig, 65, 86
Newtyle, 134

Norie-Miller, Sir Francis, 40
Norie-Miller, Sir Stanley, 41, 42
Normans Law, 14, 170

Ochil Hills, 104, 122, 126
Ochtertyre, 98, 99
Ogilvy, family of, 18, 130, 141ff, 147, 157, 163, 167, 184
Oliphants, family of, 18, 20, 32, 54, 105ff, 111

Pathstruie, 126
Perth, 17, 18, 19, 21, 30ff, 1, 2, 3
Perthshire Volunteers, 28, 29
Pictish Stones, 14ff, 59, 81, 111, 116, 124, 132-5, 140, 146, 152, 154, 161, 164-5, 172-3, 192, 4, 5, 6
Picts, 14ff, 111, 122, 133, 146, 152, 155, 161, 171, 217
Pitlessie, 178
Pitlochry, 58
Pittenweem, 224
Pow Water, 104, 106

Queen Victoria, see VICTORIA
Queen Victoria School (Dunblane), 118, 120

Rannoch, 75
Rannoch School, 75
Rattray, 53
Reekie Linn, 141
Restenneth, 17, 146
Rhynd, 123
Robert I, the Bruce, 18, 31, 49, 57, 77, 105, 157, 163, 203
Robert II, 58, 135
Robert III, 34, 36, 212
Robertson, Rev. Charles, 47
Robertsons, 18, 24, 48, 64, 75, 87
Rob Roy, 93, 126
Rollo, Lord, 113
Romans, 14, 52, 56, 85, 97, 104, 116, 161, 171
Rossie Law (Angus), 165
Rossie Law (Perthshire), 113
Rossie Priory, 152
Rothesay, Duke of, 172, 177
Ruskin, John, 45, 118
Ruthvens, Earls of Gowrie, 35, 49, 79

St Andrews, 17-9, 22, 182ff, 33
St Bride, 124
St Columba, 17, 163
St David's (Madderty), 110
St Eonan (Adamnan), 68, 69
St Fillan of Dunfillan, 19, 95
St Fillan of Strathfillan, 93
St Fillans, 96
St Leonard's College, 183, 189, 194
St Leonard's School for Girls, 194
St Madoes, 152
St Mary's College, 184, 195
St Monance, 224, 40
St Ronan, 98
St Rule, 191
St Salvator's College, 183, 185, 193
St Serf, 113, 130
St Vigeans, 163
Sandemans, 37, 86
Schiehallion, 75, 86, 11
Scone, 17, 18, 31, 49
Scot, Sir John, 181
Scott, Sir Walter, 34, 95, 97, 125, 127, 130, 165, 225
Scottish Horse, 27
Scrymgeour, 157, 173
Sharp, Archbishop, 195
Shielings, 71-3
Sheriffmuir, 18, 102, 117
Sidlaw Hills, 122, 131
Sma' Glen, 77, 85
Smythe of Methven, 79
Soutar, William, 45, 65
Souterrains, 14, 133, 140, 154, 155, 162, 22
Stewart, Alexander (author), 69, 73
Stewart, Alexander (Wolf of Badenoch), 58, 75
Stewart, Alexandra, 71
Stewart, Daniel, 22, 67

Stewart, James (Earl of Atholl), 34
Stewarts, 18, 24, 48, 59, 60, 62, 66, 75, 94, 120
Stobhall, 52
Strathallan Castle Aircraft Museum, 108
Strathallan School, 111
Strathearn, 103, 111
Strathmiglo, 175
Strathtay, 86
Struan, 64

Tayport, 173
Tentsmuir, 170
Threipland, 152
Tibbermuir, 77
Trinafour, 75
Trinity College Glenalmond, 85
Tulliallan, 199
Tullibardine Chapel, 108

Unicorn, H.M.S., 161, 162
Unna, Percy, 90

Victoria, Queen, 64, 74, 89, 125
Vikings, 17

Waid, Andrew, 22
Wallace, William, 18, 126, 166
Watson, Rev. John, 85
Wavell, Field Marshal Lord, 26
Weem, 67
Wemyss, 123
West Wemyss, 218
Wilkie, David, 178
William the Lion, King, 32, 144, 157, 163, 166
Wood, Admiral Sir Andrew, 222

Yetts of Muckhart, 116, 126